THE BOND OF LIFE
בצרור החיים

Presented to

by

in memory of

whose soul, we pray, will be bound
up forever in the bond of life

כי יי יהיה לך לאור עולם ושלמו ימי אבלך

*"The Lord will be your everlasting light and
the days of your mourning will come to an end."*

THE
BOND OF
LIFE ~~

בִּצְרוֹר הַחַיִּים

A Book for Mourners

Edited by
RABBI JULES HARLOW

THE RABBINICAL ASSEMBLY
New York

We are grateful to the publishers and authors listed below for having granted permission to print excerpts from the following works:

From *Franz Rosenzweig: His Life and Thought* by Nahum N. Glatzer. © 1953, 1961 by Schocken Books Inc. Reprinted by permission of Schocken Books Inc.

From *The Essence of Judaism* by Leo Baeck. © 1948 by Schocken Books Inc. Reprinted by permission of Schocken Books Inc.

From *May I Have a Word with You?* by Rabbi Morris Adler. © 1967, by B'nai B'rith. Used by permission of Crown Publishers, Inc.

From *A Faith for Moderns* by Rabbi Robert Gordis. © 1960 by Robert Gordis, reprinted by permission of Bloch Publishing Company.

From "Reflections on Death," by Abraham Joshua Heschel. © 1973 by Sylvia Heschel, executrix of the Estate of Abraham Joshua Heschel. Used by permission of Sylvia Heschel.

From *A Time to Search* by Ruth Brin, published by The Jonathan David Company. © 1959 by Ruth Brin. Reprinted by permission of the author.

Library of Congress Catalog Card Number: 75-14888

DESIGNED BY BETTY BINNS

❧Contents

✒ Introduction

"What person shall live and not see death?" (Psalms 89:49). The Psalmist reflects the understanding that death is part of the fate of every human being, the fate of each of us. "There is no cure for death, not even health," wrote Franz Rosenzweig. We should never try to deny death. It is futile to attempt to hide from death, and it is damaging to seek refuge in the various bizarre, dehumanizing, irrational, and escapist trappings which have been called the pornography of death.

When death is faced realistically, the severe shock is dissipated sooner. Jewish tradition prescribes for us stages of mourning and grief; a gradual and healthy separation from the dead is part of the process of healing.

We must face grief with courage and with faith. The Jewish tradition's insistence upon confronting

---

1

death directly is reflected in the requirement that the tearing of a mourner's garment (or of a symbolic ribbon) as a sign of grief must be done while the mourner is standing.

Deep despair is not an unnatural reaction to the death of one whom we have loved. As individuals and as a people, Jews have known despair. But for our own sake as well as for the sake of the dead, we must not succumb to continuing despair and self-pity.

When the ancient Temple was destroyed in Jerusalem, great numbers of Jews apparently decided to withdraw from the normal routine of life. Overwhelmed by depression as they mourned the young men and women and the elders who had been killed, as well as the destruction of the Temple, they refused to eat or drink. They were confronted by Rabbi Joshua, who said: "My children, I know that it is impossible not to mourn. But to mourn excessively is forbidden." The *shivah* period is the appropriate time to mourn and to reflect upon the past. The past, and our memories of the dead, are precious. But we do a disservice to the dead and to those memories if we focus only upon the past.

Over the centuries, Jews have been able to face death as an inevitable part of life even when they could not completely comprehend the suffering which accompanies it, and in the absence of ready answers to the question, "Why did it happen?" Death is a mystery. The Bible does not treat the subject in depth, except to record it as a reality which the patriarchs, the prophets, and succeeding generations of Jews faced. In the post-Biblical period, Judaism developed a doctrine

of the afterlife and belief in immortality while constantly stressing the meaning and importance of life in this world.

Jewish tradition has developed a regimen of mourning rites. Properly understood and practiced, they have the power to help us face the fact of death with calm and strength, while making it difficult for damaging fantasies and illusions to develop. It would be a stark and perilous experience to face the fact of death without the framework of such practices and without the faith which they imply.

Especially at a time when we mourn the death of one we loved do we need the help and comfort that other people can give us, and the sustenance and support which are part of our faith in God. Faith affirms life. It can give strength to the mourner and solace to the dying. Faith has been defined as "the courage to be," the power to enjoy life's blessings sustained by the hope that as we become better human beings we can help make the world a better place in which to live. The ability to grow in spirit makes death a less fearful experience to us. When we develop a measure of faith in ourselves, and in God who sustains life, we can find meaning for our own existence so basic and supportive that neither life nor death can overwhelm us. Then we can state with the Psalmist, "Yea, though I walk in a valley overshadowed by death, I will fear no evil, for You are with me."

Comforting the mourner is a *mitzvah*, a religious obligation. It is an act done in the total absence of any other motivation, or hope of being rewarded. This is a creative, spiritual act. Deep sensitivity is required.

What should be said by those who come to comfort? Our Sages cautioned us against entering into a polemic on the mystery of death in the presence of those who are deep in mourning. They warned against superficial philosophizing and meaningless, unreal statements calculated to ease the pain of grief. Grief is painful, and real, and its expression should not be prevented. This is not to exclude comforter and mourner from concrete discussions which can lead to a better understanding of life and death, at the proper moment.

The mourner needs sympathy, love, and care. He or she should be involved in discussions which focus upon the dignity and meaning in the life of the dead. It is most helpful to share with the mourner some incident from the life of the dead which illustrates kindness or humor or other fine attributes. The attitude toward death held by those who visit a house of mourning will have much to do with the way in which they comfort the bereaved. Our own fears and anxieties at such moments can have an effect upon those who are mourning. Discomfort and disjointed language and thoughts are bound to have an adverse effect upon those in need of consolation.

It is my hope that this addition to the liturgical creations of The Rabbinical Assembly will help us through moments of grief, guide us in the institutions of Jewish religious practice in the home and synagogue, afford us opportunities for prayer, meditation and understanding, and introduce us to the ideas and ideals of extraordinary people who have pondered over the theology and psychology of death. May those of us who mourn know that we are all cut from the same

human pattern designed by God and that we share both in the joys and sorrows of the people Israel and mankind.

Rabbi Edward T. Sandrow
Chairman, Liturgical Publications Committee
The Rabbinical Assembly

AN ACKNOWLEDGMENT

The Hebrew texts of the services, and their translation, are based upon the *Mahzor for Rosh Hashanah and Yom Kippur* published by The Rabbinical Assembly. Unless otherwise noted, all selections and translations in this volume are by the editor, Rabbi Jules Harlow, whose invaluable help and guidance made the labors of the chairman much lighter and through whose creative talents we have added a much needed volume to the spiritual legacy of The Rabbinical Assembly.

E.T.S.

✍ A guide
to practice

Since Judaism is a way of life, Jewish tradition teaches specific ways of confronting all aspects of life, including death. Our tradition's practices in this area are governed by respect for the dead and concern for the mourner. Dignity and taste are further basic assumptions of Jewish law in mourning.

Only an outline of observance can be presented in these pages. A rabbi should be consulted for further information, interpretation and guidance. A rabbi should be consulted as soon as possible after a death occurs.

Those who are interested in reading more complete works on the subject will benefit from the following:

A Guide to Life, by Rabbi H. Rabinowicz, Jewish Chronicle Publications.

The Jewish Way in Death and Mourning, by Rabbi Maurice Lamm, Jonathan David Publishers.

Shulḥan Arukh (Code of Jewish Law), *Yoreh Deah*, 340–403.

Who is a mourner?

We are obliged to mourn for a father, mother, son, daughter, brother, sister (including half-brother and half-sister), husband or wife, but not for an infant less than thirty days old. Males from the age of thirteen years and one day and females from the age of twelve years and one day should observe the laws of mourning.

We are *permitted* to observe the mourning rites for anyone, not only for the relatives listed above.

Between death and burial

During this period the mourner is known as an *onen.* The most important duty of an *onen* is arranging for the funeral and the burial of the dead. In recognition of this and of the mourner's state of mind at this time, the *onen* is exempted from fulfilling other religious duties, such as reciting prayers or putting on *tefillin,* and is not called to the Torah in the synagogue. (The *onen* is exempt from fulfilling religious duties even if others are attending to the funeral arrangements.) An *onen* should not drink wine, eat meat, or say a blessing before or after eating, nor should he or she indulge in luxuries or pleasures, or conduct business and professional activities. On Shabbat or on a Festival, an *onen* follows

the appropriate public observances of the day, which include eating meat, drinking wine, and reciting benedictions.

While one may want to offer an *onen* assistance in making the funeral arrangements, it is *not* appropriate to visit the *onen* during this time, at home or at a funeral chapel.

Respect for the dead

Human life is sacred. The human body deserves respect, even after the breath of life has left it. Respect for the dead *(k'vod hamet)* is a fundamental principle governing Jewish practice. One expression of this respect is the ritual washing *(taharah)* of the dead body which is then dressed in shrouds *(takhrikhim)*. This is done by members of the *hevrah kadishah*, a group traditionally devoted to the proper burial of the dead.

A dead body is not to be left alone before the funeral. Although some sources trace this practice to the necessity of protecting the body from harm, not leaving the body unattended is essentially another way of showing respect to the dead. It is appropriate for mourners and other members of the family and friends to be with the body. In order to maintain a constant watch, however, arrangements are made for other individuals *(shomrim, watchers)* to be with the body day and night. Those who are with the body should spend their time chanting and reading from the Book of Psalms.

Since ancient times it has been considered degrading to leave the dead unburied. Jewish tradition

A guide to practice

---

teaches that the dead must be buried as soon as possible, usually within twenty-four hours after death. A delay is permitted when it is needed to obtain shrouds or a proper coffin, or for the sake of honoring the dead by waiting for relatives and friends who must travel great distances.

The dead are not to be put on display. It is improper to apply cosmetics to the dead, just as it is improper to dress the dead in anything other than shrouds or to provide an expensive coffin. The coffin, which is covered with an appropriate cloth, is not opened at the funeral.

People who want to express their respect and their sympathy in a tangible way should contribute to a favorite cause of the deceased, rather than send flowers to the home or to the chapel. Mourners generally prefer being notified of charitable contributions made in memory of the dead to receiving specially prepared baskets or cartons of food or sweets. Jewish tradition has always emphasized concern for the living, helping the needy in this world. This is also a way of extending the influence of the dead after he or she is no longer walking this earth.

Shrouds and coffin

The body of the dead is clothed in plain white linen, cotton, or muslin shrouds *(takhrikhim).*

The Talmud records that at one time the bodies of the wealthy were brought to burial on a richly ornamented, stately bed, while the bodies of the poor were brought to burial on a plain platform (bier). This

practice brought shame and embarrassment to the poor. Therefore, we are informed, a law was instituted that all of the dead, rich and poor alike, were to be brought to burial on a plain bier. (The dead at that time were not buried in coffins, just as they are not buried in coffins in contemporary Israel.)

The Talmud also records that at one time the expense of burying the dead was harder to bear than the fact of death itself. It reached the point that families sometimes abandoned the bodies of relatives to escape the burden of an overwhelming expense. Then the distinguished Rabban Gamaliel left instructions that he be buried in plain linen shrouds rather than in the expensive garments which he and his family easily could have afforded. His act set an impressive precedent, and since that time Jewish tradition has insisted upon simple burial with a minimum expense.

Our tradition teaches that all Jews are to be buried in the same type of inexpensive garments (takhrikhim). This practice also emphasizes the fact that all people, rich and poor alike, are equal before God. The same principle is reflected in the requirement of a plain, inexpensive wooden coffin. It is customary for a dead man to be buried in a tallit which he used during his life, after one of the fringes has been cut to make it ritually unfit. Objects of value for the living are not buried with the dead.

Kriah

Kriah, a tear made in the mourner's clothing or on a ribbon attached to the clothing, is an external symbol of

inner grief and mourning. It has been so considered since ancient times. In the Bible, Jacob, David, and Job, for example, reacted to reports of death by rending their garments. *Kriah* is usually made immediately preceding the start of the funeral service. It must be done for the mourner while the mourner is standing, signifying that we should confront sorrow directly.

For a parent, *kriah* is on the left side, close to the heart. For all others, *kriah* is on the right side. A benediction is recited by the mourner just before *kriah*: *Barukh attah Adonai eloheinu melekh ha'olam, dayan ha-emet.* "Praised are You, Lord our God, King of the universe, the true judge." Like the mourner's *kaddish*, this benediction is a reaffirmation of faith, and of the value of life, made at a time of intense sorrow and pain. *Kriah* should be visible throughout the period of *shivah*, but not on Shabbat.

If one learns of a relative's death within thirty days after the fact, *kriah* is required. *Kriah* is always required whenever one learns of a parent's death, regardless of the length of time that has elapsed since the day of death.

The funeral: Levayah

The literal translation of *levayah*, "accompanying," teaches us that the nature of a Jewish funeral implies involvement. It is a *mitzvah* and an act of respect not only to attend the funeral service, but especially to actually accompany the dead, walking behind the coffin for at least a few feet immediately after the funeral or at the cemetery.

Both the funeral and the burial services are brief. The Biblical and other texts read generally emphasize human mortality, resignation to God's inscrutable will, affirmation of life, acknowledgment of God as the true judge, and immortality of the soul.

At the cemetery

The dead are buried in the earth. "For dust you are and to dust you shall return" (Genesis 3:10).

We show our respect and love for the dead through personal involvement in the funeral and burial. Members of the family and friends serve as pallbearers, carrying and escorting the coffin to the hearse after the funeral service and to the grave at the cemetery. The procession pauses several times on its way to the grave.

It is appropriate for relatives and friends to drop several spadefulls of earth on the lowered coffin, another act of involvement reflecting their constant concern for one whom they loved. Laborers may then fill the grave. (Some recite *kaddish* after the coffin is covered with earth; others wait until the grave is filled.) After reciting *kaddish*, the mourners walk between two lines formed by the others present, who say *Hamakom y'nahem etkhem b'tokh sh'ar aveilei tzion virushalayim.* "May the Almighty comfort you with all the other mourners of Zion and Jerusalem."

Before leaving the cemetery it is customary to rinse the hands. Further, it is also customary to rinse the hands before entering the home upon returning from the cemetery.

Mourner's kaddish

A mourner first recites *kaddish* at the cemetery after burial. This particular *kaddish* is known as the burial *kaddish*; thereafter the regular mourner's *kaddish* is recited. The *kaddish* is generally thought of as a prayer for the dead. But while the mourner's *kaddish* certainly is recited in that context, it does not mention death or the dead. Essentially it is an affirmation of life and faith. It confronts death with life. Reciting the mourner's *kaddish* is an act of looking to the future and all of life with faith and hope, in the presence of grief and despair.

Kaddish originally referred to a brief prayer and response recited at the close of Rabbinic lessons in the ancient synagogue and house of study. Such lessons would end with a discourse containing a message of comfort and consolation. The *kaddish* extended that message as a prayer of messianic hope. The name of God is not mentioned in the *kaddish*, which emphasizes hallowing and praising Him through redemption of life in this world and through the universal acceptance of His sovereignty. In addition to the form of *kaddish* known as mourner's *kaddish*, there are several variations recited at the conclusion of various sections of the prayer service.

Kaddish is an Aramaic word meaning holy. Recitation of *kaddish* is an act of hallowing and praising God and His name. In Jewish tradition, such an act must take place in public assembly, which is defined as at least a quorum of ten adults *(minyan)*. Thus the *kaddish*, in any variation, is recited only in the presence of a *minyan*.

The recitation of mourner's *kaddish* and other prayers is very important, but it should be kept in mind that respect for the dead is essentially shown through the quality of one's life.

Mourner's *kaddish* is recited for eleven months. In a leap year, First Adar and Second Adar are counted as two separate months. Mourner's *kaddish* is also recited on each anniversary of the death *(yahrzeit)*, and at Memorial Services on Yom Kippur, Sukkot, Pesaḥ and Shavuot.

Kaddish derabanan (page 21) is a variation of *kaddish* recited after the study or reading of a Rabbinic text.

Meal of consolation

A mourner's first meal after returning from the cemetery *(se'udat havra'ah)* is provided by friends and neighbors, who thus express their concern in a practical way. The meal generally includes hard boiled eggs, lentils or other round objects symbolizing fate and the wheel of life for some, symbolizing life and hope for others. In ancient times the egg symbolized life and resurrection. Neither wine nor meat is served at this meal.

Visiting a house of mourning

The *mitzvah* of comforting mourners *(niḥum aveilim)* is fulfilled by a personal visit to the house of mourning. Fulfilling this *mitzvah*, in Rabbinic tradition, is "one of the things which bring good to the world." The very

fact that you have come to a house of mourning is an act of consolation. Sitting with the mourner is an act of respect and comfort. One need not be mute, but neither should one feel compelled to maintain a constant flow of conversation. The most appropriate topic of conversation is the person who died, and his or her life. It is customary for a visitor to wait for the mourner to begin a conversation. A visit should not be unduly long, and certainly is not the time for general socializing.

People visiting a house of mourning should not expect to be served or even offered food by any of the mourners, who thus would be acting in the inappropriate role of hosts at a social gathering.

Upon leaving, one addresses several formal words to the mourners. *Hamakom y'nahem etkhem b'tokh sh'ar aveilei tzion virushalayim.* "May the Almighty comfort you with all the other mourners of Zion and Jerusalem."

Shivah

Shivah means seven, the number of days in the stage of mourning which begins after burial. This observance is traced to ancient times. We read in the Bible that Joseph mourned seven days after his father's death. Mourners stay together at the home of the deceased or at the home of a mourner, cut off from the normal routine of their lives which death has interrupted. They abstain from business and professional activities, sexual intercourse, bathing or anointing the body, using cosmetics, and cutting hair. If severe financial loss

would result from not working, the mourner is permitted to return to work after observing the mourning for three days, including a brief observance the third day.

Mourners sit only on low stools or benches and do not wear leather footwear. (Exceptions are made for pregnant women and others for whom this might cause difficulties.) The mourner should be seated when people offer their condolences; the mourner is not to act as a host or hostess. Mirrors (symbols of vanity) are either covered in a house of mourning or turned to the wall.

The first three days of *shivah* constitute a period of more intense mourning. During this period, mourners observing tradition strictly will not greet people. They may, however, initiate a conversation. It is customary for people visiting a mourner not to speak before the mourner begins the conversation.

The day of the burial counts as the first day of *shivah*. *Shivah* ends on the morning of the seventh day, after one hour.

Shabbat is included in counting the seven days, though on Shabbat no outward signs of mourning apply. The mourners should wear regular shoes, sit on regular chairs, and change into clothing that bears no signs of mourning. They also attend synagogue services.

On Friday (unless it is the seventh day of *shivah*) or on the day before a Festival, *shivah* is observed until two and one half hours before sunset. On Pesaḥ eve it ends at noon.

A Festival, Rosh Hashanah, or Yom Kippur, annul the remainder of *shivah*, provided that the mourner has first observed at least one hour of *shivah*.

A candle, which burns continuously for seven days, is lit upon returning home from the cemetery. The light of the candle symbolizes the soul. "The soul of man is the light of the Lord" (Proverbs 20:27).

At the end of *shivah* the mourners should take a short walk together, symbolizing their return to life's normal routine.

When speaking of the deceased, a Hebrew phrase is generally added: *alav hashalom* (may he rest in peace) or *aleha hashalom* (may she rest in peace). *Zikhrono livrakhah* (for a male) and *zikhronah livrakhah* (for a female) are also used, meaning "of blessed memory."

Shloshim

Shloshim ("thirty") ends on the morning of the thirtieth day after the funeral. The period from the end of *shivah* to the end of *shloshim* is one of transition from deep bereavement to resuming life's normal routine. A mourner during this period does not wear new clothes or cut the hair, does not participate in general festivities, and avoids public places of entertainment. A mourner does not attend parties celebrating a *brit milah*, *pidyon haben*, or a wedding, though he or she may attend the ceremonies. When mourning a parent's death, restrictions continue until twelve months after the day of death.

At the end of *shloshim* it is appropriate for family and friends to gather together to read or study appropriate texts and to speak about the dead.

If mourning has been observed for at least one hour before a Festival, *shivah* is ended by that Festival. In that event, *shloshim* ends fifteen days after the last

A guide to practice

17

day of Pesaḥ or Shavuot, and eight days after the last day of Sukkot.

When *shivah* is completed before a Festival, *shloshim* ends when the Festival begins. When *shivah* is completed before Rosh Hashanah, *shloshim* ends when Yom Kippur begins. When *shivah* ends before Yom Kippur, *shloshim* ends with Sukkot.

If burial took place during *ḥol hamo'ed*, the intermediate days of a Festival, *shivah* begins after the last day of the Festival, which counts as one of the days of *shivah* and of *shloshim*.

If one does not learn of a relative's death immediately, but within thirty days after the funeral, *shivah* and *shloshim* begin at once, and *kriah* is required. If one learns of a relative's death more than thirty days after the funeral, neither *shivah* nor *shloshim* is observed. The mourner in such an event should remove the shoes and sit on the floor or on a low stool for one hour as a sign of mourning.

Whenever one learns of a parent's death, whether after thirty days or after a full year, *kriah* is required. As in the case of other relatives, one does not observe *shivah* or *shloshim* when hearing of a parent's death more than thirty days after the fact, but mourning practices of the full year apply until twelve months after the day of burial.

Tisha B'av and Purim

It is customary for mourners to attend synagogue services to hear the Book of Lamentations *(Eikhah)* and to recite prayers and lamentations *(kinot)*. They should at-

tend Purim services to hear the reading of the Book of Esther (The *Megillah*), though they should not of course participate in any joyous celebration of the day.

Tombstone

It is customary to place a tombstone *(matzeivah)* on a grave, dedicating it in a brief ceremony which usually takes place eleven months after the death. It may take place at any time after the period of *shivah*.

There is a variety of practices concerning inscriptions, though the tendency emphasizes simplicity. Usually the Hebrew letters *pei* and *nun* appear, abbreviations for the words meaning "here lies buried" *(po nikbar/nikberah)*. The Hebrew and English names of the dead, dates of birth and death, and the Hebrew letters 'ת'נ'צ'ב'ה' are generally included. These letters are the initials of the words in the phrase *tehei nishmato/nishmatah tzerurah bitzror ha-ḥayim.* "May his/her soul be bound up in the bond of life."

While the formal unveiling of a tombstone is of significance to the family and friends, Jewish tradition has not emphasized it as a basic ceremony. Care should be taken to avoid the extremes of either another funeral or a festive reunion, at the cemetery or at home.

Respect paid to the memory of the dead is not confined to the site where the earthly remains are interred. But as the grave does symbolize a memorial for the dead it is an appropriate place for family and friends to gather in respect.

The formal unveiling itself is a symbol, signifying that we must unveil our hearts, opening them to the

memory of the dead, to the meaning of their lives, to their influence upon our lives, and to appropriate ways of perpetuating their memory.

Yahrzeit

Yahrzeit is observed on each anniversary of the day of death according to the Hebrew calendar.

One who is not certain of the day when a relative died should select an appropriate date on which to observe *yahrzeit* each year.

A candle should burn in the home during the twenty-four hour period of *yahrzeit*, sunset to sunset, starting on the evening preceding the day. Light symbolizes the soul, as it is written in the Book of Proverbs: "The soul of man is the light of the Lord."

When the *yahrzeit* coincides with Shabbat or a Festival, the *yahrzeit* candle should be lit before the candle-lighting for the day.

It is appropriate to fulfill some *mitzvah* in honor of the dead on this day. This could consist of study, acting as *ba'al tefillah* in the synagogue, or contributing to some worthy cause in memory of the deceased. It is also appropriate for family and friends to gather on the *yahrzeit* for the purpose of recalling various aspects of and events in the life of the dead, perpetuating his or her memory in a warm and intimate atmosphere.

Mourner's *kaddish* is recited at all services on the *yahrzeit*, from evening services on the night before through afternoon services on the day itself. On Shabbat before the *yahrzeit* one should receive an *aliyah* at

synagogue services and perhaps recite the *haftarah* as well.

One who is unable to recite Mourner's *kaddish* on the day of *yahrzeit* may do so at the evening service following the day of *yahrzeit*.

Yizkor

Yizkor ("May God remember") services in memory of the dead are held on Yom Kippur, the eighth day of Sukkot, the last day of Pesaḥ and the second day of Shavuot. Contrary to popular opinion, a person with a living parent may attend *yizkor* services.

৯ Grief and mourning

Our loving attachments, though we like to think of them as steady, fixed, and enduring, change a good deal over the years. Those of us who are fortunate enough to survive sixty or seventy years die out of a family which usually is entirely different from the family into which we are born. We are born to our parents and we usually die away from our children.

Over our life span we have gradually managed to outgrow our need for our parents, usually attached ourselves to husband or wife, and generally sustained a relation with our children which varies in closeness. Not only does the object of our love change, but so does its intensity. A small child who loses a parent is catastrophically overwhelmed by the loss. An adult, whose aged parents die when they have already begun to suffer the consequences of old age, even as he grieves for

them, can be sufficiently detached to feel relieved that they are spared further misery.

The nature of our love changes too. When we marry, we each love our partner because we feel we are achieving a union with the person whom we regard as the representation of one or more ideals that we hold, ideals of beauty, of character, of personality, or of virtue. As we age together as a couple, we come to realize that we have each married a real person with faults as well as virtues, and we lose the illusions which we held at first. The first love, based upon union with an ideal, is succeeded by a more realistic love based upon companionship, intimacy, and shared interests and experiences.

At times, these transitions may take place gradually, and at other times abruptly. There are long periods in our lives when these changes take place so gradually that we scarcely recognize that they occur. There are other occasions, the milestones of life, when a child becomes a *Bar* or *Bat Mitzvah*, when he graduates from school, when a son or daughter becomes engaged and then married, when a child is born, when there is a divorce or death, which remind us forcefully that a significant change is taking place and that an attachment which we have enjoyed is about to be terminated or significantly altered. When we lose someone by death, our grief marks a relatively abrupt loss. When a son or daughter marries, we are pained by our loss even as we rejoice for the enrichment of our lives which the new young family will bring. And that is why we weep at weddings as well as at funerals.

Weeping is the visible and audible expression of

Grief and mourning

23

our craving for reunion with the person from whom we are being separated. As infants, we cry to compel our mothers to return and care for us. Thereafter we weep when we are overwhelmed by a craving for reunion with someone we have loved when we have abused, alienated, or lost the love. We weep when we witness a change, as at a *Bar Mitzvah* ceremony, a wedding ceremony, or a funeral. We may also weep when illness, accident, defeat, or catastrophe make us feel helpless and force us back into the position of the infant who cries for his protecting and rescuing mother. When someone we love has died, we weep because we wish to undo that separation; and we weep also because we feel so helpless in our loss and pain.

Grief, then, is the experience of pain which occurs when we acknowledge a loss. We grieve for our deserted and abandoned selves, and we grieve the lack of fulfillment and the loss of joy which death has imposed upon the one who has died. Mourning begins after we have acknowledged our loss. It is driven by grief. Grief impels us, since we cannot really undo the loss, to review the pleasures and gratifications of the past. We feel pain as we contrast the remembered pleasures of the past with the stark loneliness and frustration of the present and of the future, in which our loved one will no longer participate. But fortunately, as this painful review proceeds, the ties gradually become relaxed, the loss seems less overwhelming, and each successive remembering of each pleasurable event in the past is a little less painful than the previous one. The process of mourning, therefore, is the process of accommodating ourselves to the new reality, to the world in which the

Grief and mourning

loved individual no longer exists. It makes it possible for us to make peace with this reality and to live with it.

As we mourn, we gradually revise the image of the world with which we live. In the new world, the loved individual no longer exists. We change our way of life so that we no longer look to the individual whom we have lost for the pleasures to which we have become accustomed. We replace that person to some extent, with one or more others, or we learn to do without the individual and the love. Just as the adolescent often finds it helpful, in the process of detaching himself from his parents, to adopt their views, their values, their standards and ideals, so many of us find it helpful to accommodate ourselves to the loss of someone we have loved, even late in life, by changing our own way of life so that it resembles more that of the individual we have lost. When our parents die, we model ourselves after them more faithfully than before. When a husband or wife dies, we adopt his or her interests more seriously than before. When a child of ours dies, we make his or her individual personality or interest a central focus of our lives. The process of mourning cannot be evaded. The more we immerse ourselves in it, the sooner it is over. If we try to ignore it, we impose upon ourselves the handicap of living in a world that no longer exists.

Grief is least intense and mourning is easiest when an adult son or daughter has lost an aged parent. The emotional disengagement actually has occurred gradually over a period of years. The importance of the parent has been eclipsed by the role of spouse and children. And the death of an aging parent spares him the

Grief and mourning

pain and humiliation which physical debility and mental senility bring. On the other hand, there are some adults who have never been able to become at all self-reliant. They have been able to live only by the emotional nourishment of another individual, whether a parent, a sibling, a spouse, or even a child. When this nourishing and supporting individual dies, and the survivor's mental equilibrium is seriously threatened, he responds to the event not so much with grief as with anger; he strives less to reconcile himself to reality than by his anger to force reality to return to him that which has been taken away, as if that were possible.

His anger is directed in many instances against the dead parent or parent-substitute who has deserted him. It may be directed against the doctor who took care of the individual who died. It may be directed against the survivor's own family. These angry feelings may be expressed openly; they may be entirely repressed, and expressed therefore only indirectly; or part of the anger may be expressed and the other part concealed. Most often perhaps, the individual turns the anger against himself, fearing that if he did willingly entertain anger against the individual by whom he feels abandoned, he would be punished. Anger turned against oneself creates guilt and a tendency to criticize and to punish oneself. One angry individual may complain that his loved one who has died was neglected by the doctor; another will complain that he himself had neglected to call the doctor soon enough or to get the right doctor.

The individual who feels guilty becomes obsessed with incidents in which he had hurt the person who

died, and he wonders whether any of these hurts could have facilitated the ultimate death. Guilt also has a positive aspect; that is, it expresses a wish for reconciliation. The survivor expresses his wish to become reconciled with the individual whom he has lost by criticizing and punishing himself, or by making sacrifices, such as generous contributions to charity. Anger and guilt are not wholesome responses, in contrast to grief, which is a wholesome response. Anger is not helpful and it may alienate otherwise friendly and important people who could help the survivor to regain some peace of mind. Anger directed against the self, if sufficiently intense, may trigger depressive illness. It should be remembered, though, that these distinctions are not hard and fast, and many otherwise normal people experience some feelings of anger or guilt in their response and bereavement. The difference between the normal and the abnormal is that in the latter instance the anger or guilt becomes an obsessive, overriding concern and does not remit.

Expression of guilt and sadness will vary with the individual's disposition and with the expectations of the community in which he lives. Some individuals permit themselves to express their feelings openly while others try to restrain the expression of feelings. A few individuals tend to exaggerate their feelings in order to elicit sympathy or some other response. In ancient times, in some communities, the survivor engaged professional mourners to display his grief in a ritualized way. In many societies today it is considered to be a sign of sophistication and especially of "manliness" to show almost no feeling. No one degree of visi-

ble expression of grief is more wholesome than another, or more useful in reaching an accommodation with the changed reality. For as we noted above, it is not grief or its expression which brings about the healing, but the silent and time-consuming process of mourning.

There is ordinarily no need for medical attention to the bereaved individual. Most of us become frightened when we see an individual displaying raw emotion, especially grief and anger. We would like to suppress such displays. But comforting the mourner does not mean that we must discourage his expression of grief. In fact, the expression of grief itself may be comforting in the sense that the process of weeping often brings relief to the individual who feels misery. Comforting the bereaved individual means helping him to pass from the world which has been destroyed, the world in which he enjoyed the love of the individual who has died, to the new world in which he must live without that individual. When we comfort the bereaved individual we are offering him our own love, in the hope that it may to some slight extent replace the love which he has lost.

If there is persistent insomnia, the individual's physician may or may not wish to prescribe sedation in small amounts. If expression of grief or the process of mourning becomes protracted so that the individual remains seriously disabled for more than a month or so, then it may be that mourning has been gradually transformed into incipient depressive illness. If that is the case, then medical attention is required. It would be wise when severe grief and mourning are unduly

Grief and mourning

protracted to arrange to have a physician, preferably a psychiatrist, attempt to assess whether and to what extent mourning has been usurped by illness.

In daily life, society requires that we attempt to protect those around us, with whom we live and work and play, from the unpleasant and potentially offensive impact of inappropriate or excessive displays of feeling. We do this by observing an etiquette, a set of rules of conduct which tell us what is appropriate and what is inappropriate in most of the situations which we ordinarily encounter. When we grieve for someone whom we have loved and lost, our feelings are generally far more intense than they are in other circumstances, and if we are angered by the loss, our anger is apt to hurt those around us. Those who come to visit us fear lest they inadvertently hurt us in our grief-stricken state, and they also fear lest our anger and resentment hurt them. Therefore, in every society and culture a special etiquette is imposed for grieving and mourning and for visiting and comforting the bereaved. In fact, because our feelings toward the individual whom we have loved but who has abandoned us are often so mixed, containing both yearning and anger in varying proportions, there is a fairly strict etiquette that determines the burial ceremony itself. In its most important features, the etiquette becomes a fixed ritual; in its less crucial aspects, it remains a preferred mode of conduct.

Jewish burial requires a frank acknowledgement of the loss by insisting that the bereaved witness and indeed participate in the burial. The act of *kriah* serves as a visible expression of grief and symbolic acceptance

of injury to oneself. Injuring oneself, we have seen, expresses the feeling of guilt, and in an unconscious way is meant to appease the protecting person who, by dying, has abandoned us, or who has failed to protect us against the tragic loss of someone else whom we have loved. The enforced abstention from work and from the ordinary activities of daily life during the period of *shivah*, facilitates the process of mourning. The obligation upon family and friends to comfort the mourner, helps him to redistribute his resources of love and encourages him to accept support and affection from others.

Immediately following the death of a close relative, the survivor is said to be an *onen*. The individual is presumed to be in a state of shock; he may be too shocked even to express grief and certainly too shocked to begin the process of mourning. This state of *aninut* lasts until the burial takes place. Immediately thereafter the period of *shivah* begins, which lasts seven days, the first three days of the period being observed as an interval of more intense mourning, so that the mourner is considered more receptive to the comfort of friends only thereafter. During the period of *aninut* the individual is considered responsible for meeting almost no obligations except those which are most urgent. During the period of *shivah* he is expected to abstain from ordinary activity but to meet minimal obligations. After the termination of *shivah*, until thirty days have elapsed from the date of burial, the individual may resume ordinary business and professional obligations, but he is expected to restrict participation in pleasures. At the end of these first thirty days

Grief and mourning

(*shloshim*), he is permitted to become somewhat more lenient with himself, though he remains technically a mourner and observes restrictions until a year has passed following the death of the individual whom he mourns. (The mourner's *kaddish* is recited for eleven months.) Every year thereafter on the anniversary of the death, he observes *yahrzeit*.

This is a schedule, then, for graduated expression of the subsiding intensity of grief and mourning. This schedule discourages us from mourning either too little or too much. It reduces our concern that we might not be showing enough respect to the memory of the one whom we have lost. It also prevents us from cutting short the period of mourning before it has been properly completed.

From the point of view of mental hygiene, we know of no procedure which can facilitate a more prompt or rapid healing of the psychic wound, nor any which deters more effectively the deterioration of mourning into depression. Well-meaning friends and family, out of their own inability to face the grief of the bereaved, attempt to protect them in one way or another from the full realization of the loss. While nothing is to be gained by reporting clinical details of the anguish of death, it is to the advantage of the bereaved that he acknowledge fully that death has occurred and that he participate as fully as he can in prescribed burial and mourning ritual. Exceptions should be considered only in the case of children, or individuals who are physically ill or mentally ill.

Rabbis and physicians are often asked whether a surviving child should be permitted to attend the fu-

neral and the burial. The injury which threatens his stability and mental health is the actual loss of his parent. He will not be protected against that loss by being shielded from the normal rituals. These rituals are painful but they are not the cause of illness. If the child is old enough to understand what is happening, he should not be shielded from the funeral ritual. The actual burial would probably be too shocking for a younger child, but one might be guided by the wishes of a child eight years old or older. In making plans for the child, one should keep in mind that what the child does not see or hear, he fills in for himself by fantasy. Since his fantasy is created in the midst of a catastrophe, it is usually a horrid fantasy, far worse than reality. The more of reality he can observe, the less opportunity there is for distressing fantasy. If the child is left at home while the other members of the family go off to the funeral service and burial ground, what must he think is going on that he is not permitted to see?

Similar considerations obtain in the case of adults who are not well. Since they cannot be protected against the loss itself, depriving them of normal ritual mourning makes the loss more painful for them to endure. However, while the shock of disclosure is extremely painful but not dangerous for the normal individual, it might be dangerous for one who is physically or mentally ill. Under such circumstances, one is best guided by the physician who is caring for the ill individual.

A word should be said about the fact that most children can neither grieve nor mourn. The thought of death is far too disturbing for them to acknowledge or

to come to terms with. To a much greater extent than most adults, they can simply ignore it. They do not revise the image of their world to correct it for the loss, but manage to ignore the discrepancy between the absence of the lost parent or relative and their silent expectation that he is still around somewhere. They will talk as though they know and have come to terms with the facts, but inwardly they cling to old images and out of date realities. Nothing can or should be done to force them to grieve or to mourn. The process of mourning will come about spontaneously some time later, during adolescence.

One would think that philosophy is of little consequence to the survivor at the time of bereavement. Yet we all feel that we have to know why things happen. Psychoanalysts speak of a "need for causality." When death is expected and prepared for, the survivor can easily see the naturalness of the event and, though he acknowledges his pain, he reconciles himself to its inevitability. But when death is unexpected or the loss too overwhelming, the survivor feels disappointed and let down by whatever kind of order he has assumed to exist in the universe. He recollects religious concepts of reward and punishment, and protests as though moral behavior guaranteed eternal life and freedom from pain and disappointment. The anger to which we have referred previously, may now be directed against God, against religion or against the rabbi. The survivor sees in the death a sign of the absence of order and constancy, a sign of chaos in the universe. Humans cannot tolerate a world without order, without cause and effect, controlled by what may seem to be a capricious

God who ignores an individual's behavior in determining his fate. But the life-death cycle, viewed from the historical rather than an individual point of view, is indeed a constant and it does reflect an orderly universe. While the experience of grief makes it difficult to retain a historical and philosophical perspective, the process of mourning leads us back to the realization that all who live must die, and that what matters for the community is *how* we have lived rather than how *long* we have lived. At a time when life seems so futile and fragile, the process of mourning and the rituals associated with it make us feel that we are not alone, but part of an enduring community. Our religion teaches us to view the world and its changes, life and death, good and bad fortune "from the viewpoint of Heaven" (*taḥat aspeklaryat ha-shamayim*) which transcends the view of any one individual.

Dr. Mortimer Ostow

Rabbinic sources

After the formal study or exposition of one or more of the following sources in the presence of a minyan, all rise as the mourners recite kaddish derabanan *(page 21 of the other section).*

One is obliged to bless God for the evil in life in the same spirit as one blesses God for the good in life, as it is written, "Love the Lord your God with all your heart, and all your soul and all your might" (Deuteronomy 6:5). In the Hebrew for "heart" in this verse, the letter *bet* is repeated *(levav)*; usually the word is written with one *bet (lev)*. From this we derive the lesson that we must love God with *both* of our impulses, the impulse to evil and the impulse to good. "And with all your soul" means, even if He takes your soul, your life; "And with all your might"—with all of your material possessions. . . .

At the close of every benediction recited at the First Temple in Jerusalem they would utter "from everlasting" *(min ha-olam)*. But after heretics had begun to pervert the truth by teaching that there is only one world *(olam)*, it was decreed that they should conclude with the words "from everlasting to everlasting" *(min ha-olam v'ad ha-olam)*.

Mishnah Berakhot 9:5

ﳥ How did they exhort witnesses in capital cases to give truthful testimony? They would admonish them as follows: You may be intending to offer as testimony that which is supposition or rumor or the repetition of evidence submitted to another court, or perhaps you may be intending to say that you heard it from a reliable person, or perhaps you are unaware that we will cross-examine you. You must realize that capital cases are not the same as cases concerning property. In cases concerning property, one who is found guilty may make atonement by paying a fine. But in capital cases, the executed person's blood and the blood of those who could have been his descendants are inseparably attached to one who gives wrong evidence, to the end of all generations. For we have seen that in the case of Cain, who slew his brother, it is written, "Your brother's bloods cry out" (Genesis 4:10). The verse does not say *blood* but *bloods*, referring to Abel's blood and the blood of his succeeding generations, who will never be born. Therefore the Bible relates that God created Adam, a single human being, as the forefather of all mankind. This teaches us that to destroy a single life is to destroy a whole world, even as to save a single

Rabbinic sources

life is to save a whole world. That all people have a common ancestor should make for peace, since no one can say to anyone else: "My father was greater than your father." That mankind began with a single human being is an answer to heretics who could claim the existence of more than one Creator. That mankind began with a single human being proclaims forever the greatness of the Holy One. For man stamps many coins with one die and they all look alike, but the Holy One stamped every human being with the stamp of Adam, yet no person is like any other. Therefore, every human being must declare, "It is for my sake that the world was created."

Sanhedrin 4:5

Hillel would say: Do not separate yourself from the community. Do not trust yourself until the day of your death. Do not judge anyone else until you are in his situation. Do not say anything that is unintelligible in the hope that it will ultimately be understood. And do not say, "When I have leisure I will study." Perhaps you will have no leisure.

Mishnah Avot 2:5

Rabbi Eliezer would say: Let the honor of your fellow be as dear to you as your own. Be not easily moved to anger. And repent one day before your death.

Mishnah Avot 2:15

Rabbi Simeon would say: Be scrupulous in reading the *sh'ma* and in saying the *amidah*. When you pray, do not regard your prayer as a fixed, mechanical form,

Rabbinic sources

but as an act of supplication and compassion in God's Presence. For as the prophet Joel has said, "He is gracious and compassionate, slow to anger and abundant in lovingkindness, repenting of evil" (Joel 2:13). Be not evil in your own eyes.

Mishnah Avot 2:18

When Akavya ben Mahalalel was on his death bed, his son asked: "Father, commend me to your colleagues." Akavya replied, "I will not commend you." His son asked, "Have you found some fault in me?" His father answered, "No. But your own good deeds will bring you near to them without any commendation, and your own bad deeds will remove you far from them despite my commendation."

Mishnah Eduyot 5:7

When Rabbi Yoḥanan finished reading the Book of Job he would say: The end of a man is death and the end of a beast is slaughter. Every creature born must die. Blessed is he who was reared in Torah and who labored in Torah, who pleased his Creator, who lived with a good name and who departed this world with a good name. Of such a person, Solomon said, "A good name is better than precious oil, and the day of death is better than the day of birth" (Ecclesiastes 8:1).

Berakhot 17a

Raba said: When a person is brought to judgment in the world to come, questions will be asked. "Did you conduct your affairs with integrity? Did you set aside fixed times for the study of Torah? Did you oc-

cupy yourself with raising a family? Did you hope for Israel's redemption and for universal peace? Did you search for wisdom? Did you acquire understanding?" If the answer to these questions is "yes," but the person did not treasure reverence for the Lord, all the learning and the fulfillment of commandments are of little value.

Shabbat 31a

ᔇ Our Rabbis taught: During the first three days, a mourner is forbidden to work, even if the mourner is poor and depends upon charity for support. After three days, a mourner in need could do work in private . . .

Our Rabbis taught: During the first three days, a mourner is forbidden to go to another house of mourning (either to a private home or to attend a funeral at a cemetery). After the first three days a mourner may go to another house of mourning. However, he is not to take a place among the comforters there but rather among those who are being comforted.

Our Rabbis taught: During the first three days a mourner is forbidden to give a greeting. After three days, a mourner may respond to a greeting, but may not give one. After seven days, a mourner may both give a greeting and respond to one, in the usual manner.

Mo'ed Katan 21b

ᔇ "Weep not for the dead, bemoan him not" (Jeremiah 22:10). This verse should be taken to mean that we should not weep for the dead in excess, that we should not bemoan the dead beyond measure.

How is this teaching applied? In the practice of

Rabbinic sources

weeping for three days, lamenting for seven days, and refraining from cutting hair or wearing pressed clothes for thirty days. After that amount of time, we are told, the Holy One says: "You are not more compassionate towards the dead than I."

Mo'ed Katan 27b

In earlier times, the expense of burying the dead was harder to bear than the fact of death itself. Families sometimes abandoned the bodies of relatives to escape the burden of the expense. But Rabban Gamaliel set an example by disregarding his own status in terms of what was then customary. He stressed simplicity by requesting that he be buried in inexpensive linen garments. This set a precedent which then was followed by everyone. Said Rav Pappa: Nowadays, people use for shrouds even rough cloth worth a few pennies.

Mo'ed Katan 27b

Said Rabbi Yohanan: You should not speak to a mourner until the mourner begins the conversation. Thus it is written, "So they sat down with him on the ground. . .and none spoke a word to him, for they saw that his grief was very great" (Job 2:13). Only later do we read that "Job opened hir mouth" (Job 3:1). And only then do we read "Then Eliphaz the Yemenite answered. . ." (Job 4:1).

Mo'ed Katan 28b

When Rabbi Shimon Ben Zavdi died, Rabbi Levi was asked to deliver the funeral oration. He selected a verse from the book of Job as his text. "There are mines

for silver and places where gold is refined. There are places where iron is taken out of the earth and where copper is smelted out of ore" (Job 28:4).

If any of these things should be lost, they can be replaced. But when a wise man dies, how can he be replaced?

Genesis Rabbah 91:19

Two ships were sailing near the shore, one headed toward the open sea and the other headed toward the harbor. Everyone was cheering the outgoing ship, but very few cheered the incoming ship.

A wise man, observing this scene, felt it to be a great contradiction. He said that the outgoing ship should not be cheered, for nobody knows what lies in wait for it, what stormy seas it may encounter, how it would weather the storms during its voyage. But, he continued, everyone should cheer the incoming ship since it clearly has reached port safely, having concluded its journey in peace.

Exodus Rabbah 48:1

THE DEATH OF MOSES

As the time approached for Moses to leave this world, the Holy One said to him: "Behold, your time is drawing near."

Said Moses: "Dear Lord! After all my efforts on behalf of Your people, You can tell *me* that my time is drawing near? 'I shall not die, but live, and proclaim the works of the Lord!' " (Psalms 118:17).

Said God: "Moses, you cannot prevail, for 'This is the destiny of all men' " (Ecclesiastes 12:13).

Rabbinic sources

Moses wanted at least to be allowed to enter the Land of Israel. Ten times it had been decreed that he would never be permitted to set foot on that soil. But Moses refused to take the decree seriously, for he reasoned as follows: "The people Israel committed serious sins, yet whenever I prayed on their behalf, God would answer my prayer at once. Since I have not sinned from the days of my youth, does it not stand to reason that God will answer me when I pray on my own behalf?"

However, Moses finally came to realize the finality of that decree, for he put on sackcloth, drew a circle on the ground and stood within that circle, declaring: "I will not move from here until You annul the decree!" Approaching God in prayer and in supplication, he finally stated: "I will not move from this spot until judgment will have been suspended!"

Heaven and earth were shaken by the power of Moses' prayer. Heaven and earth and indeed all of creation trembled, saying: "Perhaps it is God's will to destroy this world, to create a new universe." A heavenly voice assured them: "It is not God's wish to destroy the world. The soul of every living thing is in the hands of God, and the spirit of all flesh, even the spirit of Moses. Since his end is now drawing near, and he refuses to budge, there is a great commotion in the world."

At that hour, God proclaimed that every heavenly gate should be locked to prevent Moses' prayer from ascending on high, and that the heavenly court should not accept Moses' prayer, for the decree of his death had been sealed.

Rabbinic sources

When the fiery seraphim and other heavenly creatures realized that God had decided not to grant Moses longer life, they exclaimed: "Praised be the glory of the Lord, for there is no injustice in His Presence; all persons, great and small, are treated equally."

Moses sadly asked, "Is this the reward for my forty years of labor, helping the people of Israel to become faithful, to become holy? I suffered with them. Shall I be denied the privilege of sharing their joy? If You forbid me to enter the Promised Land, You will be giving the lie to Your own Torah, which states that you must give the laborer his wages. Where are my wages for the forty years I worked on behalf of Your children?"

When God responded with silence, Moses continued: "Please, if You will not allow me to enter the Land of Israel, just let me stay alive; let me live, and not die."

"But Moses," God replied, "then you would be making My Torah fraudulent, for it is written in My Torah that 'there is none who can deliver out of My hand' " (Deuteronomy 32:39).

Said Moses to God: "Lord of the universe! If You will not allow me to enter the Land of Israel, let me be a beast of the field; let me eat grass and drink water and enjoy the world."

God replied: "Moses, you have spoken enough."

Moses persisted: "Then let me be a bird, that I might fly the length and breadth of the Holy Land, let me soar above the Promised Land and be allowed to see it in that way."

Rabbinic sources

43

God replied: "Moses, you have spoken enough."

"Then at least grant me that, after my death, my bones may be carried across the Jordan, to rest in the Holy Land."

God replied: "Moses, not even your bones will cross the Jordan."

Moses continued his plea: "Lord of the universe! Do You not recall the time when You told me, 'Come now and I will send you unto Pharaoh, that you may bring the people Israel out of bondage'? Let me lead them into the land, as I led them out of bondage."

"Moses," said God, "you are going to die, because you are a descendant of Adam."

Moses was outraged. "How can You compare me to Adam? You gave him a commandment which easily could have been obeyed, and he disobeyed it. He deserved death. But I have not transgressed Your commandments. Why, then, should I die?"

"Moses, who was your father?" God asked.

"Amram."

"And who was Amram's father?"

"Yizhar."

"And who was his father?"

"Kehat."

"And who was Kehat's father?"

"Levi."

"And who was the ancestor of them all?"

"Adam," replied Moses.

"Was the life of any of these men spared?"

"No. They are all dead."

"And yet you demand to live on?"

Moses became indignant. "Lord of the universe!

Rabbinic sources

Adam ate the forbidden fruit, and as a punishment You decreed that he should die. Did I ever eat of any fruit which You forbade me? In fact, You Yourself refer to me as 'My servant Moses, faithful in all My house.' "

"Are you worthier than Noah?"

"Yes," Moses replied. "When You sent the flood, he did not beg mercy for his fellow creatures, his own generation. But when You were about to punish the people Israel, I said: 'If You will not forgive their sin, then blot me, I pray, out of Your book which You have written.' "

"Moses, did I advise you to slay the Egyptian taskmaster?"

"*You* slew all the firstborn of Egypt! Shall I die on account of the one single Egyptian that I slew while he was oppressing my brothers as slaves?"

"Moses! Do you dare compare yourself to Me? I slay and I restore to life, I sustain and I revive the dead. Furthermore, it states in My Torah which you have transmitted that whoever kills another human being shall himself be put to death."

In desperation, Moses went to his disciple Joshua to ask a favor. "My son, remember the love which I have always shown you, teaching you Torah and law, and all the arts and sciences. For my sake, Joshua, please beg for God's mercy, please pray that He take pity on me and permit me to enter the Land of Israel."

Joshua, weeping, began to pray. But the angel Sammael appeared, to stop up his mouth, saying: "Why do you presume to oppose the command of God, the Rock whose work is perfect, all of whose ways are just?" Joshua reported back to Moses. "Master, Sam-

Rabbinic sources

mael will not let me pray." At these words, Moses burst into tears and Joshua, too, wept bitterly.

Then Moses, in tears, approached every work of creation, asking, "Please implore for mercy on my behalf." But all of them replied, "We cannot even ask mercy for ourselves. God has made everything beautiful in its time, but afterward all go to one place, all are of dust and all return to dust. For the heavens shall vanish like smoke, it is written, and the earth shall wax old like a garment."

Moses returned to Joshua and said, "Question me regarding all the laws that are not quite clear to you, for soon I shall be taken away, and you shall see me no more." Joshua replied that since he had never left his master's side, he had no doubts concerning anything which he had been taught by Moses.

"Come here, Joshua," said Moses.

Joshua went over to Moses, who kissed him and wept upon his neck. Then Moses blessed him. "May you be at peace, and may the people Israel be at peace with you."

Moses then intoned a song in praise of God, blessed the people Israel, and prayed for them.

When Moses had finished his blessing, he asked the people to forgive him for the times when he had been stern with them. "You have had a great deal to bear on my account. Please forgive me now." And they forgave him. Then they said, "We have often angered you and have laid great burdens upon you. Please forgive us now." And Moses forgave them.

When God first asked the angels Gabriel and Zag-

zagel to take the soul of Moses, they refused, feeling that it would be an unseemly act. But Sammael volunteered to go. With great glee he took his sword, girded himself in cruelty, wrapped himself in wrath and soon confronted Moses. Moses, however, adamantly refused to give up his soul! Sammael, dejected, returned to report this to God.

Moses finally made his peace with the realization that nothing could possibly save him from death, though he did ask not to be delivered into the hands of Sammael. Then he declared, "The Rock, His work is perfect and all His ways are just, a faithful God who does no wrong, righteous and true is He" (Deuteronomy 32:4).

Three ministering angels came with God to take the soul of Moses. Gabriel arranged Moses' couch, Michael spread a purple cloth over it, and Zagzagel laid down a woolen pillow. God said, "Moses, close your eyes." And Moses did so. "Place your feet next to each other." And Moses did so. "Fold your hands and place them on your chest." And Moses did so.

Then the Holy One summoned the soul from the body. The soul pleaded that it be allowed to remain in the body of Moses.

When Moses realized that his soul was refusing to leave him, he asked his soul, "Do you fear the angel of death?"

The soul replied, "No."

"Will you weep when others weep at my death?"

The soul replied, "The Lord has delivered my eyes from tears."

Rabbinic sources

"Will you perchance go to hell when I am dead?"

"I will walk before the Lord in the land of the living," the soul replied.

"Then," said Moses, "return unto your rest, my soul, for the Lord has dealt bountifully with you."

Thereupon God kissed Moses; God took away his soul with a kiss on the mouth.

God wept, so to speak. "Who will stand up for Me against the workers of iniquity?" (Psalms 94:16).

The angels wept, "Where shall wisdom be found?"

The heavens lamented, "The godly man is perished from the earth" (Micah 7:2).

The earth mourned, "There is not one upright man" (Micah 7:2).

The moon, the sun and the planets wailed, "The righteous perish and no one takes it to heart" (Isaiah 57:1).

His disciple Joshua wept, "Help, O Lord, for the faithful are no more; the loyal have vanished from among men" (Psalms 12:2).

"The righteous is remembered for a blessing," (Proverbs 10:7) and his soul for life in the world to come. Amen. And thus may it be His will. Praised be the Lord forever. Amen and Amen.

Deuteronomy Rabbah 11
and other Rabbinic sources

꩜ Readings

FEAR NOT DEATH

꩜ Fear not death; we are destined to die. We share this with all other mortals, with all who ever lived, with all who ever will be. Bewail the dead, hide not your grief, do not restrain your mourning. But remember that continuing sorrow is worse than death. When the dead are at rest, let their memory rest, and be consoled when the soul departs.

Seek not to understand what is too difficult for you, search not for what is hidden from you. Be not overoccupied with what is beyond you, for you have been shown more than you can understand.

As a drop of water in the sea, as a grain of sand on the shore are man's few days in eternity. The good things in life last for limited days, but a good name endures forever.

O God, our Father, You redeem our souls from the grave, You are the Rock of our salvation. Forsake us not in time of trouble, in days of distress and desolation. Help us to endure, O Lord, for we have placed our hope in You.

Adapted from Ben Sira

A PRAYER OF THE AFFLICTED

❧ A prayer of the afflicted, overwhelmed, pouring out his complaint before the Lord.

Listen to my prayer, Lord; hear my cry. Hide not Your Presence from me in the day of my distress. For my days are consumed like smoke, my body is burning up as if with fever. I am stricken, withered like grass; I do not have the strength to eat. My skin hangs on my bones; bitterly I moan. I am like an owl in the wilderness, living in the ruins. I cannot sleep. I mourn in solitude like a lone sparrow on a rooftop. All day long my enemies taunt me; they use my name for a curse. My food is ashes on my tongue; what I drink is mixed with tears, because of Your wrath and Your fury. Once You exalted me, but now You have cast me down. My days are as brief as an evening shadow, and I am withering away like grass. But You, O Lord, are enthroned forever; Your name endures throughout all generations.

He has drained my strength, He has shortened my days, until I cry: "My God, take me not away before my days are done, You whose days endure throughout all generations."

You established the earth of old, the heavens are

Readings

the work of Your hands. They shall perish, but You shall endure. They shall wear out like a garment; You change them like clothing and they pass away. But You are eternal. Your years have no end. Your servant's children live in Your Presence; their posterity shall endure.

From Psalm 102 (1–13, 24–29)

A PRAYER OF MOSES, MAN OF GOD

O Lord, You have been our refuge
From generation to generation.

> Before the mountains were born,
> Before the earth was fashioned,

From age to age, everlastingly You are God.

> But man You turn back to dust.
> You say: "Return, O mortals."

A thousand years are in Your sight
As a passing day, an hour of night.

> You sweep men away and they sleep.
> They flourish for a day, like grass.

In the morning it sprouts afresh;
By nightfall it fades and withers.

> By Your anger we are consumed,
> By Your wrath we are overcome.

You set out our sins before You,
Our secrets before Your Presence.

Readings

Your wrath darkens our days,
Our lives expire like a sigh.

Three score and ten our years may number
Four score years if granted the vigor.

Laden with trouble and travail,
Life quickly passes and flies away.

Who can know the power of Your wrath?
Who can measure the reverence due You?

Teach us to use all of our days,
That we may attain a heart of wisdom.

Relent, O Lord! How long must we suffer?
Have compassion upon Your servants.

Grant us of Your love in the morning
That we may joyously sing all our days.

Match days of sorrow with days of joy,
Equal to the years we have suffered.

Then Your servants will see Your power,
Then their children will know Your glory.

May the Lord our God show us compassion,
And may He prosper the work of our hands.

May He prosper the work of our hands.

Psalm 90

A TIME FOR EVERYTHING

There is a time for everything,
A time for all things under heaven:

Readings

A time to be born and a time to die,
A time to plant and a time to uproot,
A time to slay and a time to heal,
A time to tear down and a time to build,
A time to weep and a time to laugh,
A time to wail and a time to dance,
A time to scatter and a time to gather,
A time to embrace and a time to shun embraces,
A time to seek and a time to lose,
A time to keep and a time to discard,
A time to tear and a time to sew,
A time for silence and a time for speech,
A time for love and a time for hate,
A time for war and a time for peace.

Ecclesiastes 3:1–8

GIVE ME THE VISION

Shall I cry out in anger, O God,
Because Thy gifts are mine but for a while?
Shall I be ungrateful for the moments of laughter,
The seasons of joy, the days of gladness and festivity,
When tears cloud my eyes and darken the world
And my heart is heavy within me?
Shall I blot from mind the love
I have known and in which I have rejoiced
When a fate beyond my understanding takes from me
Friends and kin whom I have cherished, and leaves me
Bereft of shining presences that have lit my way
Through years of companionship and affection?

Give me the vision, O God, to see and feel

Readings

That imbedded deep in each of Thy gifts
Is a core of eternity, undiminished and bright,
An eternity that survives the dread hours
of affliction and misery.
Those I have loved, though now beyond my view,
Have given form and quality to my being.
They have led me into the wide universe
I continue to inhabit, and their presence
Is more vital to me than their absence.

What Thou givest, O Lord,
Thou takest not away.
And bounties once granted
Shed their radiance evermore.

Rabbi Morris Adler

GOD OF MEN AND MOUNTAINS

God of men and mountains,
Master of people and planets,
Creator of the universe:
I am afraid.

I am afraid of the angels
Thou hast sent to wrestle with me:

The angel of success
who carries a two-edged sword

The angels of darkness
Whose names I do not know,

Readings

54

The angel of death
For whom I have no answer.

I am afraid of the touch
Of Thy great hand on my feeble heart.

Yet must I turn to Thee and praise Thee,
Awful and great though Thou art,
For there is none else.

There is no strength nor courage
But in Thee.
There is no life, no light, no joy,
But in Thee.

Ruth Brin

REFLECTION ON THE KADDISH

This is the hall, this the hush, this the hour
I rise to praise the Lord of all the living
and the lonely dead.

I rise to praise;
I raise my voice,
I lift my head,
despite the sick
despite the dead
despite the cries
of pain, I rise
to praise my Lord.

I praise the Lord
whom all men praise
with separate song.
He made the earth,
the sky, the throng
of those who raise
in prayerful phrase
their souls to Him.

This holy hour, this hush, this lull
I yield to Him whose glory is beyond all praise
and bless His name,
and say Amen.

Ruth Brin

THE GIFT OF MEMORY

We thank Thee, O God of life and love,
For the resurrecting gift of memory
Which endows Thy children fashioned in Thine image
With the Godlike sovereign power
To give immortality through love.
Blessed be Thou, O God,
Who enablest Thy children to remember.

Rabbi Morris Adler

Readings

✎ Reflections

WHEN GOD CLAIMS HIS OWN

✎ Something precious is taken from us, and we think of it as something we have lost, instead of something we have had. We remember only how empty our lives are now, we forget how full and rich they were before; we forget all the many days and years of happiness we lived while the beloved object was still with us. We praise God for our treasures while we have them; we cease to praise Him for them when they are fled. But God never gives; He only lends. What is life itself but a loan?

When God claims His own shall we rebel? Instead of murmuring because He takes our precious things from us, let us be grateful to Him for having spared them to us so long. Let us count the past happy days not as loss, but as gain. We have had them; and, now

that they are ended, let us turn the loss to glorious gain—the gain that comes with new courage, with nobler tasks, with a wider outlook on life and duty.

Rabbi Morris Joseph

ON THE DEATH OF THE YOUNG

David prayed to God for his child; he fasted, and lay all night upon the ground. The elders of his house tried to raise him from the ground, but he would not rise, nor would he eat food with them. On the seventh day the child died. The servants of King David feared to tell him that the child was dead, for they reasoned: "While his child was still alive, he did not listen to us when we spoke to him. How, then, can we tell him that the child is dead? He may do himself some harm."

When David noticed that his servants were whispering to each other, he realized that the child was dead. Then David asked his servants, "Is the child dead?" They answered, "He is dead." So David arose from the ground and washed and changed his clothes, and he went to the house of the Lord, and he worshipped. Then he went to his own house and, when he asked, they set food before him, and he ate. His servants then asked him, "What is this thing that you have done?" And David replied, "While the child was still alive, I fasted and I wept, for I said, 'Who knows whether the Lord will be gracious to me, that the child will live?' But now he is dead. Why should I fast? Can I bring him back? I shall go to him, but he will not return to me."

II Samuel 12:16–23

Reflections

༄ A righteous person, though dying early in life, shall be at rest, for an honored old age does not depend upon length of time, nor is it measured by the number of one's years. For *understanding* is gray hair, and *a blameless life* is old age. Being perfected in a little while, he fulfilled long years, for his soul pleased the Lord.

The Wisdom of Solomon

༄ And the king was deeply pained, and he went to the room which was above the gate, and as he walked he said, "My son Absalom, my son, my son Absalom. Would that I had died instead of you, Absalom my son, my son."

II Samuel 19:1

ON SUFFERING

༄ The Only God is the source of life and life is borne by Him, even in all suffering and in spite of all suffering . . . . Submission to the love of God . . . in times of suffering has nothing in common with that fatalism which finds a weary composure in the idea of everything being fixed and determined, or with that resignation which becomes paralyzed before its conviction that all events are inevitable and human volition is mere vanity. Nor does it have anything in common with that melancholy meditation which surrenders its curiosity in the face of the world's inexorability. Still less does it have any connection with the dull indifference of the person who becomes apathetic and surrenders under the blows of a fate which has broken him. The submission to the love of God, as it is felt here, is

not a banal "philosophy" and contemplation; nor does it involve an indifference to life. It is simply the yearning of man to overcome his feeling of God's remoteness by the feeling of God's nearness. It is devoutness and it is prayer; it prays by asking questions, but even in its questioning it prays. "Shall we receive good at the hand of God, and shall we not receive evil?" (Job 2:10).

One of the peculiar words of the Bible, repeatedly emphasized, is the word "why," but this "why" also remains a word of prayer. Just because that submission is a prayer is it so different from many other questionings which seem to resemble it. Its deepest characteristic is the silence of devotion. "I have stilled and quieted my soul" (Psalms 131:2). "I was dumb, I opened not my mouth; because it is Your doing" (Psalms 39:10). "It is good for a man that he sit alone and keep silence, because he has taken it upon himself" (Lamentations 3:28). . . .

Man can bless only the One God and only that man can bless Him who experiences Him as the God of all times, the God of the fathers and the children, the God of darkness and of light. The prayers of suffering could also therefore appropriate this conception. In the talmudic scripture we find the words: "Man must bless God in his affliction as well as in his joy" (*Mishnah Berakhot* 9:5). "Be not like one of the idolators: when all goes well with him, he honors his gods, but if misfortune overcomes him, he curses them. Not so with the Israelites. If God sends them happiness they bless Him, and if God afflicts them with sorrow, they bless Him" (*Mekhilta* to Exodus 20:23). The last sentence —in which is displayed a stability of attitude toward life

that is the very essence of monotheism and is its major difference from paganism— is the saying of Rabbi Akiba. He also coined the saying: "Whatever God does, is done for the best" (*Berakhot* 60b). This was his life's confession; for he had come to know suffering in all the ways that man could. He had the right to say this without sounding as if he were mocking misfortune. It was not the mere wisdom of reason, but religiousness which found this and many a similar word. In them the peculiarity of Judaism reveals itself, conveying the sense of something higher, something lasting and eternal which the soul possesses and by which it retains its assurance in the ways of God.

Rabbi Leo Baeck

ON LIFE AND DEATH

There is no cure for death. Not even health. But the healthy man has the strength to walk alive to his grave. The sick man invokes Death and lets himself be carried on his back, half-dead from fear of him. Health experiences even Death only "at the right time." It is good friends with him, and knows that when he comes he will remove the rigid mask and take the flickering torch from the hands of his frightened, weary, disappointed brother, Life. He'll dash it on the ground and extinguish it, and only then under the skies that flame up for the first time when the torch has been extinguished, he'll enfold the swooning one in his arms and only then, when Life has closed its eloquent lips, he'll open his eternally silent mouth and say: "Do you recognize me? I am your brother."

Franz Rosenzweig

Reflections

꙳ One of the most tender and poignant scenes in Biblical history is that of the last moments of Moses. He ascended Mount Nebo and viewed the Land of Promise concerning which he had spoken so often to the children of Israel and which he was himself not destined to enter.

What thoughts passed through the mind of the immortal Lawgiver as he looked out across the Jordan? He had devoted a lifetime to his people, bringing them out of Egypt and painstakingly guiding them through the wilderness. He had striven to wean them away from false gods and pagan practices. He had patiently borne their burdens and bickerings and had tried to elevate them to higher standards and sensitivities.

And now that they were about to move forward to a great fulfillment, to end their wanderings and begin life as a settled people, he was not permitted to accompany them. Moses would have been more than human had he not reflected that his efforts and sacrifices might soon belong to a forgotten past. And what of his teachings, doctrines, and ideals? Would they endure? Perhaps Moses surrendered to the feeling that he had lived and labored in vain.

Yet the subsequent history of Israel is dominated by his towering figure. The sense of commitment and the memory of the covenant were constantly being recalled to the people centuries later by the prophets and other leaders who continued to walk in the footsteps of Moses. Though he did not enter the promised land, his spirit continued to guide and direct the people whom he had served in his lifetime.

Reflections

Here is a touching parable of the immortality exercised by those who have deeply touched our lives and enriched us with their love. A dear and cherished one is taken from us. The Jordan symbol of the boundary between life and death intervenes between us. Yet as we move onward, the enduring spirit of the love we have known and the life we have shared continue to shape and inspire us. The yesterdays are beyond the reach of death as our love transforms them into current and living influences. We continue to live by a light that defies time and death.

Rabbi Morris Adler

LIVING ON

༄ In recording King David's death, the Bible states, "And David slept with his fathers" (I Kings 2:10). Why does it not state, "And David died"?

The Sages answered their own question: "David was survived by a son who followed the good ways of his father's life, continuing his father's noble deeds. Therefore, it could not be said that David was really dead, for he lived on through the good deeds of his son."

Baba Batra 116a

PEACE AND HEALING

༄ Without God, life is a lonely darkness, even for the man who is in the midst of many other men and even for the man who enjoys pleasures and power. Greater yet than the loneliness of the man who is not understood by his fellow men or who has been cast out by them is the loneliness of the man who knows only his

fellow men and only of ties with this earth. It is the loneliness of the man whose soul is far from all that is real, eternal and sublime. In this forlorn state man trembles with despair when he seeks answers to those questions about life that he cannot evade.

It is precisely from this fear — the fear of the night of infinitude and of the forlornness of the merely earthly and human— that there arises the yearning for that illumination and harmonizing One who is the creator of all eternity. The man who knows this yearning, which always also involves a finding, is lifted out of his forlornness; his night is filled with light and his soul redeemed from despair. "Thou art my lamp, O Lord; the Lord lightens my darkness" (II Samuel 22:29). "In Thy light we see light" (Psalms 36:10). Whoever knows himself to be intimately bound to the one and eternal God knows no loneliness, for his life is never solitary. No matter how intimately we may come in contact with our fellow man we still remain alone in our innermost soul, for every personality is unique upon earth, and loneliness is a part of individuality. But in God our life finds its peace. Peace —that is one of the words to which Israel gave a fresh meaning. All the struggle and striving of the world makes man weary. But in unity with God man finds his rest and his salvation: his peace. "Whom have I in heaven but Thee? And there is none upon earth that I desire beside Thee. . . . God is the strength of my heart and my portion for ever" (Psalms 73:25f.). "Blessed is the man that trusteth in the Lord, and whose hope the Lord is" (Jeremiah 17:7). And the blessing ends in the word "peace"—"The Lord . . . give thee peace" (Numbers 6:26). "Peace,

peace to him that is far off, and to him that is near, saith the Lord; and I will heal him" (Isaiah 57:19).

Rabbi Leo Baeck

REFLECTIONS ON DEATH

☙ Existence embraces both life and death, and in a way death is the test of the meaning of life. If death is devoid of meaning, then life is absurd. Life's ultimate meaning remains obscure unless it is reflected upon in the face of death. . . .

Death is grim, harsh, cruel, a source of infinite grief. Our first reaction is consternation. We are stunned, distraught. Slowly, our sense of dismay is followed by a sense of mystery. Suddenly, a whole life has veiled itself in secrecy. Our speech stops, our understanding fails. In the presence of death there is only silence, and a sense of awe.

Is death nothing but an obliteration, an absolute negation? The view of death is affected by our understanding of life. If life is sensed as a surprise, as a gift, defying explanation, then death ceases to be a radical, absolute negation of what life stands for. For both life and death are aspects of a greater mystery, the mystery of being, the mystery of creation. Over and above the preciousness of particular existence stands the marvel of its being related to the infinite mystery of being or creation.

Death, then, is not simply man's coming to an end. It is also entering a beginning. . . .

Death may be the beginning of exaltation, an ultimate celebration, a reunion of the divine image with

the divine source of being. Dust returns to dust, while the image, the divine stake in man, is restored to the bundle of life. Death is not sensed as a defeat but as a summation, an arrival, a conclusion. . . .

The meaning of death is in return, regardless of whether it results in a continuation of individual consciousness or in merging into a greater whole. We are what we are by what we come from. We achieve what we do by what we hope for. Our ultimate hope has no specific content. Our hope is God. We trust that He will not desert those who trust in Him. . . .

Death, what follows death, is a mystery defying imagination. Facing it, our language is silence. Yet while the body descends into the grave, trust remains, hope persists and enters a simile.

Marvelous and beautiful is life in the body, but more marvelous and more beautiful is life in a word. The word is greater than the world; by the word of God all was created. The Book, Scripture, is an everlasting constellation of holy words. When a good man dies, his soul becomes a word and lives in God's book.

"And many of those who sleep in the dust of the earth shall awake, some to everlasting life and some to shame and everlasting contempt" (Daniel 12:2).

The decisive message of this passage is that death is not the final act, that there will be an awakening of those who sleep in the dust.

This is the hope that in dying I become a seed and that after I decay I am born again. Must the self remain the same rather than become the seed of a new self, a new being? . . .

Reflections

The meaning of existence is in the sanctification of time, in lending eternity to the moments. Being human is a quest for the lasting.

Craving for God, longing for immediate perception of the divine, for emancipation from selfish desires and inclinations—such freedom can only be achieved beyond death.

It is a distortion to characterize the life of man as moving toward death. Death is the end of the road, and while moving along the long road of days and nights, we are really moving toward living, acting, achieving. Death is the end of the road, but not its meaning, not a refutation of living. That every moment of life is a step toward death is a mechanical view. Every moment of life is a new arrival, a new beginning. Those who say that we die every day, that every moment deprives us of a portion of life, look at moments as time past. Looking at moments as time present, every moment is a new arrival, a new beginning. . . .

Abraham Joshua Heschel

ON THE HEREAFTER

*By way of preface to a modern view of the hereafter, we would do well to recall four basic insights of particular value that are to be found in traditional religion. First is the emphasis upon living the good life for its own sake without the desire for reward or the fear of punishment. This principle must be fundamental to a living religion, irrespective of one's attitude toward the hereafter. . . .

Equally vital is the biblical conviction that this world is the arena where God manifests Himself and

where man can fulfill his destiny. This view is echoed in Rabbinic thought: "Better one hour of repentance and good deeds in this world than all the life of the world to come, but better one hour of joy in the world to come than all the life of this world" (*Abot* 4:17). For the traditional believer, the full *enjoyment of salvation* is reserved for the world to come, but the *achievement of salvation* is a task to be accomplished in this world. . . .

Third, the Bible emphasizes that children constitute a uniquely satisfying avenue of immortality for men. . . . Whatever other forms of eternal life may or may not be open to man, he does live on, both in his descendants and in the effect that his life and work can exert upon the society of which he is a part. . . .

Finally, there is a bewildering array of conceptions of the afterlife to be found in the religious and literary sources of Western religion, varying from the literal to the figurative, from the grossest and most material to the most spiritual. Yet underlying them all, one principle may be discerned: the conviction that physical death does not end all for man, that in some sense man's life is indestructible and his spirit is endowed with immortality. . . .

The belief in immortality remains an area where each individual must confront the wonder of existence for himself, and make peace on his own terms with the mystery of death. He may feel impelled to spell out in detail his hopes and fears, and draw upon the descriptions of the world-to-come to be found in many pages of religious literature. We believe that a man will be wiser to accept the limitations of existence and knowledge that are basic to the human situation, and not seek

to peer behind the veil. What form man's deathlessness may take in another realm of being we cannot discover, because it lies beyond the range of our earthly experience. To borrow an analogy from Maimonides, for us to conceive of life after death, an existence necessarily free from physical traits and attributes, is as impossible as for a color-blind person to grasp the colors of a sunset. . . .

On the issue of man's immortality, humility is the basic virtue and dogmatism the cardinal sin. That man lives on, we may affirm; how he lives on, we cannot know. Koheleth, the biblical thinker, has told us all we know or need to know: "The dust returns to the earth as it was, and the spirit returns to God who gave it."

Rabbi Robert Gordis

๑ Conclusion of shivah

At the conclusion of shivah, the following may be
said. Other selections meaningful to
members of the family may of course be sub-
stituted or added, drawing from elsewhere in this
volume or from other sources.

๑ God is our refuge, and our strength; He is always our help in adversity. Therefore, even though the earth should change, we shall not fear. In all misfortune, He is our stronghold. Sorrow has been our daily bread, and tears of grief have been our drink. May the God of compassion, the light in our midst, lead us now to life. He will heal us, time after time. He calls our life away from the grave, surrounds us with goodness and tender love. May He heal our wounds, and may He heal the wounds of all the people Israel. And let us say: Amen.

As a mother comforts her children, so shall I comfort you, says the Lord. The Lord heals the broken-hearted; He binds up their wounds. The Lord will be your enduring light, and the days of your mourning will come to an end.

Almighty God, Master of mercy, Healer of the broken-hearted, let neither death nor sorrow have dominion over us. Grant us strength as we mourn the loss of _____. May we always cherish what is imperishable in the life of _____. Bless our family with love and with peace, that we may serve You with all our heart. May the memory of _____ inspire us to deeds of lovingkindness. And let us say: Amen.

The mourners rise, and leave their home to walk a short distance together, as a symbol of their return to a more normal routine.

Conclusion of shivah

71

When visiting the cemetery

The following psalms may be recited, or other passages found elsewhere in this volume. It is not a requirement to recite any selection; one may prefer to meditate in silence briefly near the grave. Eil malei raḥamim (pages 80-83 of this section) is the appropriate prayer to be chanted before leaving the grave site.

The Lord is my shepherd, I shall not want. He gives me repose in green meadows. He leads me beside the still waters, He revives my spirit. He guides me on the right path, for that is His nature. Though I walk in the valley of the shadow of death, I fear no harm, for You are with me. Your staff and Your rod comfort me. You prepare a banquet for me in the presence of my foes. You anoint my head with oil; my cup overflows. Surely goodness and kindness shall be my portion all

the days of my life. And I shall dwell in the House of the Lord forever.

Psalm 23 (For Hebrew, see page 187)

❧ I will lift up my eyes to the mountains. What is the source of my help? The source of my help is the Lord, Creator of heaven and earth. He will not let you falter; your Guardian will not slumber. Surely the Guardian of Israel will neither slumber nor sleep. The Lord is your protector, the Lord is your shelter at your right hand. The sun will not smite you by day, nor the moon by night. The Lord will guard you from all harm; He will preserve your soul. The Lord will guard your going and your coming, now and forevermore.

Psalm 121

IN MEMORY OF A FATHER

❧ I now recall my dear father, may he rest in peace. I am grateful for the gift of his life, and for the good memories which enable me to recall the blessings of his life. May the love and kindness with which he touched my life help me to share those qualities with others.

With a contrite heart I repent of my thoughts or acts which may have caused him pain, and pray that my transgressions against him be pardoned.

May God's compassion shelter his soul and sustain my life. May his virtues be reflected in my life.

Add your own thoughts

May his soul be bound up in the bond of life. May his memory endure as a blessing. Amen.

When visiting the cemetery

˷ I now recall my dear mother, may she rest in peace. I am grateful for the gift of her life, and for the good memories which enable me to recall the blessings of her life. May the love and kindness with which she touched my life help me to share those qualities with others.

With a contrite heart I repent of my thoughts or acts which may have caused her pain, and pray that my transgressions against her be pardoned.

May God's compassion shelter her soul and sustain my life. May her virtues be reflected in my life.

Add your own thoughts

May her soul be bound up in the bond of life. May her memory endure as a blessing. Amen.

IN MEMORY OF A HUSBAND

˷ Distressed with a sense of loss, yet sustained and comforted by wonderful memories, I now recall my beloved husband, _____, may he rest in peace. Love is strong as death, and the beauty and the meaning of our life together survive the grave. I am grateful for the gift of his life, of his love, and for the many blessings which we shared. May they continue to influence my life.

With a contrite heart I repent of my thoughts or acts which may have caused him pain, and pray that my transgressions against him be pardoned.

May God's compassion shelter his soul and sustain my life.

When visiting the cemetery

May his soul be bound up in the bond of life. May his memory endure as a blessing. Amen.

IN MEMORY OF A WIFE

෴ Distressed with a sense of loss, yet sustained and comforted by wonderful memories, I now recall my beloved wife, _____, may she rest in peace. Love is strong as death, and the beauty and the meaning of our life together survive the grave. I am grateful for the gift of her life, of her love, and for the many blessings which we shared. May they continue to influence my life.

With a contrite heart I repent of my thoughts or acts which may have caused her pain, and pray that my transgressions against her be pardoned.

May God's compassion shelter her soul and sustain my life.

Add your own thoughts

May her soul be bound up in the bond of life. May her memory endure as a blessing. Amen.

IN MEMORY OF A SON

෴ I lovingly recall my dear son, _____, may he rest in peace, renewing the bond that binds my life with the memory of his life. Recalling how he enriched my life, I am grateful for the gift of his life, for its blessings which he enjoyed and for that which he accomplished. May I honor his memory by helping to

When visiting the cemetery

perpetuate that which was good and meaningful for him.

With a contrite heart I repent of my thoughts or acts which may have caused him pain, and pray that my transgressions against him be pardoned.

May God's compassion shelter his soul and sustain my life.

Add your own thoughts

May his soul be bound up in the bond of life. May his memory endure as a blessing. Amen.

IN MEMORY OF A DAUGHTER

᠀ I lovingly recall my dear daughter, _____, may she rest in peace, renewing the bond that binds my life with the memory of her life. Recalling how she enriched my life, I am grateful for the gift of her life, for its blessings which she enjoyed, and for that which she accomplished. May I honor her memory by helping to perpetuate that which was good and meaningful in her life.

With a contrite heart I repent of my thoughts or acts which may have caused her pain, and pray that my transgressions against her be pardoned.

May God's compassion shelter her soul and sustain my life.

Add your own thoughts

May her soul be bound up in the bond of life. May her memory endure as a blessing. Amen.

When visiting the cemetery

IN MEMORY OF A BROTHER

✏ Time will not erase the good which I recall in the life of my dear brother, _____, may he rest in peace. I am grateful for the memories of the blessings in his life, and for those precious shared blessings which bound us together. May I help to perpetuate that which was good and meaningful for him.

With a contrite heart I repent of my thoughts or acts which may have caused him pain and pray that my transgressions against him be pardoned.

May God's compassion shelter his soul and sustain my life. May we in the land of the living learn to turn to each other always in lovingkindness.

Add your own thoughts

May his soul be bound up in the bond of life. May his memory endure as a blessing. Amen.

IN MEMORY OF A SISTER

✏ Time will not erase the good which I recall in the life of my dear sister, _____, may she rest in peace. I am grateful for the memories of the blessings in her life, and for those precious shared blessings which bound us together. May I help to perpetuate that which was good and meaningful in her life.

With a contrite heart I repent of my thoughts or acts which may have caused her pain, and pray that my transgressions against her be pardoned.

May God's compassion shelter her soul and sus-

tain my life. May we in the land of the living learn to turn to each other always in understanding.

Add your own thoughts

May her soul be bound up in the bond of life. May her memory endure as a blessing. Amen.

IN MEMORY OF OTHER MALE RELATIVES AND FRIENDS

☙ "The dust returns to the earth, whence it came, and the soul returns unto God who gave it."

I now recall the life of _____, may he rest in peace. Grateful for the blessings of that life, I hope and pray that his good qualities will have a lasting influence upon my life.

With a contrite heart I repent of my thoughts or acts which may have caused him pain, and pray that my transgressions against him be pardoned.

May God's compassion shelter his soul and sustain my life. May I help to perpetuate that which was good and meaningful to him. And may we in the land of the living learn to turn to each other always in lovingkindness.

Add your own thoughts

May his soul be bound up in the bond of life. May his memory endure as a blessing. Amen.

IN MEMORY OF OTHER FEMALE RELATIVES AND FRIENDS

☙ "The dust returns to the earth, whence it came, and the soul returns unto God who gave it."

When visiting the cemetery

I now recall the life of _____, may she rest in peace. Grateful for the blessings of that life, I hope and pray that her good qualities will have a lasting influence upon my life.

With a contrite heart I repent of my thoughts or acts which may have caused her pain, and pray that my transgressions against her be pardoned.

May God's compassion shelter her soul and sustain my life. May I help to perpetuate that which was good and meaningful to her. And may we in the land of the living learn to turn to each other always in lovingkindness.

Add your own thoughts

May her soul be bound up in the bond of life. May her memory endure as a blessing. Amen.

REFLECTION

The earth inherits that which is mortal. But only the dust returns to the dust. The soul is not abandoned to the grave, the faithful do not suffer oblivion. For the Lord has shown us the way of life. He has planted eternity in our midst, granting us a share in His unending life. He surrounds us with lovingkindness, enabling us to cherish hopes and to perform good deeds which time cannot destroy. Goodness, love and faith endure from age to age, helping to hasten the kingdom of God in this world. He redeems our life from the grave. His ways are the source of our hope and our comfort.

When visiting the cemetery

Eil Malei Raḥamim

For male

אֵל מָלֵא רַחֲמִים, שׁוֹכֵן בַּמְּרוֹמִים, הַמְצֵא מְנוּחָה נְכוֹנָה תַּחַת כַּנְפֵי הַשְּׁכִינָה, בְּמַעֲלוֹת קְדוֹשִׁים וּטְהוֹרִים כְּזֹהַר הָרָקִיעַ מַזְהִירִים, אֶת־נִשְׁמַת _____ בֶּן _____ שֶׁהָלַךְ לְעוֹלָמוֹ, בְּגַן עֵדֶן תְּהֵא מְנוּחָתוֹ. אָנָּא, בַּעַל הָרַחֲמִים הַסְתִּירֵהוּ בְּסֵתֶר כְּנָפֶיךָ לְעוֹלָמִים, וּצְרוֹר בִּצְרוֹר הַחַיִּים אֶת־נִשְׁמָתוֹ, יְיָ הוּא נַחֲלָתוֹ, וְיָנוּחַ בְּשָׁלוֹם עַל מִשְׁכָּבוֹ, וְנֹאמַר אָמֵן.

Eil malei raḥamim sho-khein bam'romim, hamm-tzei m'nukhah n'khonah taḥat kanfei ha-sh'khinah, b'ma-alot k'doshim u-t'horim k'zohar ha-rakiya maz-hirim et nishmat _____ ben _____ sheh-halakh l'olamo, b'gan eiden t'hei m'nuḥato. Ana, ba-al ha-raḥamim, hassti-rei-hu b'seiter k'nafekha l'olamim, u-tzror bi-tzror ha-ḥayim et nishmato, Adonai hu naḥalato, v'yanu-aḥ b'shalom al mishkavo, v'nomar amen.

When visiting the cemetery

Exalted, compassionate God, grant perfect peace in Your sheltering Presence, among the holy and the pure who shine with the splendor of the firmament, to the soul of our dear _____ who has gone to his eternal home. Master of mercy, remember all his worthy deeds in the land of the living. May his soul be bound up in the bond of life. May his memory always inspire us to attain dignity and holiness in life. May he rest in peace. And let us say: Amen.

Personal meditation

Compassionate God, at this time of remembrance I offer my prayers in behalf of _____. Keep his beloved soul in Your providential care. May his memory and the goodness which he wrought in his life find continuity in my life, and unto all eternity.

Personal thoughts may be added.

Amen.

Eil Malei Raḥamim

ﷺ

For female

אֵל מָלֵא רַחֲמִים, שׁוֹכֵן בַּמְּרוֹמִים, הַמְצֵא מְנוּחָה נְכוֹנָה תַּחַת
כַּנְפֵי הַשְּׁכִינָה, בְּמַעֲלוֹת קְדוֹשִׁים וּטְהוֹרִים כְּזֹהַר הָרָקִיעַ
מַזְהִירִים אֶת־נִשְׁמַת _____ בַּת _____ שֶׁהָלְכָה
לְעוֹלָמָהּ, בְּגַן עֵדֶן תְּהֵא מְנוּחָתָהּ. אָנָּא, בַּעַל הָרַחֲמִים
הַסְתִּירֶהָ בְּסֵתֶר כְּנָפֶיךָ לְעוֹלָמִים, וּצְרוֹר בִּצְרוֹר הַחַיִּים אֶת־
נִשְׁמָתָהּ, יְיָ הוּא נַחֲלָתָהּ, וְתָנוּחַ בְּשָׁלוֹם עַל מִשְׁכָּבָהּ, וְנֹאמַר
אָמֵן.

*Eil malei raḥamim sho-khein bam'romim, hamm-tzei m'nukhah
n'khonah taḥat kanfei ha-sh'khinah, b'ma-alot k'doshim
u-t'horim k'zohar ha-rākiya maz-hirim et nishmat _____ bat
_____ sheh-halkhah l'olamah, b'gan eiden t'hei m'nuḥatah.
Ana, ba-al ha-raḥamim, hassti-reha b'seiter k'nafekha l'olamim,
u-tzror bi-tzror ha-ḥayim et nishmatah, Adonai hu naḥalatah,
v'tanu-aḥ b'shalom al mishkavah, v'nomar amen.*

When visiting the cemetery

Exalted, compassionate God, grant perfect peace in Your sheltering Presence, among the holy and the pure who shine with the splendor of the firmament, to the soul of our dear _____ who has gone to her eternal home. Master of mercy, remember all her worthy deeds in the land of the living. May her soul be bound up in the bond of life. May her memory always inspire us to attain dignity and holiness in life. May she rest in peace. And let us say: Amen.

Personal meditation

Compassionate God, at this time of remembrance I offer my prayers in behalf of _____. Keep her beloved soul in Your providential care. May her memory and the goodness which she wrought in her life find continuity in my life, and unto all eternity.

Personal thoughts may be added.

Amen.

✑ Kindling the yahrzeit light

The *yahrzeit* candle should burn from sunset to sunset, on the anniversary of the day of death according to the Hebrew calendar, starting on the evening preceding the day. A selection from Psalms or other passages found elsewhere in this book may be read. There is no special prayer or benediction to be recited. It is appropriate to meditate briefly, silently or aloud. Some suggested reflections follow.

✑ I now recall my dear _____ who has gone to his/her eternal home. May his/her soul be bound up in the bond of life, in peace. Amen.

✑ I kindle this light in loving memory of _____ , recalling words from the Book of Proverbs: "The soul of man is the light of the Lord."

Zekher tzadik livrakhah. The memory of the right-eous is a blessing. May my life continue to embrace the life and deeds, the words and thoughts of _____ who has gone to his/her eternal home. May he/she rest in peace. Amen.

 O merciful God, I turn to You in prayer on the *yahrzeit* of the death of my dear _____ . Be with me as I stand in remembrance and in loving recollection. As I light this candle in his/her memory, I put my trust in You.

 Renew my strength, O Lord. I am grateful for the years of the life of _____ . Help me to understand how my life has been formed and shaped by what he/she was and by what he/she did. Help me to make part of my life a living monument of holiness to his/her memory. May he/she rest in peace. Amen.

An introduction to the daily service

After the first period of mourning *(shivah)* mourners begin returning to the normal routine of their lives. During the period of *shivah*, members of the community come to the house of mourning for services of prayer, providing the *minyan* necessary for the public recitation of the mourner's *kaddish* (see page 169). After *shivah*, the mourner joins the daily services and recites the mourner's *kaddish* at the synagogue.

The daily service may at first seem strange and unwieldy to those unfamiliar with it. People long familiar with the service may appear to be rushing through their prayers at an impossibly fast pace. We should remember that things are not always what they seem to be. What appears to us as routine and mechanical may actually be a meaningful devotional experience to someone else. It is impossible to judge solely on the

basis of external factors. If you enter a chapel where the service is proceeding at a rapid clip, you should not be immediately discouraged. It also is not advisable for you to rush through a service merely to keep pace with others. Further, some people will say the words of the mourner's *kaddish* much faster than you can or want to say them. It is not unreasonable for you to request a slower pace, so that your recitation of *kaddish* can be more than a ritual gesture for you.

There are many paths, many ways. You must find the path proper for you. Remember that your inner involvement is more important than your reading rate. It is better to say a few words with devotion than many pages without it. But remember that these are not the only alternatives. As time goes on, you will be able to increase both the number of passages which you do recite and the depth of your devotion.

The service is formally structured, emphasizing and developing specific themes. We hope to present some of that sense of order in these limited remarks, as well as some sense of priority among and within sections of the daily service. Throughout this discussion it would be helpful to refer to the various pages of the service as printed elsewhere in this volume.

The core of the daily service is ancient, and has been recited by Jews in many parts of the world throughout the centuries. It consists primarily of the recitation of Biblical passages *(k'riat sh'ma)* as an act of accepting God's sovereignty, accompanied by benedictions praising God for Creation, Revelation, and Redemption. This is followed by the prayer *par excellence* in Jewish tradition, the *Amidah* (the Standing Prayer,

An introduction to the daily service

also known as the Silent Prayer and as the *shmoneh esreh*). It consists of benedictions of praise, petition and gratitude. Other sections of varying length and importance precede and follow this core of the service. (The page numbers given here refer to the section of this volume containing Hebrew and English services.)

Birkhot Hashaḥar *Morning Benedictions (pages 1-23)*

This is the first section of the morning service. It celebrates the renewal of life in a new day, expressing gratitude for God's gift of body and soul, as well as for His compassion, for our covenant with Him, and for the Torah. Passages from the Torah and from Rabbinic literature are recited to fulfill the minimal obligation for daily study. After the recitation of a Rabbinic passage, mourners recite *kaddish derabanan* (see page 22), a version of the *kaddish* especially associated with the study of a text.

Pesukei Dezimra *Passages of Praise (pages 25-47)*

K'riat sh'ma and the *Amidah,* the core of the service, are approached only after preparation. Part of this preparation consists of the Morning Benedictions and Prayers of Praise, composed of various benedictions and Biblical verses, mostly from the Book of Psalms. Hopefully, concentration on words of these sections will help us to approach the core of our prayer in the proper spirit, with an informed heart, freely, openly and gladly.

This section begins with *barukh sheh-amar* (page 25). Its various psalms and other passages could be read

An introduction to the daily service

in their entirety or with some selectivity, depending upon factors of time and inclination. The section concludes with *yishtabah* (page 47).

K'riat Sh'ma *(page 57)*

Hear, O Israel: The Lord our God, the Lord is One.

This familiar declaration is a verse from the Book of Deuteronomy (6:4). It is followed by a phrase which is *not* from the Bible (Praised be His glorious sovereignty throughout all time). That phrase was introduced at this point by the ancient Rabbis who are responsible for our basic service; they added it to clarify the reason why we recite the Biblical verses of *k'riat sh'ma*: to declare the acceptance of God's sovereignty in our lives (*kabbalat ol malkhut shamayim*) and our ultimate loyalty to God. The passage from Deuteronomy then continues, through Verse 9 of Chapter 6. This Biblical passage is followed by two others: Deuteronomy 11:13–21 and Numbers 15:37–41. These passages call for the unqualified love of God and the observance of His commandments (including *tallit, tefillin,* and *mezuzah*), for the study and transmission of Torah, and for remembering the spiritual goals of the ancient redemption from bondage.

The benediction following *k'riat sh'ma* in the morning service praises God as Redeemer of the people Israel in the past as well as in our lives now and in time to come. (In the evening service, a second benediction is added at this point, praising God for His peace and protection. The theme of the first benediction is the

An introduction to the daily service

89

same, morning and evening, though the words differ in each instance.)

K'riat sh'ma is always preceded by two benedictions. While the words of these benedictions are not identical in the morning and in the evening, the themes are the same. The first benediction praises God for His gift of Creation; the second praises Him for Revelation, His gift of Torah, which is a sign of His love. This love of God for the people Israel is reciprocated in the first passage of *k'riat sh'ma*, through which we declare the love of the people Israel for God.

The first benediction before *k'riat sh'ma* is itself preceded by a phrase which formally introduces the core of the service. The leader of the service calls the congregation to formal public worship as all rise and he chants *Barkhu* (Praise the Lord, Source of all blessing). After members of the congregation respond, they are seated and the service continues with the first benediction before *k'riat sh'ma*, praising God for Creation. (*Barkhu* is recited only with a *minyan*—at least a quorum of ten adults, required for acts of public worship.)

Amidah *(pages 65-77)*

The *Amidah*, recited while standing (as its Hebrew name indicates) follows *k'riat sh'ma* and its benedictions. Another name for this prayer is *shmoneh esreh*, which means "eighteen." Originally, this prayer consisted of eighteen benedictions. A nineteenth benediction was added in ancient times.

The first three benedictions continue the praise of

God reflected earlier in the service, now celebrating Him as God of history and of nature, and praising His holiness. The final three benedictions express gratitude to God and include a prayer for peace. (The words of the prayer for peace vary in the morning and the evening services.) These same six benedictions begin and conclude all versions of the *Amidah*, for daily, Shabbat and Festival services. The benedictions appearing between the first and the last three vary in number and in content, depending upon the occasion. The daily *Amidah* contains thirteen petitionary benedictions at this point, requesting knowledge, the acceptance of repentance, forgiveness, redemption, health, a productive year, the ingathering of exiles, justice, retribution for heretics and persecutors, reward for the righteous, the building of Jerusalem, messianic redemption, and God's hearing of prayer. (On Shabbat or a holiday, only one benediction reflecting the special nature of the day, is recited at this point, for a total of seven benedictions in the *Amidah*.)

On special occasions (such as Hanukkah, Purim, the first of the month, and Israel's Independence Day, or during the ten days of penitence) appropriate sections are added to the *Amidah*.

Although the *Amidah* is a formal structure of classic prayer, it is appropriate to add one's own prayers during the recitation of the petitionary benedictions, especially during the benediction *shomeia tefillah* ("Lord who hears prayer," page 73), and always after the conclusion of the *Amidah* (see page 77).

When the *Amidah* is repeated aloud by the Hazzan or other chanter of the service, in the morning or the

An introduction to the daily service

91

afternoon, *Kedushah* (proclaiming God's holiness) is inserted (page 67). This section is of mystic origin, inspired by the prophet Isaiah's vision.

Taḥanun

In ancient times it was the custom of many to continue in silent prayer without any fixed text for some minutes after the formal benedictions of the *Amidah* were concluded. Such prayers were called *taḥanun* (supplication). Over the years this custom of improvising became formalized, and gradually a fixed text was prescribed. *Taḥanun* for Monday and Thursday is longer than on other days.

Taḥanun is not recited in a house of mourning.

K'riat haTorah *Torah Reading*

The study of Torah is a central act of Jewish worship. On Monday and Thursday mornings (as on Shabbat afternoon) the first section of the prescribed reading for the following Shabbat is read. The Torah is also read on Rosh Ḥodesh (first of the month), Ḥanukkah, Purim, Intermediate Days of Passover and of Sukkot, Tisha B'av (morning and afternoon), Fast Days, and on Israel's Independence Day.

Although the Torah may be read in a house of mourning, customarily it is not. There are technical difficulties—a Sefer Torah must be acquired, and it must remain in the home to be used for at least three services.

An introduction to the daily service

Aleinu *(page 97)*

Since the fourteenth century, *Aleinu* has been included at the end of every service. Through these two paragraphs, Jews daily envision and pray for the universal recognition of God's sovereignty by a united mankind.

The daily Psalms *(pages 103-111)*

A special psalm for each day of the week was sung by the Levites in the ancient Temple in Jerusalem. These psalms are now part of the daily service. The psalm usually is added after *Aleinu*. (Some congregations insert the daily psalm earlier in the morning service.) Special psalms for other days and occasions are also added at this point. (For example, Psalm 49 in a house of mourning or Psalm 103 on Rosh Ḥodesh.)

Depending upon local custom, the mourner's *kaddish* is recited after *Aleinu* and after each of the added psalms, or it is recited one time only after *Aleinu and* the added psalm or psalms.

Kaddish

For a note on *kaddish*, see page 13. *Kaddish* is used in several forms *(ḥatzi kaddish, kaddish shalem)* to conclude sections of the service. Thus, for example, it is chanted after *yishtabaḥ* and before *barkhu*, after the Torah reading, and toward the end of the entire service, preceding *Aleinu*. It also is recited in a form known as Mourner's *kaddish* by mourners and by those observing *yahrzeit*.

An introduction to the daily service

Hallel

This collection of Psalms is added on special occasions such as Rosh Ḥodesh, the intermediate days of Passover and Sukkot, Ḥanukkah and Israel's Independence Day (as well as on Passover, Sukkot, and Shavuot).

Hallel is not recited in a house of mourning.

Musaf

An additional *Amidah* is recited on Rosh Ḥodesh (see page 195) and on the intermediate days of Passover and Sukkot. Another variation of the Musaf *Amidah* is added to the service on Shabbat and on holidays.

An introduction to the daily service

Yahrzeit

ANNIVERSARY OF THE DAY OF DEATH

Name _____

Date _____
             day   month   year

Hebrew name _____

Hebrew date _____

Name _____

Date _____
             day   month   year

Hebrew name _____

Hebrew date _____

Name _____

Date _____
             day   month   year

Hebrew name _____

Hebrew date _____

Yahrzeit

ANNIVERSARY OF THE DAY OF DEATH

Name _____

Date _____
                    day   month   year

Hebrew name _____

Hebrew date _____

Name _____

Date _____
                    day   month   year

Hebrew name _____

Hebrew date _____

Name _____

Date _____
                    day   month   year

Hebrew name _____

Hebrew date _____

בִּצְרוֹר הַחַיִּים

בִּצְרוֹר
הַחַיִּים

෴ THE BOND OF LIFE

A Book for Mourners

Edited by
RABBI JULES HARLOW

THE RABBINICAL ASSEMBLY
New York

✦ Contents

Throughout the Hebrew text, portions repeated by the Reader are indicated with a slash mark— \.

Morning service

שַׁחֲרִית ❧ ❧

מוֹדֶה אֲנִי לְפָנֶיךָ מֶלֶךְ חַי וְקַיָּם שֶׁהֶחֱזַרְתָּ בִּי נִשְׁמָתִי בְּחֶמְלָה. רַבָּה אֱמוּנָתֶךָ.

*Our morning benedictions celebrate the renewal of
life and the blessings of each day.*

*We put on the tallit, which reminds us of all the
commandments.*

בָּרוּךְ אַתָּה יְיָ אֱלֹהֵינוּ מֶלֶךְ הָעוֹלָם
אֲשֶׁר קִדְּשָׁנוּ בְּמִצְוֹתָיו וְצִוָּנוּ לְהִתְעַטֵּף בַּצִּיצִת.

בָּרְכִי נַפְשִׁי אֶת־יְיָ, יְיָ אֱלֹהַי גָּדַלְתָּ מְּאֹד, הוֹד וְהָדָר לָבָשְׁתָּ. עֹטֶה
אוֹר כַּשַּׂלְמָה, נוֹטֶה שָׁמַיִם כַּיְרִיעָה.

Meditation before putting on tefillin:

הִנְנִי מְכַוֵּן בְּהַנָּחַת תְּפִלִּין לְקַיֵּם מִצְוַת בּוֹרְאִי שֶׁצִּוָּנוּ לְהָנִיחַ
תְּפִלִּין, כַּכָּתוּב בַּתּוֹרָה: וּקְשַׁרְתָּם לְאוֹת עַל יָדֶךָ, וְהָיוּ לְטֹטָפֹת
בֵּין עֵינֶיךָ.

וְהֵם אַרְבַּע פָּרָשִׁיּוֹת אֵלּוּ: שְׁמַע, וְהָיָה אִם שָׁמֹעַ, קַדֶּשׁ, וְהָיָה
כִּי יְבִיאֲךָ, שֶׁיֵּשׁ בָּהֶם יִחוּדוֹ וְאַחְדוּתוֹ יִתְבָּרַךְ שְׁמוֹ.

Morning service

2

Birkhot Hashahar

ॐ

I thank You, eternal King, for restoring my soul in compassion. Great is Your faithfulness.

*Our morning benedictions celebrate the renewal
of life and the blessings of each day.*

We put on the tallit, *which reminds us
of all the commandments.*

Praised are You, Lord our God, King of the universe who sanctified our life with His commandments, commanding us to wear the *tallit* with fringes.

Let all my being praise the Lord who is clothed in magnificence, arrayed in majesty. He wraps Himself in light as in a garment. He unfolds the heavens as a curtain.

Meditation before putting on tefillin:

I put on tefillin in fulfillment of my Creator's commandment, written in the Torah: Bind them as a sign upon your hand, and set them as frontlets between your eyes.

The tefillin contain four passages from the Torah which teach the unity of God, recall the miracle of the Exodus, declare His dominion over all that is in the heavens and on earth, and affirm our duty to serve God with soul and heart and mind.

Morning service

3

וְצִוָּנוּ לְהָנִּיחַ עַל הַיָד לְזִכְרוֹן זְרוֹעוֹ הַנְּטוּיָה, וְשֶׁהִיא נֶגֶד הַלֵּב לְשַׁעְבֵּד בָּזֶה תַּאֲווֹת וּמַחְשְׁבוֹת לִבֵּנוּ לַעֲבוֹדָתוֹ, יִתְבָּרַךְ שְׁמוֹ, וְעַל הָרֹאשׁ נֶגֶד הַמֹּחַ, שֶׁהַנְּשָׁמָה שֶׁבְּמֹחִי עִם שְׁאָר חוּשַׁי וְכֹחוֹתַי כֻּלָּם יִהְיוּ מְשֻׁעְבָּדִים לַעֲבוֹדָתוֹ, יִתְבָּרַךְ שְׁמוֹ.

While placing tefillin *on the arm:*

בָּרוּךְ אַתָּה יְיָ אֱלֹהֵינוּ מֶלֶךְ הָעוֹלָם,
אֲשֶׁר קִדְּשָׁנוּ בְּמִצְוֹתָיו וְצִוָּנוּ לְהָנִּיחַ תְּפִלִּין.

While placing tefillin *on the head:*

בָּרוּךְ אַתָּה יְיָ אֱלֹהֵינוּ מֶלֶךְ הָעוֹלָם,
אֲשֶׁר קִדְּשָׁנוּ בְּמִצְוֹתָיו וְצִוָּנוּ עַל מִצְוַת תְּפִלִּין.

בָּרוּךְ שֵׁם כְּבוֹד מַלְכוּתוֹ לְעוֹלָם וָעֶד.

While placing the strap around the finger:

וְאֵרַשְׂתִּיךְ לִי לְעוֹלָם, וְאֵרַשְׂתִּיךְ לִי בְּצֶדֶק וּבְמִשְׁפָּט וּבְחֶסֶד וּבְרַחֲמִים. וְאֵרַשְׂתִּיךְ לִי בֶּאֱמוּנָה, וְיָדַעַתְּ אֶת־יְיָ.

We are commanded to place tefillin on the arm nearest the heart, that we may recall His outstretched arm, and be reminded to subject our impulses and desires to His service. We place tefillin also on the head to remind us of the duty to direct all the power of our mind to His service, praised be He.

While placing tefillin *on the arm:*

Praised are You, Lord our God, King of the universe who sanctified us with His commandments, commanding us to put on tefillin.

While placing tefillin *on the head:*

Praised are You, Lord our God, King of the universe who sanctified us with His commandments, commanding us concerning tefillin.

Praised be His glorious sovereignty throughout all time.

While placing the strap around the finger:

I will betroth you to Me forever. I will betroth you with righteousness, with justice, love and compassion. I will betroth you to Me in faithfulness, and you shall love the Lord.

בְּטֶרֶם כָּל־יְצִיר נִבְרָא.   אֲדוֹן עוֹלָם אֲשֶׁר מָלַךְ

אֲזַי מֶלֶךְ שְׁמוֹ נִקְרָא.   לְעֵת נַעֲשָׂה בְחֶפְצוֹ כֹּל

לְבַדּוֹ יִמְלֹךְ נוֹרָא.   וְאַחֲרֵי כִּכְלוֹת הַכֹּל

וְהוּא יִהְיֶה בְּתִפְאָרָה.   וְהוּא הָיָה וְהוּא הֹוֶה

לְהַמְשִׁיל לוֹ לְהַחְבִּירָה.   וְהוּא אֶחָד וְאֵין שֵׁנִי

וְלוֹ הָעֹז וְהַמִּשְׂרָה.   בְּלִי רֵאשִׁית בְּלִי תַכְלִית

וְצוּר חֶבְלִי בְּעֵת צָרָה.   וְהוּא אֵלִי וְחַי גּוֹאֲלִי

מְנָת כּוֹסִי בְּיוֹם אֶקְרָא.   וְהוּא נִסִּי וּמָנוֹס לִי

בְּעֵת אִישַׁן וְאָעִירָה.   בְּיָדוֹ אַפְקִיד רוּחִי

יְיָ לִי וְלֹא אִירָא.   וְעִם רוּחִי גְוִיָּתִי

הֲרֵינִי מְקַבֵּל עָלַי מִצְוַת הַבּוֹרֵא: וְאָהַבְתָּ לְרֵעֲךָ כָּמוֹךָ.

We are grateful for the gift of our body

בָּרוּךְ אַתָּה יְיָ אֱלֹהֵינוּ מֶלֶךְ הָעוֹלָם אֲשֶׁר יָצַר אֶת־הָאָדָם בְּחָכְמָה וּבָרָא בוֹ נְקָבִים נְקָבִים חֲלוּלִים חֲלוּלִים.\גָּלוּי וְיָדוּעַ לִפְנֵי כִסֵּא כְבוֹדֶךָ שֶׁאִם יִפָּתֵחַ אֶחָד מֵהֶם אוֹ יִסָּתֵם אֶחָד מֵהֶם אִי אֶפְשָׁר לְהִתְקַיֵּם וְלַעֲמֹד לְפָנֶיךָ. בָּרוּךְ אַתָּה יְיָ רוֹפֵא כָל־בָּשָׂר וּמַפְלִיא לַעֲשׂוֹת.

The Lord eternal reigned before the birth of every living thing.

When all was made, as He ordained, then only was He known as King.

When all is ended He alone will reign in awesome majesty.

He was, He is, and He will be, glorious in eternity.

Peerless and unique is He, with none at all to be compared.

Beginningless and endless, His vast dominion is not shared.

My God, my life's redeemer, He is my refuge in distress,

My shelter sure, my cup of life with goodness limitless.

When I wake, as when I sleep, my spirit in His care I place.

Body and spirit in His keep, I have no fear, held in His grace.

I hereby accept the obligation of fulfilling my Creator's commandment in the Torah: Love your neighbor as yourself.

We are grateful for the gift of our body

Praised are You, Lord our God, King of the universe who has fashioned the body with wisdom, creating veins and arteries and all vital organs, a delicately balanced complex, marvelous in structure, intricate in design. The failure of a single part can cause the collapse of this complex. Praised are You, Lord, Healer of all flesh who sustains our bodies with wondrous ways.

We are grateful for the gift of our soul

אֱלֹהַי, נְשָׁמָה שֶׁנָּתַתָּ בִּי טְהוֹרָה הִיא. אַתָּה בְרָאתָהּ אַתָּה יְצַרְתָּהּ
אַתָּה נְפַחְתָּהּ בִּי וְאַתָּה מְשַׁמְּרָהּ בְּקִרְבִּי וְאַתָּה עָתִיד לִטְּלָהּ מִמֶּנִּי
וּלְהַחֲזִירָהּ בִּי לֶעָתִיד לָבוֹא.\כָּל־זְמַן שֶׁהַנְּשָׁמָה בְּקִרְבִּי מוֹדֶה אֲנִי
לְפָנֶיךָ יְיָ אֱלֹהַי וֵאלֹהֵי אֲבוֹתַי רִבּוֹן כָּל־הַמַּעֲשִׂים אֲדוֹן כָּל־
הַנְּשָׁמוֹת. בָּרוּךְ אַתָּה יְיָ הַמַּחֲזִיר נְשָׁמוֹת לִפְגָרִים מֵתִים.

We are grateful for the renewal of each day

בָּרוּךְ אַתָּה יְיָ אֱלֹהֵינוּ מֶלֶךְ הָעוֹלָם,

אֲשֶׁר נָתַן לַשֶּׂכְוִי בִינָה לְהַבְחִין בֵּין יוֹם וּבֵין לָיְלָה.

בָּרוּךְ אַתָּה יְיָ אֱלֹהֵינוּ מֶלֶךְ הָעוֹלָם, שֶׁעָשַׂנִי בְּצַלְמוֹ.

בָּרוּךְ אַתָּה יְיָ אֱלֹהֵינוּ מֶלֶךְ הָעוֹלָם, שֶׁעָשַׂנִי יִשְׂרָאֵל.

בָּרוּךְ אַתָּה יְיָ אֱלֹהֵינוּ מֶלֶךְ הָעוֹלָם, שֶׁעָשַׂנִי בֶּן־חוֹרִין.

בָּרוּךְ אַתָּה יְיָ אֱלֹהֵינוּ מֶלֶךְ הָעוֹלָם, פּוֹקֵחַ עִוְרִים.

בָּרוּךְ אַתָּה יְיָ אֱלֹהֵינוּ מֶלֶךְ הָעוֹלָם, מַלְבִּישׁ עֲרֻמִּים.

בָּרוּךְ אַתָּה יְיָ אֱלֹהֵינוּ מֶלֶךְ הָעוֹלָם, מַתִּיר אֲסוּרִים.

בָּרוּךְ אַתָּה יְיָ אֱלֹהֵינוּ מֶלֶךְ הָעוֹלָם, זוֹקֵף כְּפוּפִים.

בָּרוּךְ אַתָּה יְיָ אֱלֹהֵינוּ מֶלֶךְ הָעוֹלָם, רוֹקַע הָאָרֶץ עַל הַמָּיִם.

בָּרוּךְ אַתָּה יְיָ אֱלֹהֵינוּ מֶלֶךְ הָעוֹלָם, שֶׁעָשָׂה לִי כָּל־צָרְכִּי.

בָּרוּךְ אַתָּה יְיָ אֱלֹהֵינוּ מֶלֶךְ הָעוֹלָם, הַמֵּכִין מִצְעֲדֵי־גָבֶר.

We are grateful for the gift of our soul

The soul You have given me is pure, my God. You created it, You formed it, You breathed it into me and You preserve it within me. You will also take it from me, and You will restore it to me in time to come. So long as this soul is within me I acknowledge You, Lord my God and God of my fathers, Master of all creation, Lord of all souls. Praised are You, Lord who restores the soul to the lifeless, exhausted body.

We are grateful for the renewal of each day

Praised are You, Lord our God, King of the universe

who enables His creatures to distinguish between night and day,

who made me in His image,

who made me a Jew,

who made me free,

who gives sight to the blind,

who clothes the naked,

who releases the bound,

who raises the downtrodden,

who creates heaven and earth,

who provides for all my needs,

who guides man on his path,

בָּרוּךְ אַתָּה יְיָ אֱלֹהֵינוּ מֶלֶךְ הָעוֹלָם, אוֹזֵר יִשְׂרָאֵל בִּגְבוּרָה.

בָּרוּךְ אַתָּה יְיָ אֱלֹהֵינוּ מֶלֶךְ הָעוֹלָם, עוֹטֵר יִשְׂרָאֵל בְּתִפְאָרָה.

בָּרוּךְ אַתָּה יְיָ אֱלֹהֵינוּ מֶלֶךְ הָעוֹלָם, הַנּוֹתֵן לַיָּעֵף כֹּחַ.

We are grateful for compassion, for which we pray

בָּרוּךְ אַתָּה יְיָ אֱלֹהֵינוּ מֶלֶךְ הָעוֹלָם הַמַּעֲבִיר שֵׁנָה מֵעֵינַי וּתְנוּמָה
מֵעַפְעַפָּי. וִיהִי רָצוֹן מִלְּפָנֶיךָ יְיָ אֱלֹהֵינוּ וֵאלֹהֵי אֲבוֹתֵינוּ שֶׁתַּרְגִּילֵנוּ
בְּתוֹרָתֶךָ וְדַבְּקֵנוּ בְּמִצְוֹתֶיךָ, וְאַל תְּבִיאֵנוּ לֹא לִידֵי חֵטְא וְלֹא לִידֵי
עֲבֵרָה וְעָוֹן וְלֹא לִידֵי נִסָּיוֹן וְלֹא לִידֵי בִזָּיוֹן, וְאַל תַּשְׁלֶט־בָּנוּ יֵצֶר
הָרָע וְהַרְחִיקֵנוּ מֵאָדָם רָע וּמֵחָבֵר רָע. וְדַבְּקֵנוּ בְּיֵצֶר הַטּוֹב
וּבְמַעֲשִׂים טוֹבִים וְכֹף אֶת־יִצְרֵנוּ לְהִשְׁתַּעְבֶּד־לָךְ.\וּתְנֵנוּ הַיּוֹם
וּבְכָל־יוֹם לְחֵן וּלְחֶסֶד וּלְרַחֲמִים בְּעֵינֶיךָ וּבְעֵינֵי כָל־רוֹאֵינוּ
וְתִגְמְלֵנוּ חֲסָדִים טוֹבִים. בָּרוּךְ אַתָּה יְיָ גּוֹמֵל חֲסָדִים טוֹבִים לְעַמּוֹ
יִשְׂרָאֵל.

יְהִי רָצוֹן מִלְּפָנֶיךָ יְיָ אֱלֹהַי וֵאלֹהֵי אֲבוֹתַי, שֶׁתַּצִּילֵנִי הַיּוֹם וּבְכָל־יוֹם
מֵעַזֵּי פָנִים וּמֵעַזּוּת פָּנִים, מֵאָדָם רָע וּמֵחָבֵר רָע וּמִשָּׁכֵן רָע וּמִפֶּגַע
רָע וּמִשָּׂטָן הַמַּשְׁחִית, מִדִּין קָשֶׁה וּמִבַּעַל דִּין קָשֶׁה, בֵּין שֶׁהוּא בֶן־
בְּרִית וּבֵין שֶׁאֵינוֹ בֶן־בְּרִית.

Aware of our mortality, we are grateful for the covenant

who strengthens the people Israel with courage,

who crowns the people Israel with glory,

who restores vigor to the weary.

We are grateful for compassion, for which we pray

Praised are You, Lord our God, King of the universe who removes sleep from my eyes and slumber from my eyelids. May we feel at home with Your Torah and cling to Your commandments. Keep us from error, from sin and transgression. Bring us not to trial or to disgrace. Let no evil impulse master us. Keep us far from wicked men and corrupt companions. Strengthen our desire to do good deeds; teach us humility, that we may serve You. May we find grace, love and compassion in Your sight and in the sight of all who look upon us, this day and every day. Grant us a full measure of lovingkindness. Praised are You, Lord who bestows lovingkindness upon His people Israel.

May it be Your will, Lord my God and God of my fathers, to protect me this day and every day from insolence in others and from arrogance in myself. Save me from vicious people, from bad neighbors, and from corrupt companions. Preserve me from misfortune and from powers of destruction. Save me from harsh judgments; spare me from ruthless opponents, be they members of the covenant or not.

Aware of our mortality, we are grateful for the covenant

לְעוֹלָם יְהֵא אָדָם יָרֵא שָׁמַיִם בַּסֵּתֶר וּבַגָּלוּי
וּמוֹדֶה עַל הָאֱמֶת וְדוֹבֵר אֱמֶת בִּלְבָבוֹ וְיַשְׁכֵּם וְיֹאמַר:

רִבּוֹן כָּל־הָעוֹלָמִים, לֹא עַל צִדְקוֹתֵינוּ אֲנַחְנוּ מַפִּילִים תַּחֲנוּנֵינוּ
לְפָנֶיךָ כִּי עַל רַחֲמֶיךָ הָרַבִּים. מָה אָנוּ, מֶה חַיֵּינוּ, מֶה חַסְדֵּנוּ, מַה־
צִּדְקֵנוּ, מַה־יְשׁוּעָתֵנוּ, מַה־כֹּחֵנוּ, מַה־גְּבוּרָתֵנוּ. מַה־נֹּאמַר לְפָנֶיךָ יְיָ
אֱלֹהֵינוּ וֵאלֹהֵי אֲבוֹתֵינוּ, הֲלֹא כָּל־הַגִּבּוֹרִים כְּאַיִן לְפָנֶיךָ וְאַנְשֵׁי הַשֵּׁם
כְּלֹא הָיוּ וַחֲכָמִים כִּבְלִי מַדָּע וּנְבוֹנִים כִּבְלִי הַשְׂכֵּל, כִּי רֹב מַעֲשֵׂיהֶם
תֹּהוּ וִימֵי חַיֵּיהֶם הֶבֶל לְפָנֶיךָ. וּמוֹתַר הָאָדָם מִן הַבְּהֵמָה אָיִן, כִּי הַכֹּל
הָבֶל.

אֲבָל אֲנַחְנוּ עַמְּךָ בְּנֵי בְרִיתֶךָ, בְּנֵי אַבְרָהָם אֹהַבְךָ שֶׁנִּשְׁבַּעְתָּ לוֹ בְּהַר
הַמֹּרִיָּה, זֶרַע יִצְחָק יְחִידוֹ שֶׁנֶּעֱקַד עַל גַּב הַמִּזְבֵּחַ, עֲדַת יַעֲקֹב בִּנְךָ
בְּכוֹרֶךָ שֶׁמֵּאַהֲבָתְךָ שֶׁאָהַבְתָּ אוֹתוֹ וּמִשִּׂמְחָתְךָ שֶׁשָּׂמַחְתָּ בּוֹ קָרָאתָ
אֶת־שְׁמוֹ יִשְׂרָאֵל וִישֻׁרוּן.

לְפִיכָךְ אֲנַחְנוּ חַיָּבִים לְהוֹדוֹת לְךָ וּלְשַׁבֵּחֲךָ וּלְפָאֶרְךָ וּלְבָרֵךְ וּלְקַדֵּשׁ
וְלָתֵת שֶׁבַח וְהוֹדָיָה לִשְׁמֶךָ. אַשְׁרֵינוּ, מַה־טּוֹב חֶלְקֵנוּ וּמַה־נָּעִים
גּוֹרָלֵנוּ וּמַה־יָּפָה יְרֻשָּׁתֵנוּ.\אַשְׁרֵינוּ שֶׁאֲנַחְנוּ מַשְׁכִּימִים וּמַעֲרִיבִים עֶרֶב
וָבֹקֶר וְאוֹמְרִים פַּעֲמַיִם בְּכָל־יוֹם:

שְׁמַע יִשְׂרָאֵל יְיָ אֱלֹהֵינוּ יְיָ אֶחָד.

בָּרוּךְ שֵׁם כְּבוֹד מַלְכוּתוֹ לְעוֹלָם וָעֶד.

A person should always revere God, in private as in public. He should acknowledge the truth and practice it in thought as in deed. On arising he should declare:

Lord of all worlds! Not upon our merit do we rely in supplication, but upon Your boundless compassion. What are we? What is our piety? What is our righteousness? What is our attainment, our power, our might? What can we say, Lord our God and God of our fathers? Compared to You, all the mighty are nothing, the famous are non-existent, the wise lack wisdom, the clever lack reason. For most of their actions are meaninglessness, the days of their lives emptiness. Man's superiority to the beast is an illusion. All life is a fleeting breath.

But we are Your people, partners to Your covenant, descendants of Your beloved Abraham to whom You made a pledge on Mount Moriah. We are the heirs of Isaac, his son bound upon the altar. We are Your firstborn people, the congregation of Isaac's son Jacob whom You named Israel and Jeshurun, because of Your love for him and Your delight in him.

Therefore it is our duty to thank You and praise You, to glorify and sanctify Your name among men. How good is our portion, how pleasant our lot, how beautiful our heritage. How blessed are we that twice each day, morning and evening, we are privileged to declare:

HEAR, O ISRAEL: THE LORD OUR GOD, THE LORD IS ONE.

Praised be His glorious sovereignty throughout all time.

Morning service

אַתָּה הוּא עַד שֶׁלֹּא נִבְרָא הָעוֹלָם, אַתָּה הוּא מִשֶּׁנִּבְרָא הָעוֹלָם, אַתָּה הוּא בָּעוֹלָם הַזֶּה וְאַתָּה הוּא לָעוֹלָם הַבָּא.\קַדֵּשׁ אֶת־שִׁמְךָ עַל מַקְדִּישֵׁי שְׁמֶךָ וְקַדֵּשׁ אֶת־שִׁמְךָ בְּעוֹלָמֶךָ. וּבִישׁוּעָתְךָ תָּרִים וְתַגְבִּיהַּ קַרְנֵנוּ. בָּרוּךְ אַתָּה יְיָ מְקַדֵּשׁ אֶת־שִׁמְךָ בָּרַבִּים.

בָּרוּךְ אַתָּה יְיָ אֱלֹהֵינוּ מֶלֶךְ הָעוֹלָם אֲשֶׁר קִדְּשָׁנוּ בְּמִצְוֹתָיו וְצִוָּנוּ לַעֲסֹק בְּדִבְרֵי תוֹרָה.

וְהַעֲרֶב־נָא יְיָ אֱלֹהֵינוּ אֶת־דִּבְרֵי תוֹרָתְךָ בְּפִינוּ וּבְפִי עַמְּךָ בֵּית יִשְׂרָאֵל, וְנִהְיֶה אֲנַחְנוּ וְצֶאֱצָאֵינוּ וְצֶאֱצָאֵי עַמְּךָ בֵּית יִשְׂרָאֵל כֻּלָּנוּ יוֹדְעֵי שְׁמֶךָ וְלוֹמְדֵי תוֹרָתֶךָ לִשְׁמָהּ.\בָּרוּךְ אַתָּה יְיָ הַמְלַמֵּד תּוֹרָה לְעַמּוֹ יִשְׂרָאֵל. בָּרוּךְ אַתָּה יְיָ אֱלֹהֵינוּ מֶלֶךְ הָעוֹלָם אֲשֶׁר בָּחַר בָּנוּ מִכָּל־הָעַמִּים וְנָתַן לָנוּ אֶת־תּוֹרָתוֹ. בָּרוּךְ אַתָּה יְיָ נוֹתֵן הַתּוֹרָה.

קְדֹשִׁים תִּהְיוּ כִּי קָדוֹשׁ אֲנִי יְיָ אֱלֹהֵיכֶם. לֹא תְקַלֵּל חֵרֵשׁ וְלִפְנֵי עִוֵּר לֹא תִתֵּן מִכְשֹׁל. לֹא תַעֲשׂוּ עָוֶל בַּמִּשְׁפָּט, לֹא תִשָּׂא פְנֵי דָל וְלֹא תֶהְדַּר פְּנֵי גָדוֹל, בְּצֶדֶק תִּשְׁפֹּט עֲמִיתֶךָ. לֹא תַעֲמֹד עַל דַּם רֵעֶךָ. לֹא תִשְׂנָא אֶת־אָחִיךָ בִּלְבָבֶךָ. וְאָהַבְתָּ לְרֵעֲךָ כָּמוֹךָ, אֲנִי יְיָ.

We are grateful for holiness

You are the Lord eternal, before Creation and since Creation, in this world and in the world to come. Manifest Your holiness through those who hallow You, raising us to dignity and strength. Praised are You, Lord who manifests His holiness to all mankind.

We are grateful for Torah, which we now study

Praised are You, Lord our God, King of the universe who sanctified our life with His commandments, commanding us to study Torah.

May the words of Torah, Lord our God, be sweet in our mouth and in the mouth of all Your people so that we, our children, and all the children of the House of Israel may come to know You and to study Your Torah with selfless devotion. Praised are You, Lord who teaches Torah to His people Israel. Praised are You, Lord our God, King of the universe who has chosen us by giving us His Torah. Praised are You, Lord who gives the Torah.

You shall be holy, for I the Lord your God am holy. You shall not insult the deaf, or put a stumbling block before the blind. You shall not render an unjust decision; do not be partial to the poor or show deference to the rich; judge your neighbor fairly. Do not stand idly by the blood of your neighbor. You shall not hate your brother in your heart. Love your neighbor as yourself; I am the Lord.

Leviticus 19:1, 14–18

אֵלּוּ דְבָרִים שֶׁאֵין לָהֶם שִׁעוּר: הַפֵּאָה וְהַבִּכּוּרִים וְהָרֵאָיוֹן וּגְמִילוּת חֲסָדִים וְתַלְמוּד תּוֹרָה.

אֵלּוּ דְבָרִים שֶׁאָדָם אוֹכֵל פֵּרוֹתֵיהֶם בָּעוֹלָם הַזֶּה וְהַקֶּרֶן קַיֶּמֶת לוֹ לָעוֹלָם הַבָּא, וְאֵלּוּ הֵן: כִּבּוּד אָב וָאֵם וּגְמִילוּת חֲסָדִים וְהַשְׁכָּמַת בֵּית הַמִּדְרָשׁ שַׁחֲרִית וְעַרְבִית וְהַכְנָסַת אוֹרְחִים וּבִקּוּר חוֹלִים וְהַכְנָסַת כַּלָּה וּלְוָיַת הַמֵּת וְעִיּוּן תְּפִלָּה וַהֲבָאַת שָׁלוֹם בֵּין אָדָם לַחֲבֵרוֹ, וְתַלְמוּד תּוֹרָה כְּנֶגֶד כֻּלָּם.

The following paragraph or one of the paragraphs on page 18 may be selected.

חַיָּב אָדָם לְבָרֵךְ עַל הָרָעָה כְּשֵׁם שֶׁהוּא מְבָרֵךְ עַל הַטּוֹבָה, שֶׁנֶּאֱמַר: וְאָהַבְתָּ אֵת יְיָ אֱלֹהֶיךָ בְּכָל־לְבָבְךָ וּבְכָל־נַפְשְׁךָ וּבְכָל־מְאֹדֶךָ. בְּכָל־לְבָבְךָ׳, בִּשְׁנֵי יְצָרֶיךָ, בְּיֵצֶר טוֹב וּבְיֵצֶר רָע. וּבְכָל־נַפְשְׁךָ׳, אֲפִלּוּ הוּא נוֹטֵל אֶת־נַפְשֶׁךָ. וּבְכָל־מְאֹדֶךָ׳, בְּכָל־מָמוֹנְךָ.

These are the commandments for which there is no prescribed measure: leaving crops at the corner of a field for the poor, offering first fruit as a gift to the Temple, bringing special offerings to the Temple on the three Festivals, doing deeds of lovingkindness, and studying Torah.

Mishnah Peah 1:1

These are the commandments which yield immediate fruit and continue to yield fruit in time to come: honoring parents, doing deeds of lovingkindness, attending the house of study punctually, morning and evening, providing hospitality, visiting the sick, helping the needy bride, attending the dead, devotion in prayer, and making peace between people. And the study of Torah is basic to them all.

Shabbat 127a

The following paragraph or one of the paragraphs
on page 19 may be selected.

One is obliged to bless God for the evil in life in the same spirit as one blesses God for the good in life, as it is written, "Love the Lord your God with all your heart, and all your soul and all your might" (Deuteronomy 6:5). In the Hebrew for "heart" in this verse, the letter *bet* is repeated *(levav)*; usually the word is written with one *bet (lev)*. From this we derive the lesson that we must love God with both of our impulses, the impulse to evil and the impulse to good. "And with all your soul"—even if He should take your soul, your life. "And with all your might"—with all of your material possessions.

Mishnah Berakhot 9:5

רַבִּי יַעֲקֹב אוֹמֵר: הָעוֹלָם הַזֶּה דּוֹמֶה לַפְּרוֹזְדוֹר בִּפְנֵי הָעוֹלָם הַבָּא. הַתְקֵן עַצְמְךָ בַּפְּרוֹזְדוֹר כְּדֵי שֶׁתִּכָּנֵס לַטְּרַקְלִין. הוּא הָיָה אוֹמֵר: יָפָה שָׁעָה אַחַת בִּתְשׁוּבָה וּמַעֲשִׂים טוֹבִים בָּעוֹלָם הַזֶּה מִכָּל־חַיֵּי הָעוֹלָם הַבָּא, וְיָפָה שָׁעָה אַחַת שֶׁל קוֹרַת רוּחַ בָּעוֹלָם הַבָּא מִכָּל־חַיֵּי הָעוֹלָם הַזֶּה.

רַבִּי יוֹחָנָן כִּי הֲוָה מְסַיֵּים סִפְרָא דְאִיּוֹב אָמַר הָכִי: סוֹף אָדָם לָמוּת וְסוֹף בְּהֵמָה לִשְׁחִיטָה וְהַכֹּל לְמִיתָה הֵם עוֹמְדִים. אַשְׁרֵי מִי שֶׁגָּדֵל בַּתּוֹרָה וַעֲמָלוֹ בַּתּוֹרָה וְעוֹשֶׂה נָחַת רוּחַ לְיוֹצְרוֹ, וְגָדֵל בְּשֵׁם טוֹב וְנִפְטָר בְּשֵׁם טוֹב מִן הָעוֹלָם, וְעָלָיו אָמַר שְׁלֹמֹה, "טוֹב שֵׁם מִשֶּׁמֶן טוֹב וְיוֹם הַמָּוֶת מִיּוֹם הִוָּלְדוֹ."

רַבִּי עֲקִיבָא אוֹמֵר: חָבִיב אָדָם שֶׁנִּבְרָא בְּצֶלֶם. חִבָּה יְתֵרָה נוֹדַעַת לוֹ שֶׁנִּבְרָא בְּצֶלֶם אֱלֹהִים, שֶׁנֶּאֱמַר: ,כִּי בְּצֶלֶם אֱלֹהִים עָשָׂה אֶת־הָאָדָם'. חֲבִיבִין יִשְׂרָאֵל שֶׁנִּקְרְאוּ בָנִים לַמָּקוֹם. חִבָּה יְתֵרָה נוֹדַעַת לָהֶם שֶׁנִּקְרְאוּ בָנִים לַמָּקוֹם, שֶׁנֶּאֱמַר: ,בָּנִים אַתֶּם לַייָ אֱלֹהֵיכֶם'. חֲבִיבִין יִשְׂרָאֵל שֶׁנִּתַּן לָהֶם כְּלִי חֶמְדָּה. חִבָּה יְתֵרָה נוֹדַעַת לָהֶם שֶׁנִּתַּן לָהֶם כְּלִי חֶמְדָּה שֶׁבּוֹ נִבְרָא הָעוֹלָם, שֶׁנֶּאֱמַר: ,כִּי לֶקַח טוֹב נָתַתִּי לָכֶם, תּוֹרָתִי אַל תַּעֲזֹבוּ'.

Rabbi Jacob said: This world is like a vestibule leading to the world to come. Prepare yourself in the vestibule so that you may enter the banquet hall. He used to say: One hour of repentance and good deeds in this world is better than the whole life of the world to come; and one hour of bliss in the world to come is better than the whole life of this world.

Mishnah Avot 4:16-17

When Rabbi Yohanan finished reading the Book of Job he would say: The end of a man is death and the end of a beast is slaughter. Every creature born must die. Blessed is he who was reared in Torah and who labored in Torah, who pleased his Creator, who lived with a good name and who departed this world with a good name. Of such a person, Solomon said, "A good name is better than precious oil, and the day of death is better than the day of birth" (Ecclesiastes 8:1).

Berakhot 17a

Rabbi Akiba would say: Beloved is man, for he was created in the image of God. Greater yet is the love which made this known to him, for it is written, "In the image of God He made man" (Genesis 9:6). Beloved are the people Israel, for they are called children of God. Greater yet is the love which made this known to them, for it is written, "You are children of the Lord your God" (Deuteronomy 14:1). Beloved are the people Israel, for they were given the precious instrument with which the world was created. Greater yet is the love which made this known to them, for it is written, "I have given you a good doctrine; forsake not My Torah" (Proverbs 4:2).

Mishnah Avot 3:18

Morning service

יְהִי רָצוֹן מִלְּפָנֶיךָ יְיָ אֱלֹהֵינוּ וֵאלֹהֵי אֲבוֹתֵינוּ, שֶׁתִּתֵּן חֶלְקֵנוּ בְּתוֹרָתֶךָ, וְנִהְיֶה מִתַּלְמִידָיו שֶׁל אַהֲרֹן הַכֹּהֵן, אוֹהֵב שָׁלוֹם וְרוֹדֵף שָׁלוֹם, אוֹהֵב אֶת־הַבְּרִיּוֹת וּמְקָרְבָן לַתּוֹרָה.

Kaddish Derabanan

Mourners and those observing Yahrzeit rise for Kaddish Derabanan.

יִתְגַּדַּל וְיִתְקַדַּשׁ שְׁמֵהּ רַבָּא בְּעָלְמָא דִּי בְרָא כִרְעוּתֵהּ, וְיַמְלִיךְ מַלְכוּתֵהּ בְּחַיֵּיכוֹן וּבְיוֹמֵיכוֹן וּבְחַיֵּי דְכָל־בֵּית יִשְׂרָאֵל בַּעֲגָלָא וּבִזְמַן קָרִיב, וְאִמְרוּ אָמֵן.

Congregation and mourner:

יְהֵא שְׁמֵהּ רַבָּא מְבָרַךְ לְעָלַם וּלְעָלְמֵי עָלְמַיָּא.

Mourner:

יִתְבָּרַךְ וְיִשְׁתַּבַּח וְיִתְפָּאַר וְיִתְרוֹמַם וְיִתְנַשֵּׂא וְיִתְהַדָּר וְיִתְעַלֶּה וְיִתְהַלָּל שְׁמֵהּ דְּקֻדְשָׁא בְּרִיךְ הוּא, לְעֵלָּא (לְעֵלָּא) מִן כָּל־בִּרְכָתָא וְשִׁירָתָא תֻּשְׁבְּחָתָא וְנֶחֱמָתָא דַּאֲמִירָן בְּעָלְמָא, וְאִמְרוּ אָמֵן.

עַל יִשְׂרָאֵל וְעַל רַבָּנָן וְעַל תַּלְמִידֵיהוֹן וְעַל כָּל־תַּלְמִידֵי תַלְמִידֵיהוֹן וְעַל כָּל־מָאן דְּעָסְקִין בְּאוֹרַיְתָא, דִּי בְאַתְרָא הָדֵין וְדִי בְכָל־אֲתַר וַאֲתַר, יְהֵא לְהוֹן וּלְכוֹן שְׁלָמָא רַבָּא, חִנָּא וְחִסְדָּא וְרַחֲמִין וְחַיִּין אֲרִיכִין וּמְזוֹנָא רְוִיחָא וּפוּרְקָנָא מִן קֳדָם אֲבוּהוֹן דִּי בִשְׁמַיָּא, וְאִמְרוּ אָמֵן.

יְהֵא שְׁלָמָא רַבָּא מִן שְׁמַיָּא וְחַיִּים טוֹבִים עָלֵינוּ וְעַל כָּל־יִשְׂרָאֵל, וְאִמְרוּ אָמֵן.

עוֹשֶׂה שָׁלוֹם בִּמְרוֹמָיו הוּא בְּרַחֲמָיו יַעֲשֶׂה שָׁלוֹם עָלֵינוּ וְעַל כָּל־יִשְׂרָאֵל, וְאִמְרוּ אָמֵן.

Morning service

May it be Your will, Lord our God and God of our fathers, to grant our portion in Your Torah. May we be disciples of Aaron the kohen, loving peace and pursuing peace, loving our fellow creatures and drawing them near to the Torah.

Kaddish Derabanan

Mourners and those observing Yahrzeit rise for Kaddish Derabanan.

Yit-gadal ve-yit-kadash shmei raba, b'alma divra khir'utei ve-yamlikh mal-khutei be-hayei-khon uve'yomei-khon uve-hayei di-khol beit yisrael ba-agala u-vizman kariv, v'imru amen.

Congregation and mourner:

Ye-hei shmei raba meva-rakh l'alam ul'almei 'almaya.

Mourner:

Yit-barakh ve-yish-tabah ve-yitpa'ar ve-yitromam ve-yitnasei ve-yit-hadar ve-yit'aleh ve-yit-halal shmei di-kudsha brikh hu, l'eila (l'eila) min kol bir-khata ve-shirata tush-be-hata ve-nehe-mata da-amiran b'alma, v'imru amen.

'Al yisrael v'al rabanan v'al talmidei-hon v'al kol talmidei talmidei-hon v'al kol man d'askin b'oraita, di v'atra ha-dein v'di v'khol atar va-atar, ye-hei le-hon ule-khon shlama raba, hina ve-hisda ve-rahamin ve-hayin arikhin u-mezona re-viha u-fur-kana min kodam avu-hon di vi-shmaya, v'imru amen.

Ye-hei shlama raba min shmaya ve-hayim tovim aleinu v'al kol yisrael, v'imru amen.

Oseh shalom bimromav hu b'rahamav ya'aseh shalom aleinu v'al kol yisrael, v'imru amen.

For translation, see the following page.

Morning service

Kaddish Derabanan

Mourner:

Hallowed and enhanced may He be throughout the world of His own creation. May He cause His sovereignty soon to be accepted, during our life and the life of all Israel. And let us say: Amen.

Congregation and mourner:

Ye-hei shmei raba mevarakh l'alam ul'almei 'almaya.

May He be praised throughout all time.

Mourner:

Glorified and celebrated, lauded and praised, acclaimed and honored, extolled and exalted may the Holy One be, far beyond all song and psalm, beyond all tributes which man can utter. And let us say: Amen.

Heavenly Father, grant lasting peace to our people and their leaders, to our teachers and their disciples, to all who engage in the study of Torah in this land and in all other lands. Let there be grace and kindness, compassion and love for them and for us all. Grant us fullness of life, and sustenance. Save us from all danger and distress. And let us say: Amen.

Let there be abundant peace from Heaven, with life's goodness for us and for all the people Israel. And let us say: Amen.

He who brings peace to His universe mercifully will bring peace to us, and to all the people Israel. And let us say: Amen.

Morning service

מִזְמוֹר שִׁיר חֲנֻכַּת הַבַּיִת לְדָוִד. אֲרוֹמִמְךָ יְיָ כִּי דִלִּיתָנִי וְלֹא שִׂמַּחְתָּ
אֹיְבַי לִי. יְיָ אֱלֹהָי, שִׁוַּעְתִּי אֵלֶיךָ וַתִּרְפָּאֵנִי. יְיָ הֶעֱלִיתָ מִן שְׁאוֹל נַפְשִׁי,
חִיִּיתַנִי מִיָּרְדִי־בוֹר. זַמְּרוּ לַיְיָ חֲסִידָיו, וְהוֹדוּ לְזֵכֶר קָדְשׁוֹ. כִּי רֶגַע
בְּאַפּוֹ חַיִּים בִּרְצוֹנוֹ, בָּעֶרֶב יָלִין בֶּכִי וְלַבֹּקֶר רִנָּה. וַאֲנִי אָמַרְתִּי
בְשַׁלְוִי, בַּל אֶמּוֹט לְעוֹלָם. יְיָ בִּרְצוֹנְךָ הֶעֱמַדְתָּה לְהַרְרִי עֹז, הִסְתַּרְתָּ
פָנֶיךָ הָיִיתִי נִבְהָל. אֵלֶיךָ יְיָ אֶקְרָא, וְאֶל אֲדֹנָי אֶתְחַנָּן. מַה־בֶּצַע
בְּדָמִי בְּרִדְתִּי אֶל שָׁחַת, הֲיוֹדְךָ עָפָר הֲיַגִּיד אֲמִתֶּךָ. שְׁמַע יְיָ וְחָנֵּנִי,
יְיָ הֱיֵה עֹזֵר לִי. הָפַכְתָּ מִסְפְּדִי לְמָחוֹל לִי, פִּתַּחְתָּ שַׂקִּי וַתְּאַזְּרֵנִי
שִׂמְחָה.\לְמַעַן יְזַמֶּרְךָ כָבוֹד וְלֹא יִדֹּם, יְיָ אֱלֹהַי לְעוֹלָם אוֹדֶךָ.

A Psalm of David. I extol You, Lord. You raised me up. You
did not permit foes to rejoice over me. I cried out to You,
Lord, and You healed me. You brought up my soul from the
grave; You saved me from the pit of death. Sing to the Lord,
you faithful. Praise the holiness of His glory. His anger lasts
a moment; His love is for a lifetime. Tears may linger for a
night, but joy comes with the dawn. I once thought, while at
ease: Nothing can shake my security. Favor me, and I am a
mountain of strength. Hide Your face, Lord, and I am ter-
rified. To You, Lord, would I call; before the Lord would I
plead. What profit is there if I am silenced? What benefit if I
go to my grave? Will the dust praise You? Will it proclaim
Your faithfulness? Hear me, Lord. Be gracious to me. Hear
me, Lord, and be my help. I shall never be silent, Lord my
God. I shall always sing of Your glory.

Psalm 30

The Mourner's Kaddish may be recited (pages 98-99)

Morning service

Pesukei De-zimra

❧

We rise.
In the benediction introducing Pesukei De-zimra
we praise the eternal, compassionate Creator
who redeems our lives. Our chanting of Psalms
proclaims His Kingship.

בָּרוּךְ שֶׁאָמַר וְהָיָה הָעוֹלָם, בָּרוּךְ הוּא
בָּרוּךְ עוֹשֶׂה בְרֵאשִׁית, בָּרוּךְ אוֹמֵר וְעוֹשֶׂה,
בָּרוּךְ גּוֹזֵר וּמְקַיֵּם, בָּרוּךְ מְרַחֵם עַל הָאָרֶץ,
בָּרוּךְ מְרַחֵם עַל הַבְּרִיּוֹת, בָּרוּךְ מְשַׁלֵּם שָׂכָר טוֹב לִירֵאָיו,
בָּרוּךְ חַי לָעַד וְקַיָּם לָנֶצַח, בָּרוּךְ פּוֹדֶה וּמַצִּיל, בָּרוּךְ שְׁמוֹ.

בָּרוּךְ אַתָּה יְיָ אֱלֹהֵינוּ מֶלֶךְ הָעוֹלָם, הָאֵל הָאָב הָרַחֲמָן הַמְהֻלָּל
בְּפִי עַמּוֹ, מְשֻׁבָּח וּמְפֹאָר בִּלְשׁוֹן חֲסִידָיו וַעֲבָדָיו. וּבְשִׁירֵי דָוִד
עַבְדֶּךָ נְהַלֶּלְךָ יְיָ אֱלֹהֵינוּ, בִּשְׁבָחוֹת וּבִזְמִירוֹת נְגַדֶּלְךָ וּנְשַׁבֵּחֲךָ
וּנְפָאֶרְךָ וְנַזְכִּיר שִׁמְךָ וְנַמְלִיכְךָ מַלְכֵּנוּ אֱלֹהֵינוּ\יָחִיד חֵי הָעוֹלָמִים.
מֶלֶךְ מְשֻׁבָּח וּמְפֹאָר עֲדֵי עַד שְׁמוֹ הַגָּדוֹל. בָּרוּךְ אַתָּה יְיָ מֶלֶךְ מְהֻלָּל
בַּתִּשְׁבָּחוֹת.

For an alternate service select one or more para-
graphs from pages 26 through 40, and then con-
tinue on page 46, last paragraph.

Morning service

24

Pesukei De-zimra

❧

We rise.
In the benediction introducing Pesukei De-zimra
we praise the eternal, compassionate Creator who
redeems our lives. Our chanting of Psalms
proclaims His Kingship.

He created the world with His word.

Praise Him.

Praise Him, Author of beginnings.

His word is performance.

His decree is fulfillment. Praise Him.

His mercy embraces the world and all creatures.

Praise Him. He rewards those who revere Him.

He redeems, He rescues. Praise Him.

Praise Him. He lives forever.

We praise You, Lord our God, King of the universe, compassionate Father. We laud You with the Psalms of Your servant David. We extol You in song, we celebrate Your fame in melody. We proclaim You King, singular, eternal God. Praised are You, Lord, King extolled with songs of praise.

For an alternate service select one or more paragraphs from pages 27 through 41, and then continue on page 47, last paragraph.

Morning service

25

הוֹדוּ לַיְיָ, קִרְאוּ בִשְׁמוֹ, הוֹדִיעוּ בָעַמִּים עֲלִילֹתָיו. שִׁירוּ לוֹ זַמְּרוּ־
לוֹ, שִׂיחוּ בְּכָל־נִפְלְאוֹתָיו. הִתְהַלְלוּ בְּשֵׁם קָדְשׁוֹ, יִשְׂמַח לֵב מְבַקְשֵׁי
יְיָ. דִּרְשׁוּ יְיָ וְעֻזּוֹ, בַּקְּשׁוּ פָנָיו תָּמִיד. זִכְרוּ נִפְלְאֹתָיו אֲשֶׁר עָשָׂה,
מֹפְתָיו וּמִשְׁפְּטֵי־פִיהוּ. זֶרַע יִשְׂרָאֵל עַבְדּוֹ, בְּנֵי יַעֲקֹב בְּחִירָיו. הוּא
יְיָ אֱלֹהֵינוּ, בְּכָל־הָאָרֶץ מִשְׁפָּטָיו. זִכְרוּ לְעוֹלָם בְּרִיתוֹ, דָּבָר צִוָּה
לְאֶלֶף דּוֹר. אֲשֶׁר כָּרַת אֶת־אַבְרָהָם, וּשְׁבוּעָתוֹ לְיִצְחָק. וַיַּעֲמִידֶהָ
לְיַעֲקֹב לְחֹק, לְיִשְׂרָאֵל בְּרִית עוֹלָם. לֵאמֹר לְךָ אֶתֵּן אֶרֶץ כְּנָעַן,
חֶבֶל נַחֲלַתְכֶם. בִּהְיוֹתְכֶם מְתֵי מִסְפָּר, כִּמְעַט וְגָרִים בָּהּ. וַיִּתְהַלְכוּ
מִגּוֹי אֶל גּוֹי, וּמִמַּמְלָכָה אֶל עַם אַחֵר. לֹא הִנִּיחַ לְאִישׁ לְעָשְׁקָם
וַיּוֹכַח עֲלֵיהֶם מְלָכִים. אַל תִּגְּעוּ בִמְשִׁיחָי, וּבִנְבִיאַי אַל תָּרֵעוּ.
שִׁירוּ לַיְיָ כָּל־הָאָרֶץ, בַּשְּׂרוּ מִיּוֹם אֶל יוֹם יְשׁוּעָתוֹ. סַפְּרוּ בַגּוֹיִם
אֶת־כְּבוֹדוֹ, בְּכָל־הָעַמִּים נִפְלְאֹתָיו.\כִּי גָדוֹל יְיָ וּמְהֻלָּל מְאֹד וְנוֹרָא
הוּא עַל כָּל־אֱלֹהִים. כִּי כָּל־אֱלֹהֵי הָעַמִּים אֱלִילִים, וַיְיָ שָׁמַיִם
עָשָׂה.

הוֹד וְהָדָר לְפָנָיו, עֹז וְחֶדְוָה בִּמְקֹמוֹ. הָבוּ לַיְיָ מִשְׁפְּחוֹת עַמִּים,
הָבוּ לַיְיָ כָּבוֹד וָעֹז. הָבוּ לַיְיָ כְּבוֹד שְׁמוֹ, שְׂאוּ מִנְחָה וּבֹאוּ לְפָנָיו,
הִשְׁתַּחֲווּ לַיְיָ בְּהַדְרַת־קֹדֶשׁ. חִילוּ מִלְּפָנָיו כָּל־הָאָרֶץ, אַף תִּכּוֹן
תֵּבֵל בַּל תִּמּוֹט. יִשְׂמְחוּ הַשָּׁמַיִם וְתָגֵל הָאָרֶץ וְיֹאמְרוּ בַגּוֹיִם יְיָ
מָלָךְ. יִרְעַם הַיָּם וּמְלֹאוֹ, יַעֲלֹץ הַשָּׂדֶה וְכָל־אֲשֶׁר בּוֹ. אָז יְרַנְּנוּ
עֲצֵי הַיָּעַר מִלְּפְנֵי יְיָ כִּי בָא לִשְׁפּוֹט אֶת־הָאָרֶץ. הוֹדוּ לַיְיָ כִּי טוֹב,
כִּי לְעוֹלָם חַסְדּוֹ. וְאִמְרוּ הוֹשִׁיעֵנוּ אֱלֹהֵי יִשְׁעֵנוּ וְקַבְּצֵנוּ וְהַצִּילֵנוּ מִן
הַגּוֹיִם, לְהֹדוֹת לְשֵׁם קָדְשֶׁךָ לְהִשְׁתַּבֵּחַ בִּתְהִלָּתֶךָ. בָּרוּךְ יְיָ אֱלֹהֵי
יִשְׂרָאֵל מִן הָעוֹלָם וְעַד הָעֹלָם, וַיֹּאמְרוּ כָל־הָעָם אָמֵן וְהַלֵּל לַיְיָ.

Give thanks to the Lord, call upon Him, make His deeds known among all people. Sing to Him, sing His praise, and recount all His wonders. Exult in His holiness, let those who seek the Lord rejoice. Turn to the Lord and His grandeur; seek His Presence continually. Children of Israel His servant, chosen people of Jacob, remember the wonders that He has done, His marvels and His judgments. He is the Lord our God; His judgments fill the earth. Remember His covenant always, His promise to a thousand generations, the covenant He made with Abraham, His oath to Isaac, the unchanging compact with Jacob, the everlasting covenant with Israel: "I will give you the land of Canaan," He said, "as your portion of inheritance." When you were but few in number, little more than strangers in the land, wandering from country to country, from one kingdom to another, He permitted no man to oppress you. He rebuked kings for your sake, saying: "Touch not My anointed ones, harm not My prophets." Sing to the Lord, all the earth; proclaim His saving power. Tell the nations of His glory, tell all people of His marvels. Great is the Lord, and worthy of praise; revered is He beyond all gods. The heathen gods are only idols, but the Lord has made the heavens.

Grandeur and glory are in His Presence, majesty and joy are in His holy place. Families of mankind, acclaim the Lord, acclaim His glory; come before Him with an offering, worship the Lord in the beauty of holiness. Let all men on earth tremble before Him; He has fashioned the world, and it is immovable. Let the heavens rejoice, let the earth exult, let the nations declare: The Lord is King! Let the sea roar, and all that is in it; let the fields exult, and all they contain. Let the trees of the forest sing for joy before the Lord when He comes to judge the earth. Give thanks to the Lord, for He is good;

רוֹמְמוּ יְיָ אֱלֹהֵינוּ וְהִשְׁתַּחֲווּ לַהֲדֹם רַגְלָיו, קָדוֹשׁ הוּא. רוֹמְמוּ יְיָ אֱלֹהֵינוּ וְהִשְׁתַּחֲווּ לְהַר קָדְשׁוֹ, כִּי קָדוֹשׁ יְיָ אֱלֹהֵינוּ.

וְהוּא רַחוּם יְכַפֵּר עָוֹן וְלֹא יַשְׁחִית, וְהִרְבָּה לְהָשִׁיב אַפּוֹ וְלֹא יָעִיר כָּל־חֲמָתוֹ. אַתָּה יְיָ לֹא תִכְלָא רַחֲמֶיךָ מִמֶּנִּי, חַסְדְּךָ וַאֲמִתְּךָ תָּמִיד יִצְּרוּנִי. זְכֹר רַחֲמֶיךָ יְיָ וַחֲסָדֶיךָ, כִּי מֵעוֹלָם הֵמָּה. תְּנוּ עֹז לֵאלֹהִים, עַל יִשְׂרָאֵל גַּאֲוָתוֹ, וְעֻזּוֹ בַּשְּׁחָקִים. נוֹרָא אֱלֹהִים מִמִּקְדָּשֶׁיךָ, אֵל יִשְׂרָאֵל הוּא נֹתֵן עֹז וְתַעֲצֻמוֹת לָעָם, בָּרוּךְ אֱלֹהִים. אֵל נְקָמוֹת יְיָ, אֵל נְקָמוֹת הוֹפִיעַ. הִנָּשֵׂא שֹׁפֵט הָאָרֶץ, הָשֵׁב גְּמוּל עַל גֵּאִים. לַיְיָ הַיְשׁוּעָה, עַל עַמְּךָ בִרְכָתֶךָ סֶּלָה. יְיָ צְבָאוֹת עִמָּנוּ, מִשְׂגָּב לָנוּ אֱלֹהֵי יַעֲקֹב סֶלָה.\יְיָ צְבָאוֹת, אַשְׁרֵי אָדָם בֹּטֵחַ בָּךְ. יְיָ הוֹשִׁיעָה, הַמֶּלֶךְ יַעֲנֵנוּ בְיוֹם קָרְאֵנוּ.

הוֹשִׁיעָה אֶת־עַמֶּךָ וּבָרֵךְ אֶת־נַחֲלָתֶךָ וּרְעֵם וְנַשְּׂאֵם עַד הָעוֹלָם. נַפְשֵׁנוּ חִכְּתָה לַיְיָ, עֶזְרֵנוּ וּמָגִנֵּנוּ הוּא. כִּי בוֹ יִשְׂמַח לִבֵּנוּ, כִּי בְשֵׁם קָדְשׁוֹ בָטָחְנוּ. יְהִי חַסְדְּךָ יְיָ עָלֵינוּ כַּאֲשֶׁר יִחַלְנוּ לָךְ. הַרְאֵנוּ יְיָ חַסְדֶּךָ, וְיֶשְׁעֲךָ תִּתֶּן־לָנוּ. קוּמָה עֶזְרָתָה לָּנוּ וּפְדֵנוּ לְמַעַן חַסְדֶּךָ. אָנֹכִי יְיָ אֱלֹהֶיךָ הַמַּעַלְךָ מֵאֶרֶץ מִצְרָיִם, הַרְחֶב־פִּיךָ וַאֲמַלְאֵהוּ. אַשְׁרֵי הָעָם שֶׁכָּכָה לּוֹ, אַשְׁרֵי הָעָם שֶׁיְיָ אֱלֹהָיו.\וַאֲנִי בְּחַסְדְּךָ בָטַחְתִּי, יָגֵל לִבִּי בִּישׁוּעָתֶךָ, אָשִׁירָה לַיְיָ כִּי גָמַל עָלָי.

His lovingkindness endures forever. Declare: Save us, our God of salvation. Gather us, and deliver us from oppression, that we may acknowledge Your holiness, that we may be exalted in praising You. Praised be the Lord God of Israel from everlasting to everlasting. And all the people said "Amen" and "Praise the Lord."

I Chronicles 16:8–36

Exalt the Lord our God, worship Him in His sanctuary; He is holy. Exalt the Lord our God, worship Him at His holy mountain; for the Lord our God is holy.

And He, being merciful, forgives iniquity and does not destroy; often He restrains His anger and does not give full vent to His fury. Lord, withhold not Your compassion from me; may Your unfailing love always guard me. Lord, remember Your compassion and Your lovingkindness, for they are eternal. Acclaim the power of God, whose pride is in the people Israel, whose majesty is in the heavens. Awesome is God in His holy place, the God of the people Israel gives courage and strength to His people. Praised be God. God of vengeance, Lord, God of vengeance, appear. Rise up, judge of the earth, punish the arrogant as they deserve. Salvation is Yours, Lord; may Your blessing be upon Your people. Lord of hosts, be with us. God of Jacob, be our protection. Lord of hosts, blessed is he who trusts in You. O Lord, help us. Answer us, O King, when we call.

Save Your people, bless Your heritage; tend Your flock and sustain them forever. We wait hopefully for the Lord; He is our help and our shield. In Him our hearts rejoice, for in His holy name do we trust. May Your lovingkindness be extended to us, Lord, for we have placed our hope in You. Show us Your lovingkindness, grant us Your saving power.

Morning service

מִזְמוֹר לְתוֹדָה: הָרִיעוּ לַיְיָ כָּל־הָאָרֶץ. עִבְדוּ אֶת־יְיָ בְּשִׂמְחָה, בְּאוּ לְפָנָיו בִּרְנָנָה. דְּעוּ כִּי יְיָ הוּא אֱלֹהִים, הוּא עָשָׂנוּ וְלוֹ אֲנַחְנוּ, עַמּוֹ וְצֹאן מַרְעִיתוֹ. בְּאוּ שְׁעָרָיו בְּתוֹדָה, חֲצֵרֹתָיו בִּתְהִלָּה, הוֹדוּ לוֹ בָּרְכוּ שְׁמוֹ. \כִּי טוֹב יְיָ, לְעוֹלָם חַסְדּוֹ, וְעַד דֹּר וָדֹר אֱמוּנָתוֹ.

יְהִי כְבוֹד יְיָ לְעוֹלָם, יִשְׂמַח יְיָ בְּמַעֲשָׂיו. יְהִי שֵׁם יְיָ מְבֹרָךְ מֵעַתָּה וְעַד עוֹלָם. מִמִּזְרַח שֶׁמֶשׁ עַד מְבוֹאוֹ מְהֻלָּל שֵׁם יְיָ. רָם עַל כָּל־ גּוֹיִם יְיָ, עַל הַשָּׁמַיִם כְּבוֹדוֹ. יְיָ שִׁמְךָ לְעוֹלָם, יְיָ זִכְרְךָ לְדֹר וָדֹר. יְיָ בַּשָּׁמַיִם הֵכִין כִּסְאוֹ וּמַלְכוּתוֹ בַּכֹּל מָשָׁלָה. יִשְׂמְחוּ הַשָּׁמַיִם וְתָגֵל הָאָרֶץ וְיֹאמְרוּ בַגּוֹיִם יְיָ מָלָךְ. יְיָ מֶלֶךְ יְיָ מָלָךְ יְיָ יִמְלֹךְ לְעֹלָם וָעֶד. יְיָ מֶלֶךְ עוֹלָם וָעֶד, אָבְדוּ גוֹיִם מֵאַרְצוֹ. יְיָ הֵפִיר עֲצַת גּוֹיִם, הֵנִיא מַחְשְׁבוֹת עַמִּים. רַבּוֹת מַחֲשָׁבוֹת בְּלֶב־אִישׁ וַעֲצַת יְיָ הִיא תָקוּם. עֲצַת יְיָ לְעוֹלָם תַּעֲמֹד, מַחְשְׁבוֹת לִבּוֹ לְדֹר וָדֹר. כִּי הוּא אָמַר וַיֶּהִי, הוּא צִוָּה וַיַּעֲמֹד. כִּי בָחַר יְיָ בְּצִיּוֹן, אִוָּה לְמוֹשָׁב לוֹ. כִּי יַעֲקֹב בָּחַר לוֹ יָהּ, יִשְׂרָאֵל לִסְגֻלָּתוֹ. כִּי לֹא יִטֹּשׁ יְיָ עַמּוֹ וְנַחֲלָתוֹ לֹא יַעֲזֹב. \וְהוּא רַחוּם יְכַפֵּר עָוֹן וְלֹא יַשְׁחִית, וְהִרְבָּה לְהָשִׁיב אַפּוֹ וְלֹא יָעִיר כָּל־חֲמָתוֹ. יְיָ הוֹשִׁיעָה, הַמֶּלֶךְ יַעֲנֵנוּ בְיוֹם קָרְאֵנוּ.

Arise and come to our help; redeem us because of Your love. "I am the Lord your God who brought you out of the land of Egypt. Speak your desire and I will fulfill it." Blessed the people who are so privileged, blessed the people whose God is the Lord. I have trusted in Your love; may I rejoice in Your saving power. I shall sing to the Lord, for He has been bountiful to me.

A Psalm of thanksgiving. Acclaim the Lord, all people on earth. Worship the Lord in gladness, come before Him with joyous song. Know that the Lord is God. He fashioned us and we are His, His people, the flock that He shepherds. Enter His gates with thanksgiving, His courts with praise. Give thanks to Him, and praise Him. For the Lord is good, His lovingkindness is eternal, His faithfulness endures for all generations.

Psalm 100

May the Lord's glory endure forever; may the Lord rejoice in His works. Praised be the Lord, now and forever. Praised be He from East to West. The Lord is exalted beyond all nations, His glory is beyond the heavens. Your glory, Lord, endures forever, Your fame endures throughout all generations. The Lord established His throne on high, the Lord established His rule over all. The heavens rejoice and the earth is glad. The nations proclaim: "The Lord is King." The Lord is King, the Lord was King, the Lord will be King throughout all time. The Lord will be King for ever and ever, the heathen will vanish from His land. The Lord thwarts the designs of nations, He foils the plans of peoples. Many plans crowd a man's heart, but the designs of the Lord are fulfilled. The designs of the Lord endure forever, His plans throughout all generations. For He spoke and the world came into being;

Morning service

אַשְׁרֵי יוֹשְׁבֵי בֵיתֶךָ, עוֹד יְהַלְלוּךָ סֶּלָה.

אַשְׁרֵי הָעָם שֶׁכָּכָה לּוֹ, אַשְׁרֵי הָעָם שֶׁיְיָ אֱלֹהָיו.

תְּהִלָּה לְדָוִד.

אֲרוֹמִמְךָ אֱלוֹהַי הַמֶּלֶךְ וַאֲבָרְכָה שִׁמְךָ לְעוֹלָם וָעֶד.

בְּכָל ־יוֹם אֲבָרְכֶךָ וַאֲהַלְלָה שִׁמְךָ לְעוֹלָם וָעֶד.

גָּדוֹל יְיָ וּמְהֻלָּל מְאֹד וְלִגְדֻלָּתוֹ אֵין חֵקֶר.

דּוֹר לְדוֹר יְשַׁבַּח מַעֲשֶׂיךָ וּגְבוּרֹתֶיךָ יַגִּידוּ.

הֲדַר כְּבוֹד הוֹדֶךָ וְדִבְרֵי נִפְלְאֹתֶיךָ אָשִׂיחָה.

וֶעֱזוּז נוֹרְאוֹתֶיךָ יֹאמֵרוּ וּגְדוּלָּתְךָ אֲסַפְּרֶנָּה.

זֵכֶר רַב טוּבְךָ יַבִּיעוּ וְצִדְקָתְךָ יְרַנֵּנוּ.

חַנּוּן וְרַחוּם יְיָ, אֶרֶךְ אַפַּיִם וּגְדָל ־חָסֶד.

טוֹב יְיָ לַכֹּל וְרַחֲמָיו עַל כָּל ־מַעֲשָׂיו.

יוֹדוּךָ יְיָ כָּל ־מַעֲשֶׂיךָ וַחֲסִידֶיךָ יְבָרְכוּכָה.

כְּבוֹד מַלְכוּתְךָ יֹאמֵרוּ וּגְבוּרָתְךָ יְדַבֵּרוּ.

לְהוֹדִיעַ לִבְנֵי הָאָדָם גְּבוּרֹתָיו וּכְבוֹד הֲדַר מַלְכוּתוֹ.

He issued a command and the world took form. The Lord has chosen Zion, He desired it for His dwelling place. The Lord has chosen Jacob for Himself, the people Israel as His treasure. The Lord will not abandon His people, He will not forsake His heritage. And He, being merciful, forgives iniquity and does not destroy. Often He restrains His anger and does not give full vent to His fury. O Lord, help us. Answer us, O King, when we call.

Blessed are they who dwell in Your house; they shall praise You forever.

Blessed the people who are so favored; blessed the people whose God is the Lord.

David sang: I glorify You, my God, my King;
I praise You throughout all time.

> Every day do I praise You, exalting Your glory forever.

Great is the Lord, and praiseworthy;
His greatness exceeds definition.

> One generation lauds Your works to another,
> Declaring Your mighty deeds.

They tell of Your wonders, and of Your glorious splendor.

> They speak of Your greatness, and of Your awesome power.

They recall Your goodness; they sing of Your faithfulness.

> Gracious and compassionate is the Lord;
> Patient, and abounding in love.

To all the Lord is good; His compassion embraces all.

מַלְכוּתְךָ מַלְכוּת כָּל־עֹלָמִים וּמֶמְשַׁלְתְּךָ בְּכָל־דּוֹר וָדֹר.

סוֹמֵךְ יְיָ לְכָל־הַנֹּפְלִים וְזוֹקֵף לְכָל־הַכְּפוּפִים.

עֵינֵי כֹל אֵלֶיךָ יְשַׂבֵּרוּ וְאַתָּה נוֹתֵן לָהֶם אֶת־אָכְלָם בְּעִתּוֹ.

פּוֹתֵחַ אֶת־יָדֶךָ וּמַשְׂבִּיעַ לְכָל־חַי רָצוֹן.

צַדִּיק יְיָ בְּכָל־דְּרָכָיו וְחָסִיד בְּכָל־מַעֲשָׂיו.

קָרוֹב יְיָ לְכָל־קֹרְאָיו, לְכֹל אֲשֶׁר יִקְרָאֻהוּ בֶאֱמֶת.

רְצוֹן יְרֵאָיו יַעֲשֶׂה וְאֶת־שַׁוְעָתָם יִשְׁמַע וְיוֹשִׁיעֵם.

שׁוֹמֵר יְיָ אֶת־כָּל־אֹהֲבָיו וְאֵת כָּל־הָרְשָׁעִים יַשְׁמִיד.

תְּהִלַּת יְיָ יְדַבֶּר־פִּי וִיבָרֵךְ כָּל־בָּשָׂר שֵׁם קָדְשׁוֹ לְעוֹלָם וָעֶד.

וַאֲנַחְנוּ נְבָרֵךְ יָהּ מֵעַתָּה וְעַד עוֹלָם. הַלְלוּיָהּ.

All of Your creatures shall praise You;
The faithful shall repeatedly bless You.

They shall describe Your glorious kingdom, declaring Your power;

And men will know of Your might, the splendor of Your dominion.

Your kingdom is an everlasting kingdom;
Your dominion endures for all generations.

The Lord supports all who stumble,
He raises all who are bowed down.

All eyes look hopefully to You, to receive their food in due time.

You open Your hand, and all the living feast upon Your favor.

In all His paths the Lord is faithful,
In all His deeds He is loving.

To all who call the Lord is near,
To all who call upon Him in truth.

He fulfills the desire of those who revere Him;
He hears their cry and delivers them.

All who love the Lord He preserves,
but all the wicked He destroys.

My mouth shall praise the Lord.

Let all flesh praise His name throughout all time.

We shall praise the Lord now and always. Halleluyah!

Psalm 145

Morning service

35

הַלְלוּיָהּ. הַלְלִי נַפְשִׁי אֶת־יְיָ. אֲהַלְלָה יְיָ בְּחַיָּי, אֲזַמְּרָה לֵאלֹהַי
בְּעוֹדִי. אַל תִּבְטְחוּ בִנְדִיבִים, בְּבֶן־אָדָם שֶׁאֵין לוֹ תְשׁוּעָה. תֵּצֵא
רוּחוֹ יָשֻׁב לְאַדְמָתוֹ, בַּיּוֹם הַהוּא אָבְדוּ עֶשְׁתֹּנֹתָיו. אַשְׁרֵי שֶׁאֵל יַעֲקֹב
בְּעֶזְרוֹ, שִׂבְרוֹ עַל יְיָ אֱלֹהָיו. עֹשֶׂה שָׁמַיִם וָאָרֶץ אֶת־הַיָּם וְאֶת־כָּל־
אֲשֶׁר בָּם, הַשֹּׁמֵר אֱמֶת לְעוֹלָם. עֹשֶׂה מִשְׁפָּט לַעֲשׁוּקִים, נֹתֵן לֶחֶם
לָרְעֵבִים, יְיָ מַתִּיר אֲסוּרִים. יְיָ פֹּקֵחַ עִוְרִים, יְיָ זֹקֵף כְּפוּפִים,
יְיָ אֹהֵב צַדִּיקִים.\יְיָ שֹׁמֵר אֶת־גֵּרִים, יָתוֹם וְאַלְמָנָה יְעוֹדֵד וְדֶרֶךְ
רְשָׁעִים יְעַוֵּת. יִמְלֹךְ יְיָ לְעוֹלָם, אֱלֹהַיִךְ צִיּוֹן לְדֹר וָדֹר. הַלְלוּיָהּ.

הַלְלוּיָהּ. כִּי טוֹב זַמְּרָה אֱלֹהֵינוּ, כִּי נָעִים נָאוָה תְהִלָּה. בּוֹנֵה
יְרוּשָׁלַיִם יְיָ, נִדְחֵי יִשְׂרָאֵל יְכַנֵּס. הָרֹפֵא לִשְׁבוּרֵי לֵב וּמְחַבֵּשׁ
לְעַצְּבוֹתָם. מוֹנֶה מִסְפָּר לַכּוֹכָבִים, לְכֻלָּם שֵׁמוֹת יִקְרָא. גָּדוֹל
אֲדוֹנֵינוּ וְרַב כֹּחַ, לִתְבוּנָתוֹ אֵין מִסְפָּר. מְעוֹדֵד עֲנָוִים יְיָ, מַשְׁפִּיל
רְשָׁעִים עֲדֵי אָרֶץ. עֱנוּ לַיְיָ בְּתוֹדָה, זַמְּרוּ לֵאלֹהֵינוּ בְכִנּוֹר.
הַמְכַסֶּה שָׁמַיִם בְּעָבִים, הַמֵּכִין לָאָרֶץ מָטָר, הַמַּצְמִיחַ הָרִים חָצִיר.
נוֹתֵן לִבְהֵמָה לַחְמָהּ, לִבְנֵי עֹרֵב אֲשֶׁר יִקְרָאוּ. לֹא בִגְבוּרַת הַסּוּס
יֶחְפָּץ, לֹא בְשׁוֹקֵי הָאִישׁ יִרְצֶה. רוֹצֶה יְיָ אֶת־יְרֵאָיו, אֶת־הַמְיַחֲלִים
לְחַסְדּוֹ. שַׁבְּחִי יְרוּשָׁלַיִם אֶת־יְיָ, הַלְלִי אֱלֹהַיִךְ צִיּוֹן. כִּי חִזַּק בְּרִיחֵי
שְׁעָרָיִךְ, בֵּרַךְ בָּנַיִךְ בְּקִרְבֵּךְ. הַשָּׂם גְּבוּלֵךְ שָׁלוֹם, חֵלֶב חִטִּים
יַשְׂבִּיעֵךְ. הַשֹּׁלֵחַ אִמְרָתוֹ אָרֶץ, עַד מְהֵרָה יָרוּץ דְּבָרוֹ. הַנֹּתֵן שֶׁלֶג

Halleluyah! Let my life praise the Lord. I shall praise the Lord all my days, I shall sing to God while I live. Put not your trust in princes, in mortal man who cannot save. His breath departs, he returns to dust, and there is the end of all his plans. Happy is he whose help is the God of Jacob, whose hope is the Lord our God. He created heaven, earth and sea, and all they contain. He keeps faith forever, bringing justice to the oppressed, providing food for the hungry. The Lord frees the bound. He gives sight to the blind. The Lord raises those bowed down. He loves the just. The Lord protects the stranger. He supports the orphan and the widow, He frustrates the designs of the wicked. The Lord will reign through all generations; Your God, Zion, will reign forever. Halleluyah!

Psalm 146

Halleluyah! It is good to sing psalms to our God; it is pleasant to praise Him. The Lord rebuilds Jerusalem, and gathers the dispersed of the people Israel. He heals the broken hearted and binds up their wounds. He knows the number of the stars, He calls each one of them by name. Great is our Lord, mighty His power; His wisdom is beyond measure. The Lord encourages the humble, and casts evildoers to the ground. Lift your voice in thanks to the Lord; sound the harp in praise of our God. He covers the heavens with clouds, He provides the earth with rain. He causes the hills to bear food for bird and beast, when they call. He cares not for the might of the war horse; He delights not in man's vaunted strength. The Lord delights in those who revere Him, in those who trust in His goodness. Praise the Lord, Jerusalem! Glorify

כַּצֶּמֶר, כְּפוֹר כָּאֵפֶר יְפַזֵּר. מַשְׁלִיךְ קַרְחוֹ כְפִתִּים, לִפְנֵי קָרָתוֹ מִי יַעֲמֹד. יִשְׁלַח דְּבָרוֹ וְיַמְסֵם, יַשֵּׁב רוּחוֹ יִזְּלוּ־מָיִם.\מַגִּיד דְּבָרָיו לְיַעֲקֹב, חֻקָּיו וּמִשְׁפָּטָיו לְיִשְׂרָאֵל. לֹא עָשָׂה כֵן לְכָל־גּוֹי וּמִשְׁפָּטִים בַּל יְדָעוּם. הַלְלוּיָהּ.

הַלְלוּיָהּ. הַלְלוּ אֶת־יְיָ מִן הַשָּׁמַיִם, הַלְלוּהוּ בַּמְּרוֹמִים. הַלְלוּהוּ כָל־מַלְאָכָיו, הַלְלוּהוּ כָּל־צְבָאָו. הַלְלוּהוּ שֶׁמֶשׁ וְיָרֵחַ, הַלְלוּהוּ כָּל־כּוֹכְבֵי אוֹר. הַלְלוּהוּ שְׁמֵי הַשָּׁמָיִם וְהַמַּיִם אֲשֶׁר מֵעַל הַשָּׁמָיִם. יְהַלְלוּ אֶת־שֵׁם יְיָ כִּי הוּא צִוָּה וְנִבְרָאוּ. וַיַּעֲמִידֵם לָעַד לְעוֹלָם, חָק־נָתַן וְלֹא יַעֲבוֹר. הַלְלוּ אֶת־יְיָ מִן הָאָרֶץ, תַּנִּינִים וְכָל־תְּהֹמוֹת. אֵשׁ וּבָרָד שֶׁלֶג וְקִיטוֹר רוּחַ סְעָרָה עֹשָׂה דְבָרוֹ, הֶהָרִים וְכָל־גְּבָעוֹת, עֵץ פְּרִי וְכָל־אֲרָזִים, הַחַיָּה וְכָל־בְּהֵמָה, רֶמֶשׂ וְצִפּוֹר כָּנָף, מַלְכֵי־אֶרֶץ וְכָל־לְאֻמִּים שָׂרִים וְכָל־שֹׁפְטֵי אָרֶץ, בַּחוּרִים וְגַם בְּתוּלוֹת, זְקֵנִים עִם נְעָרִים. יְהַלְלוּ אֶת־שֵׁם יְיָ כִּי נִשְׂגָּב שְׁמוֹ לְבַדּוֹ, הוֹדוֹ עַל אֶרֶץ וְשָׁמָיִם.\וַיָּרֶם קֶרֶן לְעַמּוֹ, תְּהִלָּה לְכָל־חֲסִידָיו, לִבְנֵי יִשְׂרָאֵל עַם קְרֹבוֹ. הַלְלוּיָהּ.

your God, Zion! He has fortified your gates, and blessed your people within. He has assured the peace of your borders, and satisfied your hunger with finest wheat. He gives His command to the earth; with speed does His word issue forth. He sends down snow white as wool, and spreads frost thick as ashes. He pelts the earth with a storm of ice. No one can withstand His wintry blasts. He issues a command and the ice melts. He stirs the winds and the waters flow. He makes His commandments known to Jacob, His statutes and decrees to the people Israel. This He has not done for other nations; nor has He taught them His decrees. Halleluyah!

Psalm 147

Halleluyah! Praise the Lord from the heavens; praise Him, angels on high. Praise Him, all shining stars, the sun, the moon, and all His hosts. Praise Him, highest heavens; praise Him, waters above the heavens. Let them all praise the glory of the Lord, for they were created by His command. He established them to endure forever. It is His decree, never to be changed. Praise the Lord, all who share the earth: monsters of the sea and all its depths, fire and hail, snow and mist, storms which obey His command, all mountains and hills, all fruitbearing trees and cedars, all wild beasts and cattle, creeping creatures, birds, kings of all the people of the world, princes and all the judges of the earth, men and women, young and old! Let all creatures praise the glory of God. He alone is supreme. His glory is over heaven and earth. He exalted the fame of His people, He called for praise for all His faithful. He exalted the people Israel, the people drawn close to Him. Halleluyah!

Psalm 148

הַלְלוּיָהּ. שִׁירוּ לַיְיָ שִׁיר חָדָשׁ, תְּהִלָּתוֹ בִּקְהַל חֲסִידִים. יִשְׂמַח יִשְׂרָאֵל בְּעֹשָׂיו, בְּנֵי צִיּוֹן יָגִילוּ בְמַלְכָּם. יְהַלְלוּ שְׁמוֹ בְמָחוֹל, בְּתֹף וְכִנּוֹר יְזַמְּרוּ־לוֹ. כִּי רוֹצֶה יְיָ בְּעַמּוֹ, יְפָאֵר עֲנָוִים בִּישׁוּעָה. יַעְלְזוּ חֲסִידִים בְּכָבוֹד, יְרַנְּנוּ עַל מִשְׁכְּבוֹתָם. רוֹמְמוֹת אֵל בִּגְרוֹנָם וְחֶרֶב פִּיפִיּוֹת בְּיָדָם. לַעֲשׂוֹת נְקָמָה בַּגּוֹיִם, תּוֹכֵחוֹת בַּלְאֻמִּים.\לֶאְסֹר מַלְכֵיהֶם בְּזִקִּים וְנִכְבְּדֵיהֶם בְּכַבְלֵי בַרְזֶל. לַעֲשׂוֹת בָּהֶם מִשְׁפָּט כָּתוּב, הָדָר הוּא לְכָל־חֲסִידָיו. הַלְלוּיָהּ.

הַלְלוּיָהּ. הַלְלוּ אֵל בְּקָדְשׁוֹ, הַלְלוּהוּ בִּרְקִיעַ עֻזּוֹ. הַלְלוּהוּ בִגְבוּרֹתָיו, הַלְלוּהוּ כְּרֹב גֻּדְלוֹ. הַלְלוּהוּ בְּתֵקַע שׁוֹפָר, הַלְלוּהוּ בְּנֵבֶל וְכִנּוֹר. הַלְלוּהוּ בְּתֹף וּמָחוֹל, הַלְלוּהוּ בְּמִנִּים וְעֻגָב. הַלְלוּהוּ בְצִלְצְלֵי־שָׁמַע, הַלְלוּהוּ בְּצִלְצְלֵי תְרוּעָה. \כֹּל הַנְּשָׁמָה תְּהַלֵּל יָהּ. הַלְלוּיָהּ. כֹּל הַנְּשָׁמָה תְּהַלֵּל יָהּ. הַלְלוּיָהּ.

*For an alternate service, continue on
page 46, last paragraph.*

Halleluyah! Sing to the Lord a new song; praise Him in the assembly of the faithful. Let the people Israel rejoice in their Maker, let the people of Zion delight in their King. Let them praise Him with dancing, with the music of drum and harp. For the Lord is pleased with His people; He crowns the humble with victory. Let the faithful sing in triumph, and rejoice both night and day. Let the praise of God be on their lips and a two-edged sword in their hand, to execute judgment on the godless, to bring punishment upon the nations, binding their kings in chains and their princes in irons, executing the judgment decreed against them. He is the glory of all His faithful. Halleluyah!

Psalm 149

Halleluyah! Praise God in His sanctuary, in His mighty heavens praise Him. Praise Him for His mighty deeds, for His infinite greatness praise Him. Praise Him with trumpet calls, with harp and lyre praise Him. Praise Him with timbrel and dance, with flute and strings praise Him. Praise Him with resounding cymbals, with clashing cymbals praise Him. Praise Him, every living soul. Let everything that breathes praise the Lord. Halleluyah!

Psalm 150

For an alternate service, continue on page 47, last paragraph.

בָּרוּךְ יְיָ לְעוֹלָם, אָמֵן וְאָמֵן. בָּרוּךְ יְיָ מִצִּיּוֹן, שֹׁכֵן יְרוּשָׁלָיִם. הַלְלוּיָהּ.\בָּרוּךְ יְיָ אֱלֹהִים אֱלֹהֵי יִשְׂרָאֵל, עֹשֵׂה נִפְלָאוֹת לְבַדּוֹ. וּבָרוּךְ שֵׁם כְּבוֹדוֹ לְעוֹלָם וְיִמָּלֵא כְבוֹדוֹ אֶת־כָּל־הָאָרֶץ, אָמֵן וְאָמֵן.

וַיְבָרֶךְ דָּוִיד אֶת־יְיָ לְעֵינֵי כָּל־הַקָּהָל וַיֹּאמֶר דָּוִיד: בָּרוּךְ אַתָּה יְיָ אֱלֹהֵי יִשְׂרָאֵל אָבִינוּ מֵעוֹלָם וְעַד עוֹלָם. לְךָ יְיָ הַגְּדֻלָּה וְהַגְּבוּרָה וְהַתִּפְאֶרֶת וְהַנֵּצַח וְהַהוֹד, כִּי כֹל בַּשָּׁמַיִם וּבָאָרֶץ, לְךָ יְיָ הַמַּמְלָכָה וְהַמִּתְנַשֵּׂא לְכֹל לְרֹאשׁ. וְהָעֹשֶׁר וְהַכָּבוֹד מִלְּפָנֶיךָ וְאַתָּה מוֹשֵׁל בַּכֹּל וּבְיָדְךָ כֹּחַ וּגְבוּרָה, וּבְיָדְךָ לְגַדֵּל וּלְחַזֵּק לַכֹּל. וְעַתָּה אֱלֹהֵינוּ מוֹדִים אֲנַחְנוּ לָךְ וּמְהַלְלִים לְשֵׁם תִּפְאַרְתֶּךָ.

אַתָּה הוּא יְיָ לְבַדֶּךָ, אַתָּה עָשִׂיתָ אֶת־הַשָּׁמַיִם, שְׁמֵי הַשָּׁמַיִם וְכָל־צְבָאָם, הָאָרֶץ וְכָל־אֲשֶׁר עָלֶיהָ, הַיַּמִּים וְכָל־אֲשֶׁר בָּהֶם, וְאַתָּה מְחַיֶּה אֶת־כֻּלָּם, וּצְבָא הַשָּׁמַיִם לְךָ מִשְׁתַּחֲוִים.\אַתָּה הוּא יְיָ הָאֱלֹהִים אֲשֶׁר בָּחַרְתָּ בְּאַבְרָם וְהוֹצֵאתוֹ מֵאוּר כַּשְׂדִּים וְשַׂמְתָּ שְּׁמוֹ אַבְרָהָם, וּמָצָאתָ אֶת־לְבָבוֹ נֶאֱמָן לְפָנֶיךָ

וְכָרוֹת עִמּוֹ הַבְּרִית לָתֵת אֶת־אֶרֶץ הַכְּנַעֲנִי הַחִתִּי הָאֱמֹרִי וְהַפְּרִזִּי וְהַיְבוּסִי וְהַגִּרְגָּשִׁי לָתֵת לְזַרְעוֹ, וַתָּקֶם אֶת־דְּבָרֶיךָ כִּי צַדִּיק אָתָּה.

We rise.

Praised be the Lord forever. Amen and Amen. Praised from Zion be the Lord who abides in Jerusalem. Halleluyah. Praised be the Lord, God of the people Israel, who alone works wonders. Praised be His glory throughout all time. May His glory fill the whole world. Amen and Amen.

David praised the Lord in the presence of all the assembled people, saying: Praised are You, God of our father Israel, throughout all time. Yours are greatness and power, Lord, glory and victory and majesty, for everything in heaven and on earth is Yours. Sovereignty is Yours, You are exalted as Ruler of all. You are the Source of wealth and honor; dominion over all the earth is Yours. Might and courage come from You, greatness and strength are Your gifts. Therefore, Lord, we thank You, and we praise Your glory.

I Chronicles 29:10–13

You alone are the Lord. You created the heavens, the high heavens and all their array, the land and all that is on it, the seas and all they contain. And You sustain them all; the array of the heavens reveres You. You, Lord God, chose Abram and brought him out of Ur of the Chaldees, naming him Abraham, finding in him a faithful servant.

You made a covenant with him, to give the Land of•the Canaanites, Hittites, Amorites, Perizzites, Jebusites and Girgashites to his descendants; and You did keep Your promise, for You are just. You saw the suffering of our ancestors in Egypt, You heard their cry at the Sea of Reeds. You sent signs and portents against Pharaoh, all of his servants

Morning service

43

וַתֵּרֶא אֶת־עֳנִי אֲבוֹתֵינוּ בְּמִצְרָיִם וְאֶת־זַעֲקָתָם שָׁמַעְתָּ עַל יַם סוּף.
וַתִּתֵּן אֹתֹת וּמֹפְתִים בְּפַרְעֹה וּבְכָל־עֲבָדָיו וּבְכָל־עַם אַרְצוֹ כִּי
יָדַעְתָּ כִּי הֵזִידוּ עֲלֵיהֶם, וַתַּעַשׂ לְךָ שֵׁם כְּהַיּוֹם הַזֶּה. \וְהַיָּם
בָּקַעְתָּ לִפְנֵיהֶם וַיַּעַבְרוּ בְתוֹךְ הַיָּם בַּיַּבָּשָׁה, וְאֶת־רֹדְפֵיהֶם הִשְׁלַכְתָּ
בִמְצוֹלֹת כְּמוֹ אֶבֶן בְּמַיִם עַזִּים.

וַיּוֹשַׁע יְיָ בַּיּוֹם הַהוּא אֶת־יִשְׂרָאֵל מִיַּד מִצְרָיִם, וַיַּרְא יִשְׂרָאֵל אֶת־
מִצְרַיִם מֵת עַל שְׂפַת הַיָּם.\וַיַּרְא יִשְׂרָאֵל אֶת־הַיָּד הַגְּדֹלָה אֲשֶׁר
עָשָׂה יְיָ בְּמִצְרַיִם וַיִּירְאוּ הָעָם אֶת־יְיָ וַיַּאֲמִינוּ בַּיְיָ וּבְמֹשֶׁה עַבְדּוֹ.

אָז יָשִׁיר מֹשֶׁה וּבְנֵי יִשְׂרָאֵל אֶת־הַשִּׁירָה הַזֹּאת לַיְיָ וַיֹּאמְרוּ לֵאמֹר:
אָשִׁירָה לַיְיָ כִּי גָאֹה גָּאָה, סוּס וְרֹכְבוֹ רָמָה בַיָּם. עָזִּי וְזִמְרָת יָהּ וַיְהִי
לִי לִישׁוּעָה. זֶה אֵלִי וְאַנְוֵהוּ, אֱלֹהֵי אָבִי וַאֲרֹמְמֶנְהוּ. יְיָ אִישׁ מִלְחָמָה,
יְיָ שְׁמוֹ. מַרְכְּבֹת פַּרְעֹה וְחֵילוֹ יָרָה בַיָּם וּמִבְחַר שָׁלִשָׁיו טֻבְּעוּ בְיַם
סוּף. תְּהֹמֹת יְכַסְיֻמוּ, יָרְדוּ בִמְצוֹלֹת כְּמוֹ אָבֶן. יְמִינְךָ יְיָ נֶאְדָּרִי
בַּכֹּחַ, יְמִינְךָ יְיָ תִּרְעַץ אוֹיֵב. וּבְרֹב גְּאוֹנְךָ תַּהֲרֹס קָמֶיךָ, תְּשַׁלַּח
חֲרֹנְךָ יֹאכְלֵמוֹ כַּקַּשׁ. וּבְרוּחַ אַפֶּיךָ נֶעֶרְמוּ מַיִם, נִצְּבוּ כְמוֹ נֵד
נֹזְלִים, קָפְאוּ תְהֹמֹת בְּלֶב־יָם. אָמַר אוֹיֵב: אֶרְדֹּף אַשִּׂיג אֲחַלֵּק
שָׁלָל, תִּמְלָאֵמוֹ נַפְשִׁי אָרִיק חַרְבִּי תּוֹרִישֵׁמוֹ יָדִי. נָשַׁפְתָּ בְרוּחֲךָ
כִּסָּמוֹ יָם, צָלֲלוּ כַּעוֹפֶרֶת בְּמַיִם אַדִּירִים. מִי־כָמֹכָה בָּאֵלִם יְיָ,

and all the people of his land, because You knew of their shamelessness against our ancestors, and You gained for Yourself a name that lives on to this day. You divided the sea for our ancestors, and they passed through its middle as on dry land. But You cast their pursuers into the depths, like a stone into turbulent waters.

Nehemiah 9:6–11

The Lord saved the people Israel from the hand of the Egyptians on that day. When the people Israel saw the Egyptians lying dead on the sea-shore, when they saw the mighty power which the Lord has used against Egypt, the people feared the Lord; they had faith in him and in His servant Moses.

Then Moses and the people Israel sang this song to the Lord: I will sing to the Lord, for He has gloriously triumphed. Horse and rider He has hurled into the sea. The Lord is my strength and my song; He is my deliverance. He is my God and I glorify Him, the God of my father and I exalt Him. The Lord, the Warrior, Lord is His name. Pharaoh's chariots and his army He has hurled into the sea; the pick of his officers have sunk in the Sea of Reeds. The watery depths have covered them; down they sank in the deep like a stone. Your right hand, Lord, glorious in power, Your right hand, Lord, shatters the enemy. With Your great powers You crush Your foes; You let loose Your fury, it consumes them like straw. At the blast of Your anger the waters piled up, flowing waters stood motionless like a wall, the waters of the deep congealed. The enemy had said, "I will pursue and overtake them, I will divide the spoil, I will wreak my will on them, I will bare my sword, my power will destroy them." You loosed the wind, the sea covered them; like lead they sank in

Morning service

45

מִי כָמְכָה נֶאְדָּר בַּקֹּדֶשׁ, נוֹרָא תְהִלֹּת עֹשֵׂה פֶלֶא. נָטִיתָ יְמִינְךָ תִּבְלָעֵמוֹ אָרֶץ. נָחִיתָ בְחַסְדְּךָ עַם זוּ גָּאָלְתָּ, נֵהַלְתָּ בְעָזְּךָ אֶל נְוֵה קָדְשֶׁךָ. שָׁמְעוּ עַמִּים יִרְגָּזוּן, חִיל אָחַז יֹשְׁבֵי פְּלָשֶׁת. אָז נִבְהֲלוּ אַלּוּפֵי אֱדוֹם, אֵילֵי מוֹאָב יֹאחֲזֵמוֹ רָעַד, נָמֹגוּ כֹּל יֹשְׁבֵי כְנָעַן. תִּפֹּל עֲלֵיהֶם אֵימָתָה וָפַחַד, בִּגְדֹל זְרוֹעֲךָ יִדְּמוּ כָּאָבֶן, עַד יַעֲבֹר עַמְּךָ יְיָ, עַד יַעֲבֹר עַם זוּ קָנִיתָ. תְּבִאֵמוֹ וְתִטָּעֵמוֹ בְּהַר נַחֲלָתְךָ, מָכוֹן לְשִׁבְתְּךָ פָּעַלְתָּ יְיָ, מִקְּדָשׁ אֲדֹנָי כּוֹנֲנוּ יָדֶיךָ. יְיָ יִמְלֹךְ לְעֹלָם וָעֶד. (יְיָ יִמְלֹךְ לְעֹלָם וָעֶד.)

כִּי לַיְיָ הַמְּלוּכָה וּמֹשֵׁל בַּגּוֹיִם. וְעָלוּ מוֹשִׁעִים בְּהַר צִיּוֹן לִשְׁפֹּט אֶת־הַר עֵשָׂו וְהָיְתָה לַיְיָ הַמְּלוּכָה. וְהָיָה יְיָ לְמֶלֶךְ עַל כָּל־הָאָרֶץ, בַּיּוֹם הַהוּא יִהְיֶה יְיָ אֶחָד וּשְׁמוֹ אֶחָד.

יִשְׁתַּבַּח שִׁמְךָ לָעַד, מַלְכֵּנוּ הָאֵל הַמֶּלֶךְ הַגָּדוֹל וְהַקָּדוֹשׁ בַּשָּׁמַיִם וּבָאָרֶץ. כִּי לְךָ נָאֶה, יְיָ אֱלֹהֵינוּ וֵאלֹהֵי אֲבוֹתֵינוּ, שִׁיר וּשְׁבָחָה הַלֵּל וְזִמְרָה עֹז וּמֶמְשָׁלָה נֶצַח גְּדֻלָּה וּגְבוּרָה תְּהִלָּה וְתִפְאֶרֶת קְדֻשָּׁה וּמַלְכוּת בְּרָכוֹת וְהוֹדָאוֹת מֵעַתָּה וְעַד עוֹלָם.\בָּרוּךְ אַתָּה יְיָ אֵל מֶלֶךְ גָּדוֹל בַּתִּשְׁבָּחוֹת, אֵל הַהוֹדָאוֹת אֲדוֹן הַנִּפְלָאוֹת הַבּוֹחֵר בְּשִׁירֵי זִמְרָה, מֶלֶךְ אֵל חֵי הָעוֹלָמִים.

the mighty waters. Who is like You, Lord, among all that is worshipped? Who is like You, majestic in holiness, awesome in splendor, working wonders? You put out Your right hand, the earth swallowed them. In Your lovingkindness You lead the people You redeemed, with Your strength You guide them to Your holy dwelling place. Nations heard and trembled. Panic gripped the dwellers of Philistia. The chieftains of Edom were dismayed, trembling seized the leaders of Moab, all of the people of Canaan were horrified. Let terror and dread fall upon them, let the threat of Your might numb them into stony silence, until Your people, Lord, pass through, until the people pass through whom You have redeemed. Bring them to Your own mountain; plant them there, Your dwelling place of Your own making, Lord, at the sanctuary, Lord, which you have established. The Lord will reign for ever and ever. (The Lord will reign for ever and ever.)

Exodus 14:30; 15:1–18

For sovereignty is the Lord's, and He rules the nations. Deliverers shall rise on Mount Zion to judge the mountain of Esau, and sovereignty will be the Lord's. The Lord shall be King of all the earth. On that day the Lord shall be One and His name One.

May You be praised forever, great and holy God, our King in heaven and on earth. Songs of praise and psalms of gratitude become You, acknowledging Your might and Your dominion. Yours are strength and sovereignty, Yours are glory and grandeur and holiness. Always we look to You for our blessings; always we offer You our thanksgiving. Praised are You, exalted God, Lord of wonders delighting in song and psalm, eternal King of the universe.

Morning service

Hatzi Kaddish

Reader:

יִתְגַּדַּל וְיִתְקַדַּשׁ שְׁמֵהּ רַבָּא בְּעָלְמָא דִּי בְרָא כִרְעוּתֵהּ, וְיַמְלִיךְ מַלְכוּתֵהּ בְּחַיֵּיכוֹן וּבְיוֹמֵיכוֹן וּבְחַיֵּי דְכָל־בֵּית יִשְׂרָאֵל בַּעֲגָלָא וּבִזְמַן קָרִיב, וְאִמְרוּ אָמֵן.

Congregation and Reader:

יְהֵא שְׁמֵהּ רַבָּא מְבָרַךְ לְעָלַם וּלְעָלְמֵי עָלְמַיָּא.

Reader:

יִתְבָּרַךְ וְיִשְׁתַּבַּח וְיִתְפָּאַר וְיִתְרוֹמַם וְיִתְנַשֵּׂא וְיִתְהַדָּר וְיִתְעַלֶּה וְיִתְהַלָּל שְׁמֵהּ דְּקֻדְשָׁא בְּרִיךְ הוּא, לְעֵלָּא (לְעֵלָּא) מִן כָּל־בִּרְכָתָא וְשִׁירָתָא תֻּשְׁבְּחָתָא וְנֶחֱמָתָא דַּאֲמִירָן בְּעָלְמָא, וְאִמְרוּ אָמֵן.

Morning service

48

Ḥatzi Kaddish

Reader:

Hallowed and enhanced may He be throughout the world of His own creation. May He cause His sovereignty soon to be accepted, during our life and the life of all Israel. And let us say: Amen.

Congregation and Reader:

Ye-hei shmei raba meva-rakh l'alam ul'almei 'almaya.

May He be praised throughout all time.

Reader:

Glorified and celebrated, lauded and praised, acclaimed and honored, extolled and exalted may the Holy One be, far beyond all song and psalm, beyond all tributes which man can utter. And let us say: Amen.

Barkhu

☙

We rise for the call to public worship.

Reader:

בָּרְכוּ אֶת־יְיָ הַמְבֹרָךְ.

Congregation and Reader:

בָּרוּךְ יְיָ הַמְבֹרָךְ לְעוֹלָם וָעֶד.

We are seated.

בָּרוּךְ אַתָּה יְיָ אֱלֹהֵינוּ מֶלֶךְ הָעוֹלָם, יוֹצֵר אוֹר וּבוֹרֵא חֹשֶׁךְ, עוֹשֶׂה שָׁלוֹם וּבוֹרֵא אֶת־הַכֹּל.

הַמֵּאִיר לָאָרֶץ וְלַדָּרִים עָלֶיהָ בְּרַחֲמִים וּבְטוּבוֹ מְחַדֵּשׁ בְּכָל־יוֹם תָּמִיד מַעֲשֵׂה בְרֵאשִׁית. מָה רַבּוּ מַעֲשֶׂיךָ יְיָ, כֻּלָּם בְּחָכְמָה עָשִׂיתָ, מָלְאָה הָאָרֶץ קִנְיָנֶךָ. הַמֶּלֶךְ הַמְרוֹמָם לְבַדּוֹ מֵאָז, הַמְשֻׁבָּח וְהַמְפֹאָר וְהַמִּתְנַשֵּׂא מִימוֹת עוֹלָם, אֱלֹהֵי עוֹלָם בְּרַחֲמֶיךָ הָרַבִּים רַחֵם עָלֵינוּ, אֲדוֹן עֻזֵּנוּ צוּר מִשְׂגַּבֵּנוּ מָגֵן יִשְׁעֵנוּ מִשְׂגָּב בַּעֲדֵנוּ. אֵל בָּרוּךְ גְּדוֹל דֵּעָה. הֵכִין וּפָעַל זָהֳרֵי חַמָּה. טוֹב יָצַר כָּבוֹד לִשְׁמוֹ. מְאוֹרוֹת נָתַן סְבִיבוֹת עֻזּוֹ. פִּנּוֹת צְבָאָיו קְדוֹשִׁים רוֹמְמֵי שַׁדַּי תָּמִיד מְסַפְּרִים כְּבוֹד אֵל וּקְדֻשָּׁתוֹ.\תִּתְבָּרַךְ יְיָ אֱלֹהֵינוּ עַל שֶׁבַח מַעֲשֵׂה יָדֶיךָ וְעַל מְאוֹרֵי אוֹר שֶׁעָשִׂיתָ יְפָאֲרוּךָ סֶּלָה.

Morning service

Barkhu

We rise for the call to public worship.

Reader:

PRAISE THE LORD, SOURCE OF BLESSING.

Congregation and Reader:

PRAISED BE THE LORD, SOURCE OF BLESSING, THROUGHOUT ALL
TIME.

We are seated.

Praised are You, Lord our God, King of the universe, form-
ing light and creating darkness, ordaining the order of all
creation.

With mercy You give light to the world and to its inhabitants. In Your goodness You renew creation day after day.
How manifold Your works, O Lord. With wisdom You
fashioned them all. The earth abounds with Your creations.
You alone are worthy of praise and glory since the world
began. Eternal God, our shield and protection, Lord of our
strength, Rock of our defense, with Your infinite mercy continue to love us. You created the sun and sent forth its rays,
magnificently reflecting Your splendor. The lights of the
heavens radiate Your glory. The hosts of heaven exalt You,
always recounting Your holiness. For the stars so radiant
with light, for the wonder of all that You have created, we
glorify You, Lord our God.

Morning service

תִּתְבָּרַךְ צוּרֵנוּ מַלְכֵּנוּ וְגוֹאֲלֵנוּ בּוֹרֵא קְדוֹשִׁים, יִשְׁתַּבַּח שִׁמְךָ לָעַד מַלְכֵּנוּ יוֹצֵר מְשָׁרְתִים וַאֲשֶׁר מְשָׁרְתָיו כֻּלָּם עוֹמְדִים בְּרוּם עוֹלָם וּמַשְׁמִיעִים בְּיִרְאָה יַחַד בְּקוֹל דִּבְרֵי אֱלֹהִים חַיִּים וּמֶלֶךְ עוֹלָם. כֻּלָּם אֲהוּבִים כֻּלָּם בְּרוּרִים כֻּלָּם גִּבּוֹרִים וְכֻלָּם עוֹשִׂים בְּאֵימָה וּבְיִרְאָה רְצוֹן קוֹנָם,\וְכֻלָּם פּוֹתְחִים אֶת־פִּיהֶם בִּקְדֻשָּׁה וּבְטָהֳרָה בְּשִׁירָה וּבְזִמְרָה, וּמְבָרְכִים וּמְשַׁבְּחִים וּמְפָאֲרִים וּמַעֲרִיצִים וּמַקְדִּישִׁים וּמַמְלִיכִים

אֶת־שֵׁם הָאֵל הַמֶּלֶךְ הַגָּדוֹל הַגִּבּוֹר וְהַנּוֹרָא קָדוֹשׁ הוּא.\וְכֻלָּם מְקַבְּלִים עֲלֵיהֶם עֹל מַלְכוּת שָׁמַיִם זֶה מִזֶּה, וְנוֹתְנִים רְשׁוּת זֶה לָזֶה לְהַקְדִּישׁ לְיוֹצְרָם בְּנַחַת רוּחַ בְּשָׂפָה בְרוּרָה וּבִנְעִימָה קְדוֹשָׁה כֻּלָּם כְּאֶחָד עוֹנִים וְאוֹמְרִים בְּיִרְאָה:

קָדוֹשׁ קָדוֹשׁ קָדוֹשׁ יְיָ צְבָאוֹת, מְלֹא כָל־הָאָרֶץ כְּבוֹדוֹ.

\וְהָאוֹפַנִּים וְחַיּוֹת הַקֹּדֶשׁ בְּרַעַשׁ גָּדוֹל מִתְנַשְּׂאִים לְעֻמַּת שְׂרָפִים, לְעֻמָּתָם מְשַׁבְּחִים וְאוֹמְרִים:

בָּרוּךְ כְּבוֹד יְיָ מִמְּקוֹמוֹ.

לְאֵל בָּרוּךְ נְעִימוֹת יִתֵּנוּ, לַמֶּלֶךְ אֵל חַי וְקַיָּם זְמִירוֹת יֹאמֵרוּ וְתִשְׁבָּחוֹת יַשְׁמִיעוּ כִּי הוּא לְבַדּוֹ פּוֹעֵל גְּבוּרוֹת עוֹשֶׂה חֲדָשׁוֹת בַּעַל מִלְחָמוֹת זוֹרֵעַ צְדָקוֹת מַצְמִיחַ יְשׁוּעוֹת בּוֹרֵא רְפוּאוֹת נוֹרָא תְהִלּוֹת אֲדוֹן הַנִּפְלָאוֹת, הַמְחַדֵּשׁ בְּטוּבוֹ בְּכָל־יוֹם תָּמִיד מַעֲשֵׂה בְרֵאשִׁית, כָּאָמוּר: לְעֹשֵׂה אוֹרִים גְּדֹלִים, כִּי לְעוֹלָם חַסְדּוֹ.\אוֹר חָדָשׁ עַל צִיּוֹן תָּאִיר וְנִזְכֶּה כֻלָּנוּ מְהֵרָה לְאוֹרוֹ. בָּרוּךְ אַתָּה יְיָ יוֹצֵר הַמְּאוֹרוֹת.

Our King, our Rock, our Redeemer, Creator of celestial creatures, You shall be praised forever. You fashion angelic seraphim who await Your word beyond the heavens. In chorus they proclaim with awe the words of living God, eternal King. Beloved, pure and mighty are they, reverently doing the will of their Creator. In purity and holiness they raise their voices, singing praise and adoration. One to another they vow loyalty to His kingship; one to another they join to hallow their Creator. With clear, sweet tones they all sing in harmony, proclaiming:

HOLY, HOLY, HOLY IS THE LORD OF HOSTS;
THE WHOLE WORLD IS FILLED WITH HIS GLORY.

As in the prophet's vision, soaring celestial creatures respond with a chorus of praise:

PRAISED BE THE LORD'S GLORY THROUGHOUT THE UNIVERSE.

To hallowed God they sweetly sing, to living God they render melody, to eternal God they sound praise. He is singular, performing mighty deeds, creating all that is new. He is the champion of justice, sowing righteousness, reaping victory. He brings healing, He is beyond all praise. He is the Lord of wonders, renewing creation day after day. So sang the Psalmist: "Give thanks to the Creator of the great lights, for His love is everlasting." Cause a new light to shine on Zion. May we all soon be worthy of its radiance. Praised are You, Lord, Creator of lights.

אַהֲבָה רַבָּה אֲהַבְתָּנוּ יְיָ אֱלֹהֵינוּ, חֶמְלָה גְדוֹלָה וִיתֵרָה חָמַלְתָּ עָלֵינוּ. אָבִינוּ מַלְכֵּנוּ, בַּעֲבוּר אֲבוֹתֵינוּ שֶׁבָּטְחוּ בְךָ וַתְּלַמְּדֵם חֻקֵּי חַיִּים כֵּן תְּחָנֵּנוּ וּתְלַמְּדֵנוּ. אָבִינוּ הָאָב הָרַחֲמָן, הַמְרַחֵם, רַחֵם עָלֵינוּ וְתֵן בְּלִבֵּנוּ לְהָבִין וּלְהַשְׂכִּיל לִשְׁמֹעַ לִלְמֹד וּלְלַמֵּד לִשְׁמֹר וְלַעֲשׂוֹת וּלְקַיֵּם אֶת־כָּל־דִּבְרֵי תַלְמוּד תּוֹרָתֶךָ בְּאַהֲבָה. וְהָאֵר עֵינֵינוּ בְּתוֹרָתֶךָ וְדַבֵּק לִבֵּנוּ בְּמִצְוֹתֶיךָ וְיַחֵד לְבָבֵנוּ לְאַהֲבָה וּלְיִרְאָה שְׁמֶךָ וְלֹא נֵבוֹשׁ לְעוֹלָם וָעֶד. כִּי בְשֵׁם קָדְשְׁךָ הַגָּדוֹל וְהַנּוֹרָא בָּטָחְנוּ, נָגִילָה וְנִשְׂמְחָה בִּישׁוּעָתֶךָ. וַהֲבִיאֵנוּ לְשָׁלוֹם מֵאַרְבַּע כַּנְפוֹת הָאָרֶץ וְתוֹלִיכֵנוּ קוֹמְמִיּוּת לְאַרְצֵנוּ כִּי אֵל פּוֹעֵל יְשׁוּעוֹת אָתָּה,\וּבָנוּ בָחַרְתָּ מִכָּל־עַם וְלָשׁוֹן וְקֵרַבְתָּנוּ לְשִׁמְךָ הַגָּדוֹל סֶלָה בֶּאֱמֶת לְהוֹדוֹת לְךָ וּלְיַחֶדְךָ בְּאַהֲבָה. בָּרוּךְ אַתָּה יְיָ הַבּוֹחֵר בְּעַמּוֹ יִשְׂרָאֵל בְּאַהֲבָה.

God's love for the people Israel is reflected in His gift of Torah, His revelation. Our love for Him is reflected in our acceptance of this gift with joy, and in our acceptance of His sovereignty which we declare by reciting the verses which follow, contained in that revelation. In an imperfect world, daily faced with choices, we must choose to show our love and our acceptance through the quality of our lives as together we bear witness to our Father, our King, the King of all humanity. Daily He renews creation; daily we must renew our allegiance to Him.

Morning service

Deep is Your love for us, Lord our God, boundless Your tender compassion. You taught our fathers the laws of life. They trusted in You, our Father and King. For their sake graciously teach us. Father, merciful Father, show us mercy; grant us discernment and understanding. Then will we study Your Torah, heed its words, teach its precepts and follow its instruction, lovingly fulfilling all its teachings. Open our eyes to Your Torah, help our hearts cleave to Your commandments. Unite all our thoughts to love and revere You. Then shall we never be brought to shame. For we trust in Your awesome holiness. We will delight in Your deliverance. Bring us safely from the corners of the earth, and lead us in dignity to our holy land. You are the Source of deliverance. You have called us from all peoples and tongues, constantly drawing us nearer to You, that we may lovingly offer You praise, proclaiming Your Oneness. Praised are You, Lord who loves His people Israel.

> *God's love for the people Israel is reflected in His gift of Torah, His revelation. Our love for Him is reflected in our acceptance of this gift with joy, and in our acceptance of His sovereignty which we declare by reciting the verses which follow, contained in that revelation. In an imperfect world, daily faced with choices, we must choose to show our love and our acceptance through the quality of our lives as together we bear witness to our Father, our King, the King of all humanity. Daily He renews creation; daily we must renew our allegiance to Him.*

K'riat Sh'ma

ॐ

If there is no minyan, add:

אֵל מֶלֶךְ נֶאֱמָן

*We formally affirm God's sovereignty, freely
pledging Him our loyalty. We are
His witnesses.*

שְׁמַע יִשְׂרָאֵל יְהוָֹה אֱלֹהֵינוּ יְהוָֹה | אֶחָד׃

Silently:

בָּרוּךְ שֵׁם כְּבוֹד מַלְכוּתוֹ לְעוֹלָם וָעֶד.

וְאָהַבְתָּ אֵת יְהוָֹה אֱלֹהֶיךָ בְּכָל־לְבָבְךָ וּבְכָל־נַפְשְׁךָ וּבְכָל־
מְאֹדֶךָ׃ וְהָיוּ הַדְּבָרִים הָאֵלֶּה אֲשֶׁר אָנֹכִי מְצַוְּךָ הַיּוֹם עַל־לְבָבֶךָ׃
וְשִׁנַּנְתָּם לְבָנֶיךָ וְדִבַּרְתָּ בָּם בְּשִׁבְתְּךָ בְּבֵיתֶךָ וּבְלֶכְתְּךָ בַדֶּרֶךְ
וּבְשָׁכְבְּךָ וּבְקוּמֶךָ׃ וּקְשַׁרְתָּם לְאוֹת עַל־יָדֶךָ וְהָיוּ לְטֹטָפֹת בֵּין
עֵינֶיךָ׃ וּכְתַבְתָּם עַל־מְזֻזוֹת בֵּיתֶךָ וּבִשְׁעָרֶיךָ׃

וְהָיָה אִם־שָׁמֹעַ תִּשְׁמְעוּ אֶל־מִצְוֹתַי אֲשֶׁר אָנֹכִי מְצַוֶּה אֶתְכֶם
הַיּוֹם לְאַהֲבָה אֶת־יְהוָֹה אֱלֹהֵיכֶם וּלְעָבְדוֹ בְּכָל־לְבַבְכֶם וּבְכָל־
נַפְשְׁכֶם׃ וְנָתַתִּי מְטַר־אַרְצְכֶם בְּעִתּוֹ יוֹרֶה וּמַלְקוֹשׁ וְאָסַפְתָּ דְגָנֶךָ
וְתִירֹשְׁךָ וְיִצְהָרֶךָ׃ וְנָתַתִּי עֵשֶׂב בְּשָׂדְךָ לִבְהֶמְתֶּךָ וְאָכַלְתָּ וְשָׂבָעְתָּ׃

Morning service

56

K'riat Sh'ma

If there is no minyan, add:
God is a faithful king.

We formally affirm God's sovereignty, freely
pledging Him our loyalty. We are
His witnesses.

HEAR, O ISRAEL: THE LORD OUR GOD, THE LORD IS ONE.

Silently:
Praised be His glorious sovereignty throughout all time.

Love the Lord Your God with all your heart, with all your soul, with all your might. And these words which I command you this day shall you take to heart. You shall diligently teach them to your children. You shall repeat them at home and away, morning and night. You shall bind them as a sign upon your hand, they shall be a symbol above your eyes, and you shall inscribe them upon the doorposts of your homes and upon your gates.

Deuteronomy 6:4–9

If you will earnestly heed the commandments I give you this day, to love the Lord your God and to serve Him with all your heart and all your soul, then I will favor your land with rain at the proper season—rain in autumn and rain in spring—and you will have an ample harvest of grain and wine and oil. I will assure abundance in the fields for your cattle. You will eat to contentment. Take care lest you be

Morning service

57

הִשָּׁמְרוּ לָכֶם פֶּן־יִפְתֶּה לְבַבְכֶם וְסַרְתֶּם וַעֲבַדְתֶּם אֱלֹהִים אֲחֵרִים
וְהִשְׁתַּחֲוִיתֶם לָהֶם: וְחָרָה אַף־יְהֹוָה בָּכֶם וְעָצַר אֶת־הַשָּׁמַיִם
וְלֹא־יִהְיֶה מָטָר וְהָאֲדָמָה לֹא תִתֵּן אֶת־יְבוּלָהּ וַאֲבַדְתֶּם מְהֵרָה
מֵעַל הָאָרֶץ הַטֹּבָה אֲשֶׁר יְהֹוָה נֹתֵן לָכֶם: וְשַׂמְתֶּם אֶת־דְּבָרַי אֵלֶּה
עַל־לְבַבְכֶם וְעַל־נַפְשְׁכֶם וּקְשַׁרְתֶּם אֹתָם לְאוֹת עַל־יֶדְכֶם וְהָיוּ
לְטוֹטָפֹת בֵּין עֵינֵיכֶם: וְלִמַּדְתֶּם אֹתָם אֶת־בְּנֵיכֶם לְדַבֵּר בָּם
בְּשִׁבְתְּךָ בְּבֵיתֶךָ וּבְלֶכְתְּךָ בַדֶּרֶךְ וּבְשָׁכְבְּךָ וּבְקוּמֶךָ: וּכְתַבְתָּם
עַל־מְזוּזוֹת בֵּיתֶךָ וּבִשְׁעָרֶיךָ: לְמַעַן יִרְבּוּ יְמֵיכֶם וִימֵי בְנֵיכֶם עַל
הָאֲדָמָה אֲשֶׁר נִשְׁבַּע יְהֹוָה לַאֲבֹתֵיכֶם לָתֵת לָהֶם כִּימֵי הַשָּׁמַיִם
עַל־הָאָרֶץ:

וַיֹּאמֶר יְהֹוָה אֶל־מֹשֶׁה לֵּאמֹר: דַּבֵּר אֶל־בְּנֵי יִשְׂרָאֵל וְאָמַרְתָּ
אֲלֵהֶם וְעָשׂוּ לָהֶם צִיצִת עַל־כַּנְפֵי בִגְדֵיהֶם לְדֹרֹתָם וְנָתְנוּ עַל־
צִיצִת הַכָּנָף פְּתִיל תְּכֵלֶת: וְהָיָה לָכֶם לְצִיצִת וּרְאִיתֶם אֹתוֹ
וּזְכַרְתֶּם אֶת־כָּל־מִצְוֹת יְהֹוָה וַעֲשִׂיתֶם אֹתָם וְלֹא תָתוּרוּ אַחֲרֵי
לְבַבְכֶם וְאַחֲרֵי עֵינֵיכֶם אֲשֶׁר־אַתֶּם זֹנִים אַחֲרֵיהֶם: לְמַעַן תִּזְכְּרוּ
וַעֲשִׂיתֶם אֶת־כָּל־מִצְוֹתָי וִהְיִיתֶם קְדֹשִׁים לֵאלֹהֵיכֶם: אֲנִי יְהֹוָה
אֱלֹהֵיכֶם אֲשֶׁר הוֹצֵאתִי אֶתְכֶם מֵאֶרֶץ מִצְרַיִם לִהְיוֹת לָכֶם לֵאלֹהִים
אֲנִי יְהֹוָה אֱלֹהֵיכֶם:

\יְיָ אֱלֹהֵיכֶם אֱמֶת.

אֱמֶת וְיַצִּיב וְנָכוֹן וְקַיָּם וְיָשָׁר וְנֶאֱמָן וְאָהוּב וְחָבִיב וְנֶחְמָד וְנָעִים וְנוֹרָא
וְאַדִּיר וּמְתֻקָּן וּמְקֻבָּל וְטוֹב וְיָפֶה הַדָּבָר הַזֶּה עָלֵינוּ לְעוֹלָם וָעֶד.

Morning service

58

tempted to forsake God and turn to false gods in worship. For then the wrath of the Lord will be directed against you. He will close the heavens and hold back the rain; the earth will not yield its produce. You will soon disappear from the good land which the Lord is giving you.

Therefore, impress these words of Mine upon your very heart. You shall bind them as a sign upon your hand, and they shall be a symbol above your eyes. Teach them to your children. Repeat them at home and away, morning and night. Inscribe them upon the doorposts of your homes and upon your gates. Then your days and the days of your children will endure as the days of the heavens over the earth, on the land which the Lord swore to give to your fathers.

Deuteronomy 11:13–21

The Lord said to Moses: Instruct the people Israel that in every generation they shall put fringes on the corners of their garments, and bind a thread of blue to the fringe of each corner. Looking upon these fringes you will be reminded of all the commandments of the Lord and fulfill them, and not be seduced by your heart or led astray by your eyes. Then you will remember and observe all My commandments and be holy before your God. I am the Lord your God who brought you out of the land of Egypt to be your God. I, the Lord, am your God.

Numbers 15:37–41

The Lord your God is Faithful.

Your teaching is true and enduring, Your words are established forever. Awesome and revered are they, eternally right; well ordered are they, always acceptable. They are

\אֱמֶת אֱלֹהֵי עוֹלָם מַלְכֵּנוּ, צוּר יַעֲקֹב מָגֵן יִשְׁעֵנוּ. לְדֹר וָדֹר הוּא קַיָּם וּשְׁמוֹ קַיָּם וְכִסְאוֹ נָכוֹן וּמַלְכוּתוֹ וֶאֱמוּנָתוֹ לָעַד קַיֶּמֶת. וּדְבָרָיו חָיִים וְקַיָּמִים נֶאֱמָנִים וְנֶחֱמָדִים לָעַד וּלְעוֹלְמֵי עוֹלָמִים, עַל אֲבוֹתֵינוּ וְעָלֵינוּ עַל בָּנֵינוּ וְעַל דּוֹרוֹתֵינוּ וְעַל כָּל־דּוֹרוֹת זֶרַע יִשְׂרָאֵל עֲבָדֶיךָ.

עַל הָרִאשׁוֹנִים וְעַל הָאַחֲרוֹנִים דָּבָר טוֹב וְקַיָּם לְעוֹלָם וָעֶד. אֱמֶת וֶאֱמוּנָה, חֹק וְלֹא יַעֲבֹר. \אֱמֶת שָׁאַתָּה הוּא יְיָ אֱלֹהֵינוּ וֵאלֹהֵי אֲבוֹתֵינוּ, מַלְכֵּנוּ מֶלֶךְ אֲבוֹתֵינוּ גּוֹאֲלֵנוּ גּוֹאֵל אֲבוֹתֵינוּ יוֹצְרֵנוּ צוּר יְשׁוּעָתֵנוּ פּוֹדֵנוּ וּמַצִּילֵנוּ, מֵעוֹלָם שְׁמֶךָ, אֵין אֱלֹהִים זוּלָתֶךָ.

עֶזְרַת אֲבוֹתֵינוּ אַתָּה הוּא מֵעוֹלָם, מָגֵן וּמוֹשִׁיעַ לִבְנֵיהֶם אַחֲרֵיהֶם בְּכָל־דּוֹר וָדוֹר. בְּרוּם עוֹלָם מוֹשָׁבֶךָ וּמִשְׁפָּטֶיךָ וְצִדְקָתְךָ עַד אַפְסֵי־אָרֶץ. אַשְׁרֵי אִישׁ שֶׁיִּשְׁמַע לְמִצְוֹתֶיךָ, וְתוֹרָתְךָ וּדְבָרְךָ יָשִׂים עַל לִבּוֹ. אֱמֶת אַתָּה הוּא אָדוֹן לְעַמֶּךָ, וּמֶלֶךְ גִּבּוֹר לָרִיב רִיבָם. אֱמֶת אַתָּה הוּא רִאשׁוֹן וְאַתָּה הוּא אַחֲרוֹן, וּמִבַּלְעָדֶיךָ אֵין לָנוּ מֶלֶךְ גּוֹאֵל וּמוֹשִׁיעַ. מִמִּצְרַיִם גְּאַלְתָּנוּ יְיָ אֱלֹהֵינוּ וּמִבֵּית עֲבָדִים פְּדִיתָנוּ. כָּל־בְּכוֹרֵיהֶם הָרַגְתָּ וּבְכוֹרְךָ גָּאָלְתָּ וְיַם סוּף בָּקַעְתָּ וְזֵדִים טִבַּעְתָּ וִידִידִים הֶעֱבַרְתָּ וַיְכַסּוּ מַיִם צָרֵיהֶם, אֶחָד מֵהֶם לֹא נוֹתָר. עַל זֹאת שִׁבְּחוּ אֲהוּבִים וְרוֹמְמוּ אֵל וְנָתְנוּ יְדִידִים זְמִירוֹת שִׁירוֹת וְתִשְׁבָּחוֹת בְּרָכוֹת וְהוֹדָאוֹת לַמֶּלֶךְ אֵל חַי וְקַיָּם. רָם וְנִשָּׂא גָּדוֹל וְנוֹרָא, מַשְׁפִּיל גֵּאִים וּמַגְבִּיהַּ שְׁפָלִים מוֹצִיא אֲסִירִים וּפוֹדֶה עֲנָוִים וְעוֹזֵר דַּלִּים וְעוֹנֶה לְעַמּוֹ בְּעֵת שַׁוְּעָם אֵלָיו. \תְּהִלּוֹת לְאֵל עֶלְיוֹן בָּרוּךְ הוּא וּמְבֹרָךְ. מֹשֶׁה וּבְנֵי יִשְׂרָאֵל לְךָ עָנוּ שִׁירָה בְּשִׂמְחָה רַבָּה, וְאָמְרוּ כֻלָּם:

sweet and pleasant and precious, good and beautiful and beloved. True it is that eternal God is our King, the Rock of Jacob is our protecting shield. He is eternal and His glory is eternal. He is God for all generations. His sovereign throne is firmly established, His faithfulness endures for all time.

His teachings are precious and abiding. They live forever. For our forefathers, for us, for our children, for every generation of the people Israel, for all ages from the first to the last, His teachings are true, everlasting. True it is that You are the Lord our God, even as You were the God of our fathers. Our King and our fathers' King, our Redeemer and our fathers' Redeemer, our Creator, our victorious stronghold, You have always helped us and saved us. Your name endures forever. There is no God but You.

You always were our fathers' help, shield for them and for their children, our Deliverer in every generation. Though You abide on the pinnacle of the universe, Your just decrees extend to the ends of the earth. Happy the man who obeys Your commandments, who takes to heart the words of Your Torah. You are, in truth, Lord of Your people, their Defender and mighty King. You are first and You are last. We have no King or Redeemer but You. You rescued us from Egypt; You redeemed us from the house of bondage. The firstborn of the Egyptians were slain, Your firstborn were saved. You split the waters of the sea. The faithful You rescued, the wicked drowned. The waters engulfed Israel's enemies; not one of the arrogant remained alive. Then Your beloved sang hymns of thanksgiving, extolling You with psalms of adoration. They acclaimed God King, great and awesome Source of all blessing, the everliving God, exalted in majesty. He humbles

מִי־כָמְכָה בָּאֵלִם יְיָ,

מִי כָּמְכָה נֶאְדָּר בַּקֹּדֶשׁ,

נוֹרָא תְהִלֹת, עֹשֵׂה פֶלֶא.

שִׁירָה חֲדָשָׁה שִׁבְּחוּ גְאוּלִים לְשִׁמְךָ עַל שְׂפַת הַיָּם. יַחַד כֻּלָּם הוֹדוּ
וְהִמְלִיכוּ וְאָמְרוּ:

יְיָ יִמְלֹךְ לְעֹלָם וָעֶד.

צוּר יִשְׂרָאֵל, קוּמָה בְּעֶזְרַת יִשְׂרָאֵל וּפְדֵה כִנְאֻמְךָ יְהוּדָה וְיִשְׂרָאֵל.
גֹּאֲלֵנוּ יְיָ צְבָאוֹת שְׁמוֹ קְדוֹשׁ יִשְׂרָאֵל. בָּרוּךְ אַתָּה יְיָ גָּאַל יִשְׂרָאֵל.

the proud and raises the lowly. He frees the captive and redeems the meek. He helps the needy and answers His people's call. Praises to God supreme, ever praised is He. Moses and the people Israel sang with great joy this song to the Lord:

Mi khamokha ba-eilim Adonai, mi kamokha nedar bakodesh nora te-hilot oseh feleh.

Who is like You, Lord, among all that is worshipped?
Who is like You, majestic in holiness,
awesome in splendor, working wonders?

The redeemed sang a new song for You. They sang in chorus at the shore of the sea, acclaiming Your sovereignty with thanksgiving:

Adonai yimlokh l'olam va'ed.
The Lord shall reign throughout all time.

Rock of Israel, arise to Israel's defense. Fulfill Your promise to deliver Judah and Israel. Our Redeemer is the Holy One of Israel, the Lord of hosts is His name. Praised are You, Lord, Redeemer of the people Israel.

Amidah

&

We stand in silent prayer, which ends on page 76.

אֲדֹנָי שְׂפָתַי תִּפְתָּח וּפִי יַגִּיד תְּהִלָּתֶךָ.

בָּרוּךְ אַתָּה יְיָ אֱלֹהֵינוּ וֵאלֹהֵי אֲבוֹתֵינוּ, אֱלֹהֵי אַבְרָהָם אֱלֹהֵי יִצְחָק
וֵאלֹהֵי יַעֲקֹב, הָאֵל הַגָּדוֹל הַגִּבּוֹר וְהַנּוֹרָא אֵל עֶלְיוֹן גּוֹמֵל חֲסָדִים
טוֹבִים וְקוֹנֵה הַכֹּל, וְזוֹכֵר חַסְדֵי אָבוֹת וּמֵבִיא גוֹאֵל לִבְנֵי בְנֵיהֶם
לְמַעַן שְׁמוֹ בְּאַהֲבָה.

From Rosh Hashanah through Yom Kippur:

זָכְרֵנוּ לְחַיִּים מֶלֶךְ חָפֵץ בְּחַיִּים,
וְכָתְבֵנוּ בְּסֵפֶר הַחַיִּים לְמַעַנְךָ אֱלֹהִים חַיִּים.

מֶלֶךְ עוֹזֵר וּמוֹשִׁיעַ וּמָגֵן. בָּרוּךְ אַתָּה יְיָ מָגֵן אַבְרָהָם.

אַתָּה גִבּוֹר לְעוֹלָם אֲדֹנָי מְחַיֵּה מֵתִים אַתָּה רַב לְהוֹשִׁיעַ.

From Shmini Atzeret to Pesaḥ:

מַשִּׁיב הָרוּחַ וּמוֹרִיד הַגָּשֶׁם.

מְכַלְכֵּל חַיִּים בְּחֶסֶד מְחַיֵּה מֵתִים בְּרַחֲמִים רַבִּים, סוֹמֵךְ נוֹפְלִים
וְרוֹפֵא חוֹלִים וּמַתִּיר אֲסוּרִים וּמְקַיֵּם אֱמוּנָתוֹ לִישֵׁנֵי עָפָר. מִי כָמוֹךָ
בַּעַל גְּבוּרוֹת וּמִי דוֹמֶה לָּךְ, מֶלֶךְ מֵמִית וּמְחַיֵּה וּמַצְמִיחַ יְשׁוּעָה.

Morning service

64

Amidah

We stand in silent prayer, which ends on page 77.

Open my mouth, O Lord, and my lips will proclaim Your praise.

Praised are You, Lord our God and God of our fathers, God of Abraham, of Isaac and of Jacob, great, mighty, awesome, exalted God, bestowing lovingkindness and creating all things. You remember the pious deeds of our fathers, and will send a redeemer to their children's children because of Your love and for the sake of Your glory.

From Rosh Hashanah through Yom Kippur:

Remember us that we may live, O King who delights in life. Inscribe us in the Book of Life, for Your sake, living God.

You are the King who helps and saves and shields. Praised are You, Lord, Shield of Abraham.

Your might, O Lord, is boundless. You give life to the dead; great is Your saving power.

From Shmini Atzeret to Pesaḥ:

You cause the wind to blow and the rain to fall.

Your lovingkindness sustains the living, Your great mercies give life to the dead. You support the falling, heal the ailing, free the fettered. You keep Your faith with those who sleep in dust. Whose power can compare with Yours? You are the master of life and death and deliverance.

Morning service

From Rosh Hashanah through Yom Kippur:

מִי כָמְוֹךָ אַב הָרַחֲמִים, זוֹכֵר יְצוּרָיו לְחַיִּים בְּרַחֲמִים.

וְנֶאֱמָן אַתָּה לְהַחֲיוֹת מֵתִים. בָּרוּךְ אַתָּה יְיָ מְחַיֵּה הַמֵּתִים.

The Silent Amidah continues on page 68.

Kedushah

*When the Reader chants the Amidah aloud,
Kedushah is added. The congregation chants the
indented portions aloud.*

נְקַדֵּשׁ אֶת־שִׁמְךָ בָּעוֹלָם כְּשֵׁם שֶׁמַּקְדִּישִׁים אוֹתוֹ בִּשְׁמֵי מָרוֹם כַּכָּתוּב
עַל יַד נְבִיאֶךָ, וְקָרָא זֶה אֶל זֶה וְאָמַר:

קָדוֹשׁ קָדוֹשׁ קָדוֹשׁ יְיָ צְבָאוֹת, מְלֹא כָל־הָאָרֶץ כְּבוֹדוֹ.

לְעֻמָּתָם בָּרוּךְ יֹאמֵרוּ:

בָּרוּךְ כְּבוֹד יְיָ מִמְּקוֹמוֹ.

וּבְדִבְרֵי קָדְשְׁךָ כָּתוּב לֵאמֹר:

יִמְלֹךְ יְיָ לְעוֹלָם אֱלֹהַיִךְ צִיּוֹן לְדֹר וָדֹר, הַלְלוּיָהּ.

לְדוֹר וָדוֹר נַגִּיד גָּדְלֶךָ, וּלְנֵצַח נְצָחִים קְדֻשָּׁתְךָ נַקְדִּישׁ, וְשִׁבְחֲךָ
אֱלֹהֵינוּ מִפִּינוּ לֹא יָמוּשׁ לְעוֹלָם וָעֶד כִּי אֵל מֶלֶךְ גָּדוֹל וְקָדוֹשׁ אָתָּה.

From Rosh Hashanah through Yom Kippur:

Whose mercy can compare with Yours, merciful Father?
In mercy You remember Your creatures with life.

Faithful are You in giving life to the dead. Praised are You,
Lord, Master of life and death.

The Silent Amidah continues on page 69.

Kedushah

*When the Reader chants the Amidah aloud,
Kedushah is added. The congregation chants
the indented portions aloud.*

We proclaim Your holiness on earth as it is proclaimed in the
heavens above. We sing the words of heavenly voices as
recorded in Your prophet's vision:
    *Ka-dosh ka-dosh ka-dosh Ado-nai tz'va-ot, m'lo khol ha-
    aretz k'vodo.*
    Holy, holy, holy Lord of hosts. The whole world is filled
    with His glory.
Heavenly voices respond with praise:
    Barukh k'vod Ado-nai mi-m'komo.
    Praised is the Lord's glory throughout the universe.
And in Your holy psalms it is written:
    *Yim-lokh Ado-nai l'olam Elo-ha-yikh tzi-yon ledor va-dor
    ha-le-lu-yah.*
    The Lord shall reign through all generations; your God,
    Zion, shall reign forever. Halleluyah.
We declare Your greatness through all generations, hallow
Your holiness to all eternity. Your praise will never leave our
lips, for You are God and King, great and holy.

From Rosh Hashanah through Yom Kippur:

בָּרוּךְ אַתָּה יְיָ הַמֶּלֶךְ הַקָּדוֹשׁ.

בָּרוּךְ אַתָּה יְיָ הָאֵל הַקָּדוֹשׁ.

The Silent Amidah continues here:

אַתָּה קָדוֹשׁ וְשִׁמְךָ קָדוֹשׁ וּקְדוֹשִׁים בְּכָל־יוֹם יְהַלְלוּךָ סֶּלָה.

From Rosh Hashanah through Yom Kippur:

בָּרוּךְ אַתָּה יְיָ הַמֶּלֶךְ הַקָּדוֹשׁ.

בָּרוּךְ אַתָּה יְיָ הָאֵל הַקָּדוֹשׁ.

אַתָּה חוֹנֵן לְאָדָם דַּעַת וּמְלַמֵּד לֶאֱנוֹשׁ בִּינָה. חָנֵּנוּ מֵאִתְּךָ דֵּעָה בִּינָה וְהַשְׂכֵּל. בָּרוּךְ אַתָּה יְיָ חוֹנֵן הַדָּעַת.

הֲשִׁיבֵנוּ אָבִינוּ לְתוֹרָתֶךָ וְקָרְבֵנוּ מַלְכֵּנוּ לַעֲבוֹדָתֶךָ, וְהַחֲזִירֵנוּ בִּתְשׁוּבָה שְׁלֵמָה לְפָנֶיךָ. בָּרוּךְ אַתָּה יְיָ הָרוֹצֶה בִּתְשׁוּבָה.

סְלַח לָנוּ אָבִינוּ כִּי חָטָאנוּ, מְחַל לָנוּ מַלְכֵּנוּ כִּי פָשָׁעְנוּ, כִּי מוֹחֵל וְסוֹלֵחַ אָתָּה. בָּרוּךְ אַתָּה יְיָ חַנּוּן הַמַּרְבֶּה לִסְלֹחַ.

רְאֵה נָא בְעָנְיֵנוּ וְרִיבָה רִיבֵנוּ וּגְאָלֵנוּ מְהֵרָה לְמַעַן שְׁמֶךָ, כִּי גּוֹאֵל חָזָק אָתָּה. בָּרוּךְ אַתָּה יְיָ גּוֹאֵל יִשְׂרָאֵל.

From Rosh Hashanah through Yom Kippur:

Praised are You, Lord and holy King.

Praised are You, Lord and holy God.

The Silent Amidah continues here:

Holy are you and holy is Your name. Holy are those who praise you daily.

From Rosh Hashanah through Yom Kippur:

Praised are You, Lord and holy King.

Praised are You, Lord and holy God.

You graciously endow man with intelligence, You teach him wisdom and understanding. Grant us knowledge, discernment and wisdom. Praised are You, Lord, for the gift of knowledge.

Our Father, bring us back to Your Torah. Our King, draw us near to Your service. Lead us back to You, truly repentant. Praised are You, Lord who welcomes repentance.

Forgive us, our Father, for we have sinned; pardon us, our King, for we have transgressed, for You forgive and pardon. Praised are You, gracious and forgiving Lord.

Behold our affliction and deliver us. Redeem us soon for the sake of Your name, for You are the mighty Redeemer. Praised are You, Lord, Redeemer of the people Israel.

Morning service

On Fast Days, Reader only continues on page 212.

רְפָאֵנוּ יְיָ וְנֵרָפֵא, הוֹשִׁיעֵנוּ וְנִוָּשֵׁעָה, כִּי תְהִלָּתֵנוּ אָתָּה. וְהַעֲלֵה רְפוּאָה שְׁלֵמָה לְכָל־מַכּוֹתֵינוּ, כִּי אֵל מֶלֶךְ רוֹפֵא נֶאֱמָן וְרַחֲמָן אָתָּה. בָּרוּךְ אַתָּה יְיָ רוֹפֵא חוֹלֵי עַמּוֹ יִשְׂרָאֵל.

בָּרֵךְ עָלֵינוּ יְיָ אֱלֹהֵינוּ אֶת־הַשָּׁנָה הַזֹּאת וְאֶת־כָּל־מִינֵי תְבוּאָתָה לְטוֹבָה

Summer (Between Pesaḥ and December fourth):

וְתֵן בְּרָכָה עַל פְּנֵי הָאֲדָמָה

Winter (Between December fourth and Pesaḥ):

וְתֵן טַל וּמָטָר לִבְרָכָה עַל פְּנֵי הָאֲדָמָה

וְשַׂבְּעֵנוּ מִטּוּבֶךָ וּבָרֵךְ שְׁנָתֵנוּ כַּשָּׁנִים הַטּוֹבוֹת. בָּרוּךְ אַתָּה יְיָ מְבָרֵךְ הַשָּׁנִים.

תְּקַע בְּשׁוֹפָר גָּדוֹל לְחֵרוּתֵנוּ וְשָׂא נֵס לְקַבֵּץ גָּלֻיּוֹתֵינוּ וְקַבְּצֵנוּ יַחַד מֵאַרְבַּע כַּנְפוֹת הָאָרֶץ. בָּרוּךְ אַתָּה יְיָ מְקַבֵּץ נִדְחֵי עַמּוֹ יִשְׂרָאֵל.

הָשִׁיבָה שׁוֹפְטֵינוּ כְּבָרִאשׁוֹנָה וְיוֹעֲצֵינוּ כְּבַתְּחִלָּה, וְהָסֵר מִמֶּנּוּ יָגוֹן וַאֲנָחָה, וּמְלֹךְ עָלֵינוּ אַתָּה יְיָ לְבַדְּךָ בְּחֶסֶד וּבְרַחֲמִים וְצַדְּקֵנוּ בַּמִּשְׁפָּט.

From Rosh Hashanah through Yom Kippur:

בָּרוּךְ אַתָּה יְיָ הַמֶּלֶךְ הַמִּשְׁפָּט.

בָּרוּךְ אַתָּה יְיָ מֶלֶךְ אוֹהֵב צְדָקָה וּמִשְׁפָּט.

Morning service

On Fast Days, Reader only continues on page 213.

Heal us, O Lord, and we shall be healed. Help us and save us, for You are our glory. Grant perfect healing for all our afflictions, faithful and merciful God of healing. Praised are You, Lord, Healer of His people.

Lord our God, make this a blessed year. May its varied produce bring us happiness.

Summer (Between Pesaḥ and December fourth):

Bring blessing upon the whole earth.

Winter (Between December fourth and Pesaḥ):

Bless the earth with dew and rain.

Bless the year with Your abounding goodness. Praised are You, Lord who blesses the years.

Sound the great shofar to herald our freedom, raise high the banner to gather all exiles. Gather the dispersed from the corners of the earth. Praised are You, Lord who gathers our exiles.

Restore our judges as in days of old, restore our counsellors as in former times. Remove from us sorrow and anguish. Reign alone over us with loving-kindness; with justice and mercy sustain our cause.

From Rosh Hashanah through Yom Kippur:

Praised are You, Lord, King of judgment.

Praised are You, Lord, King who loves justice.

Morning service

71

וְלַמַּלְשִׁינִים אַל תְּהִי תִקְוָה וְכָל־הָרִשְׁעָה כְּרֶגַע תֹּאבֵד. וְכָל־
אוֹיְבֶיךָ מְהֵרָה יִכָּרֵתוּ וּמַלְכוּת זָדוֹן מְהֵרָה תְעַקֵּר וּתְשַׁבֵּר וּתְמַגֵּר
וְתַכְנִיעַ בִּמְהֵרָה בְיָמֵינוּ. בָּרוּךְ אַתָּה יְיָ שׁוֹבֵר אוֹיְבִים וּמַכְנִיעַ
זֵדִים.

עַל הַצַּדִּיקִים וְעַל הַחֲסִידִים וְעַל זִקְנֵי עַמְּךָ בֵּית יִשְׂרָאֵל וְעַל
פְּלֵיטַת סוֹפְרֵיהֶם וְעַל גֵּרֵי הַצֶּדֶק וְעָלֵינוּ יֶהֱמוּ נָא רַחֲמֶיךָ יְיָ
אֱלֹהֵינוּ, וְתֵן שָׂכָר טוֹב לְכָל הַבּוֹטְחִים בְּשִׁמְךָ בֶּאֱמֶת, וְשִׂים
חֶלְקֵנוּ עִמָּהֶם לְעוֹלָם וְלֹא נֵבוֹשׁ כִּי בְךָ בָּטָחְנוּ. בָּרוּךְ אַתָּה יְיָ
מִשְׁעָן וּמִבְטָח לַצַּדִּיקִים.

וְלִירוּשָׁלַיִם עִירְךָ בְּרַחֲמִים תָּשׁוּב וְתִשְׁכֹּן בְּתוֹכָהּ כַּאֲשֶׁר דִּבַּרְתָּ,
וּבְנֵה אוֹתָהּ בְּקָרוֹב בְּיָמֵינוּ בִּנְיַן עוֹלָם וְכִסֵּא דָוִד מְהֵרָה לְתוֹכָהּ
תָּכִין. בָּרוּךְ אַתָּה יְיָ בּוֹנֵה יְרוּשָׁלָיִם.

אֶת־צֶמַח דָּוִד עַבְדְּךָ מְהֵרָה תַצְמִיחַ וְקַרְנוֹ תָּרוּם בִּישׁוּעָתֶךָ,
כִּי לִישׁוּעָתְךָ קִוִּינוּ כָּל־הַיּוֹם. בָּרוּךְ אַתָּה יְיָ מַצְמִיחַ קֶרֶן יְשׁוּעָה.

שְׁמַע קוֹלֵנוּ יְיָ אֱלֹהֵינוּ, חוּס וְרַחֵם עָלֵינוּ, וְקַבֵּל בְּרַחֲמִים וּבְרָצוֹן
אֶת־תְּפִלָּתֵנוּ, כִּי אֵל שׁוֹמֵעַ תְּפִלּוֹת וְתַחֲנוּנִים אָתָּה. וּמִלְּפָנֶיךָ
מַלְכֵּנוּ רֵיקָם אַל תְּשִׁיבֵנוּ. כִּי אַתָּה שׁוֹמֵעַ תְּפִלַּת עַמְּךָ יִשְׂרָאֵל
בְּרַחֲמִים. בָּרוּךְ אַתָּה יְיָ שׁוֹמֵעַ תְּפִלָּה.

Frustrate the hopes of those who malign us; let all evil very soon disappear. Let all Your enemies soon be destroyed. May You quickly uproot and crush the arrogant; may You subdue and humble them in our time. Praised are You, Lord who humbles the arrogant.

Let Your tender mercies be stirred for the righteous, the pious and the leaders of the House of Israel, toward devoted scholars and faithful proselytes. Be merciful to us of the House of Israel. Reward all who trust in You, cast our lot with those who are faithful to You. May we never come to despair, for our trust is in You. Praised are You, Lord who sustains the righteous.

Have mercy, Lord, and return to Jerusalem, Your city. May Your Presence dwell there as You promised. Rebuild it now, in our days and for all time. Re-establish there the majesty of David, Your servant. Praised are You, Lord who rebuilds Jerusalem.

Bring to flower the shoot of Your servant David. Hasten the advent of Messianic redemption. Each and every day we hope for Your deliverance. Praised are You, Lord who assures our deliverance.

Lord our God, hear our voice. Have compassion upon us, pity us, accept our prayer with loving favor. You listen to entreaty and prayer. Do not turn us away unanswered, our King, for You mercifully heed Your people's supplication. Praised are You, Lord who hears prayer.

רְצֵה יְיָ אֱלֹהֵינוּ בְּעַמְּךָ יִשְׂרָאֵל וּבִתְפִלָּתָם וְהָשֵׁב אֶת־הָעֲבוֹדָה לִדְבִיר בֵּיתֶךָ וּתְפִלָּתָם בְּאַהֲבָה תְקַבֵּל בְּרָצוֹן וּתְהִי לְרָצוֹן תָּמִיד עֲבוֹדַת יִשְׂרָאֵל עַמֶּךָ.

On Rosh Ḥodesh:

אֱלֹהֵינוּ וֵאלֹהֵי אֲבוֹתֵינוּ, יַעֲלֶה וְיָבוֹא וְיַגִּיעַ וְיֵרָאֶה וְיֵרָצֶה וְיִשָּׁמַע וְיִפָּקֵד וְיִזָּכֵר זִכְרוֹנֵנוּ וּפִקְדוֹנֵנוּ, וְזִכְרוֹן אֲבוֹתֵינוּ וְזִכְרוֹן מָשִׁיחַ בֶּן־דָּוִד עַבְדֶּךָ וְזִכְרוֹן יְרוּשָׁלַיִם עִיר קָדְשֶׁךָ, וְזִכְרוֹן כָּל־עַמְּךָ בֵּית יִשְׂרָאֵל לְפָנֶיךָ, לִפְלֵיטָה וּלְטוֹבָה וּלְחֵן וּלְחֶסֶד וּלְרַחֲמִים וּלְחַיִּים וּלְשָׁלוֹם בְּיוֹם רֹאשׁ הַחֹדֶשׁ הַזֶּה. זָכְרֵנוּ יְיָ אֱלֹהֵינוּ בּוֹ לְטוֹבָה, וּפָקְדֵנוּ בוֹ לִבְרָכָה, וְהוֹשִׁיעֵנוּ בוֹ לְחַיִּים. וּבִדְבַר יְשׁוּעָה וְרַחֲמִים חוּס וְחָנֵּנוּ וְרַחֵם עָלֵינוּ וְהוֹשִׁיעֵנוּ כִּי אֵלֶיךָ עֵינֵינוּ, כִּי אֵל מֶלֶךְ חַנּוּן וְרַחוּם אָתָּה.

וְתֶחֱזֶינָה עֵינֵינוּ בְּשׁוּבְךָ לְצִיּוֹן בְּרַחֲמִים. בָּרוּךְ אַתָּה יְיָ הַמַּחֲזִיר שְׁכִינָתוֹ לְצִיּוֹן.

During repetition of Amidah, read this paragraph
silently while Reader chants the next paragraph.

מוֹדִים אֲנַחְנוּ לָךְ שָׁאַתָּה הוּא יְיָ אֱלֹהֵינוּ וֵאלֹהֵי אֲבוֹתֵינוּ אֱלֹהֵי כָל־בָּשָׂר יוֹצְרֵנוּ יוֹצֵר בְּרֵאשִׁית. בְּרָכוֹת וְהוֹדָאוֹת לְשִׁמְךָ הַגָּדוֹל וְהַקָּדוֹשׁ עַל שֶׁהֶחֱיִיתָנוּ וְקִיַּמְתָּנוּ. כֵּן תְּחַיֵּנוּ וּתְקַיְּמֵנוּ וְתֶאֱסֹף גָּלֻיּוֹתֵינוּ לְחַצְרוֹת קָדְשֶׁךָ לִשְׁמֹר חֻקֶּיךָ וְלַעֲשׂוֹת רְצוֹנֶךָ וּלְעָבְדְּךָ בְּלֵבָב שָׁלֵם עַל שֶׁאֲנַחְנוּ מוֹדִים לָךְ. בָּרוּךְ אֵל הַהוֹדָאוֹת.

מוֹדִים אֲנַחְנוּ לָךְ שָׁאַתָּה הוּא יְיָ אֱלֹהֵינוּ וֵאלֹהֵי אֲבוֹתֵינוּ לְעוֹלָם וָעֶד, צוּר חַיֵּינוּ מָגֵן יִשְׁעֵנוּ אַתָּה הוּא. לְדוֹר וָדוֹר נוֹדֶה לְךָ וּנְסַפֵּר תְּהִלָּתֶךָ עַל חַיֵּינוּ הַמְּסוּרִים בְּיָדֶךָ וְעַל נִשְׁמוֹתֵינוּ הַפְּקוּדוֹת לָךְ וְעַל נִסֶּיךָ שֶׁבְּכָל־יוֹם עִמָּנוּ וְעַל נִפְלְאוֹתֶיךָ וְטוֹבוֹתֶיךָ שֶׁבְּכָל־עֵת

Morning service

Accept the prayer of Your people Israel as lovingly as it is offered. Restore worship to Your sanctuary. May the worship of Your people Israel always be acceptable to You.

On Rosh Ḥodesh:

Our God and God of our fathers, on this Rosh Ḥodesh remember our fathers and be gracious to us. Consider the people standing before You praying for the days of Messiah and for Jerusalem Your holy city. Grant us life, well-being, lovingkindness and peace. Bless us, Lord our God, with all that is good. Remember Your promise of mercy and redemption. Be merciful to us and save us, for we place our hope in You, gracious and merciful God and King.

May we bear witness to Your merciful return to Zion. Praised are You, Lord who restores His Presence to Zion.

During repetition of Amidah, read this paragraph silently, while Reader chants the next paragraph.

We proclaim that You are the Lord our God and God of our fathers, Creator of all who created us, God of all flesh. We praise You and thank You for granting us life and for sustaining us. May You continue to do so, and may You gather our exiles, that we may all fulfill Your commandments and serve You wholeheartedly, doing Your will. For this shall we thank You. Praised be God to whom thanksgiving is due.

We proclaim that You are the Lord our God and God of our fathers throughout all time. You are the Rock of our lives, the Shield of our salvation. We thank You and praise You through all generations, for our lives are in Your hand, our souls are in Your charge. We thank You for Your miracles which daily attend us, for Your wondrous kindness, morn-

עֶרֶב וָבֹקֶר וְצָהֳרָיִם. הַטּוֹב כִּי לֹא כָלוּ רַחֲמֶיךָ וְהַמְרַחֵם כִּי לֹא תַמּוּ חֲסָדֶיךָ מֵעוֹלָם קִוִּינוּ לָךְ.

On Ḥanukkah, turn to page 204.

On Purim, turn to page 206.

On Israel's Independence Day, turn to page 208.

וְעַל כֻּלָּם יִתְבָּרַךְ וְיִתְרוֹמַם שִׁמְךָ מַלְכֵּנוּ תָּמִיד לְעוֹלָם וָעֶד.

From Rosh Hashanah through Yom Kippur:

וּכְתֹב לְחַיִּים טוֹבִים כָּל־בְּנֵי בְרִיתֶךָ.

וְכֹל הַחַיִּים יוֹדוּךָ סֶּלָה וִיהַלְלוּ אֶת־שִׁמְךָ בֶּאֱמֶת הָאֵל יְשׁוּעָתֵנוּ וְעֶזְרָתֵנוּ סֶלָה. בָּרוּךְ אַתָּה יְיָ הַטּוֹב שִׁמְךָ וּלְךָ נָאֶה לְהוֹדוֹת.

שִׂים שָׁלוֹם בָּעוֹלָם, טוֹבָה וּבְרָכָה חֵן וָחֶסֶד וְרַחֲמִים עָלֵינוּ וְעַל כָּל־יִשְׂרָאֵל עַמֶּךָ. בָּרְכֵנוּ אָבִינוּ כֻּלָּנוּ כְּאֶחָד בְּאוֹר פָּנֶיךָ, כִּי בְאוֹר פָּנֶיךָ נָתַתָּ לָּנוּ, יְיָ אֱלֹהֵינוּ, תּוֹרַת חַיִּים וְאַהֲבַת חֶסֶד וּצְדָקָה וּבְרָכָה וְרַחֲמִים וְחַיִּים וְשָׁלוֹם. וְטוֹב בְּעֵינֶיךָ לְבָרֵךְ אֶת־עַמְּךָ יִשְׂרָאֵל בְּכָל־עֵת וּבְכָל־שָׁעָה בִּשְׁלוֹמֶךָ.

From Rosh Hashanah through Yom Kippur:

בְּסֵפֶר חַיִּים בְּרָכָה וְשָׁלוֹם וּפַרְנָסָה טוֹבָה נִזָּכֵר וְנִכָּתֵב לְפָנֶיךָ אֲנַחְנוּ וְכָל־עַמְּךָ בֵּית יִשְׂרָאֵל לְחַיִּים טוֹבִים וּלְשָׁלוֹם. בָּרוּךְ אַתָּה יְיָ עוֹשֵׂה הַשָּׁלוֹם.

בָּרוּךְ אַתָּה יְיָ הַמְבָרֵךְ אֶת־עַמּוֹ יִשְׂרָאֵל בַּשָּׁלוֹם.

At the conclusion of the Amidah, personal prayers may be added, before or instead of the following.

Morning service

ing, noon and night. Your mercy and love are boundless. We have always placed our hope in You.

On Ḥanukkah, turn to page 205.
On Purim, turn to page 207.
On Israel's Independence Day, turn to page 209.

For all these blessings we shall ever praise and exalt You.

From Rosh Hashanah through Yom Kippur:

Inscribe all the people of Your covenant for a good life.

May every living creature thank You and praise You faithfully, our deliverance and our help. Praised are You, beneficent Lord to whom all praise is due.

Grant peace, happiness and blessing to the world, with grace, love and mercy for us and for all the people Israel. Bless us, our Father, one and all, with Your light; for by that light did You teach us Torah and life, love and tenderness, justice, mercy and peace. May it please You to bless Your people Israel in every season and at all times with Your gift of peace.

From Rosh Hashanah through Yom Kippur:

May we and the entire House of Israel be remembered and recorded in the Book of life, blessing, sustenance and peace. Praised are You, Lord, Source of peace.

Praised are You, Lord who blesses His people Israel with peace.

At the conclusion of the Amidah, personal prayers
may be added, before or instead of the following.

Morning service

אֱלֹהַי, נְצֹר לְשׁוֹנִי מֵרָע וּשְׂפָתַי מִדַּבֵּר מִרְמָה, וְלִמְקַלְלַי נַפְשִׁי תִדֹּם
וְנַפְשִׁי כֶּעָפָר לַכֹּל תִּהְיֶה. פְּתַח לִבִּי בְּתוֹרָתֶךָ וּבְמִצְוֹתֶיךָ תִּרְדֹּף
נַפְשִׁי. וְכֹל הַחוֹשְׁבִים עָלַי רָעָה, מְהֵרָה הָפֵר עֲצָתָם וְקַלְקֵל
מַחֲשַׁבְתָּם. עֲשֵׂה לְמַעַן שְׁמֶךָ, עֲשֵׂה לְמַעַן יְמִינֶךָ, עֲשֵׂה לְמַעַן
קְדֻשָּׁתֶךָ, עֲשֵׂה לְמַעַן תּוֹרָתֶךָ, לְמַעַן יֵחָלְצוּן יְדִידֶיךָ הוֹשִׁיעָה יְמִינְךָ
וַעֲנֵנִי. יִהְיוּ לְרָצוֹן אִמְרֵי־פִי וְהֶגְיוֹן לִבִּי לְפָנֶיךָ, יְיָ צוּרִי וְגֹאֲלִי.
עוֹשֶׂה שָׁלוֹם בִּמְרוֹמָיו הוּא יַעֲשֶׂה שָׁלוֹם עָלֵינוּ וְעַל כָּל־יִשְׂרָאֵל,
וְאִמְרוּ אָמֵן.

Our Father, Our King

*Recite only from Rosh Hashanah through Yom Kippur
and on Fast Days. On other days, turn to page 82.*

אָבִינוּ מַלְכֵּנוּ, חָטָאנוּ לְפָנֶיךָ.
אָבִינוּ מַלְכֵּנוּ, אֵין לָנוּ מֶלֶךְ אֶלָּא אָתָּה.
אָבִינוּ מַלְכֵּנוּ, עֲשֵׂה עִמָּנוּ לְמַעַן שְׁמֶךָ.
אָבִינוּ מַלְכֵּנוּ, חַדֵּשׁ עָלֵינוּ שָׁנָה טוֹבָה.

אָבִינוּ מַלְכֵּנוּ, בַּטֵּל מֵעָלֵינוּ כָּל־גְּזֵרוֹת קָשׁוֹת.
אָבִינוּ מַלְכֵּנוּ, בַּטֵּל מַחְשְׁבוֹת שׂוֹנְאֵינוּ.
אָבִינוּ מַלְכֵּנוּ, הָפֵר עֲצַת אוֹיְבֵינוּ.
אָבִינוּ מַלְכֵּנוּ, כַּלֵּה כָּל־צַר וּמַשְׂטִין מֵעָלֵינוּ.
אָבִינוּ מַלְכֵּנוּ, כַּלֵּה דֶּבֶר וְחֶרֶב וְרָעָב, וּשְׁבִי וּמַשְׁחִית וְעָוֹן וּשְׁמָד
מִבְּנֵי בְרִיתֶךָ.

My God, keep my tongue from telling evil, my lips from speaking lies. Help me ignore those who slander me. Let me be humble before all. Open my heart to Your Torah, so that I may pursue Your commandments. Frustrate the designs of those who plot evil against me. Make nothing of their schemes. Do so for the sake of Your power, Your holiness and Your Torah. Answer my prayer for the deliverance of Your people. May the words of my mouth and the meditations of my heart be acceptable to You, my Rock and my Redeemer. He who brings peace to His universe will bring peace to us, to the people Israel and to all mankind. Amen.

Our Father, Our King

Recite only from Rosh Hashanah through Yom Kippur and on Fast Days. On other days, turn to page 83.

Avinu malkeinu, we have sinned against You.

Avinu malkeinu, we have no King but You.

Avinu malkeinu, help us for Your own sake.

Avinu malkeinu, grant us a blessed New Year.

Avinu malkeinu, annul all evil decrees against us.

Avinu malkeinu, annul the plots of our enemies.

Avinu malkeinu, frustrate the designs of our foes.

Avinu malkeinu, rid us of tyrants.

Avinu malkeinu, rid us of pestilence, sword, famine, captivity, sin and destruction.

Morning service

79

אָבִינוּ מַלְכֵּנוּ, סְלַח וּמְחַל לְכָל־עֲוֹנוֹתֵינוּ.
אָבִינוּ מַלְכֵּנוּ, מְחֵה וְהַעֲבֵר פְּשָׁעֵינוּ וְחַטֹּאתֵינוּ מִנֶּגֶד עֵינֶיךָ.

אָבִינוּ מַלְכֵּנוּ, הַחֲזִירֵנוּ בִּתְשׁוּבָה שְׁלֵמָה לְפָנֶיךָ.
אָבִינוּ מַלְכֵּנוּ, שְׁלַח רְפוּאָה שְׁלֵמָה לְחוֹלֵי עַמֶּךָ.
אָבִינוּ מַלְכֵּנוּ, זָכְרֵנוּ בְּזִכָּרוֹן טוֹב לְפָנֶיךָ.

אָבִינוּ מַלְכֵּנוּ, כָּתְבֵנוּ בְּסֵפֶר חַיִּים טוֹבִים.
אָבִינוּ מַלְכֵּנוּ, כָּתְבֵנוּ בְּסֵפֶר גְּאֻלָּה וִישׁוּעָה.
אָבִינוּ מַלְכֵּנוּ, כָּתְבֵנוּ בְּסֵפֶר פַּרְנָסָה וְכַלְכָּלָה.
אָבִינוּ מַלְכֵּנוּ, כָּתְבֵנוּ בְּסֵפֶר זְכֻיּוֹת.
אָבִינוּ מַלְכֵּנוּ, כָּתְבֵנוּ בְּסֵפֶר סְלִיחָה וּמְחִילָה.

אָבִינוּ מַלְכֵּנוּ, הַצְמַח לָנוּ יְשׁוּעָה בְּקָרוֹב.
אָבִינוּ מַלְכֵּנוּ, הָרֵם קֶרֶן יִשְׂרָאֵל עַמֶּךָ.
אָבִינוּ מַלְכֵּנוּ, שְׁמַע קוֹלֵנוּ, חוּס וְרַחֵם עָלֵינוּ.
אָבִינוּ מַלְכֵּנוּ, קַבֵּל בְּרַחֲמִים וּבְרָצוֹן אֶת־תְּפִלָּתֵנוּ.
אָבִינוּ מַלְכֵּנוּ, נָא אַל תְּשִׁיבֵנוּ רֵיקָם מִלְּפָנֶיךָ.

אָבִינוּ מַלְכֵּנוּ, זְכֹר כִּי עָפָר אֲנָחְנוּ.
אָבִינוּ מַלְכֵּנוּ, חֲמֹל עָלֵינוּ וְעַל עוֹלָלֵינוּ וְטַפֵּנוּ.

אָבִינוּ מַלְכֵּנוּ, עֲשֵׂה לְמַעַן הֲרוּגִים עַל שֵׁם קָדְשֶׁךָ.
אָבִינוּ מַלְכֵּנוּ, עֲשֵׂה לְמַעַן טְבוּחִים עַל יִחוּדֶךָ.

Avinu malkeinu, forgive and pardon all our sins.

Avinu malkeinu, ignore the record of our transgressions.

Avinu malkeinu, help us return to You fully repentant.

Avinu malkeinu, send complete healing to the sick.

Avinu malkeinu, remember us with favor.

Avinu malkeinu, inscribe us in the Book of happiness.

Avinu malkeinu, inscribe us in the Book of deliverance.

Avinu malkeinu, inscribe us in the Book of prosperity.

Avinu malkeinu, inscribe us in the Book of merit.

Avinu malkeinu, inscribe us in the Book of forgiveness.

Avinu malkeinu, hasten our deliverance.

Avinu malkeinu, exalt Your people Israel.

Avinu malkeinu, hear us; show us mercy and compassion.

Avinu malkeinu, accept our prayer with favor and mercy.

Avinu malkeinu, do not turn us away unanswered.

Avinu malkeinu, remember that we are dust.

Avinu malkeinu, have pity for us and for our children.

Avinu malkeinu, act for those slain for Your holy name.

Avinu malkeinu, act for those slaughtered for proclaiming Your unique holiness.

אָבִינוּ מַלְכֵּנוּ, עֲשֵׂה לְמַעַן בָּאֵי בָאֵשׁ וּבַמַּיִם עַל קִדּוּשׁ שְׁמֶךָ.

אָבִינוּ מַלְכֵּנוּ, עֲשֵׂה לְמַעַנְךָ אִם לֹא לְמַעֲנֵנוּ.

אָבִינוּ מַלְכֵּנוּ, חָנֵּנוּ וַעֲנֵנוּ, כִּי אֵין בָּנוּ מַעֲשִׂים,
עֲשֵׂה עִמָּנוּ צְדָקָה וָחֶסֶד וְהוֹשִׁיעֵנוּ.

Ḥatzi Kaddish

Reader:

יִתְגַּדַּל וְיִתְקַדַּשׁ שְׁמֵהּ רַבָּא בְּעָלְמָא דִּי בְרָא כִרְעוּתֵהּ, וְיַמְלִיךְ
מַלְכוּתֵהּ בְּחַיֵּיכוֹן וּבְיוֹמֵיכוֹן וּבְחַיֵּי דְכָל־בֵּית יִשְׂרָאֵל בַּעֲגָלָא
וּבִזְמַן קָרִיב, וְאִמְרוּ אָמֵן.

Congregation and Reader:

יְהֵא שְׁמֵהּ רַבָּא מְבָרַךְ לְעָלַם וּלְעָלְמֵי עָלְמַיָּא.

Reader:

יִתְבָּרַךְ וְיִשְׁתַּבַּח וְיִתְפָּאַר וְיִתְרוֹמַם וְיִתְנַשֵּׂא וְיִתְהַדָּר וְיִתְעַלֶּה
וְיִתְהַלָּל שְׁמֵהּ דְּקֻדְשָׁא בְּרִיךְ הוּא, לְעֵלָּא (לְעֵלָּא) מִן כָּל־
בִּרְכָתָא וְשִׁירָתָא תֻּשְׁבְּחָתָא וְנֶחֱמָתָא דַּאֲמִירָן בְּעָלְמָא, וְאִמְרוּ אָמֵן.

Avinu malkeinu, act for those who went through fire and water to sanctify You.

Avinu malkeinu, act for Your sake if not for ours.

Avinu malkeinu, answer us though we have no deeds to plead our cause; save us with mercy and lovingkindness.

Avinu malkeinu, honeinu va'aneinu, kee ein banu ma'asim Asei eemanu tzedakah vahesed vehoshee-einu.

Hatzi Kaddish

Reader:

Hallowed and enhanced may He be throughout the world of His own creation. May He cause His sovereignty soon to be accepted during our life and the life of all Israel. And let us say: Amen.

Congregation and Reader:

Ye-hei shmei raba meva-rakh l'alam ul'almei 'almaya.

May He be praised throughout all time.

Reader:

Glorified and celebrated, lauded and praised, acclaimed and honored, extolled and exalted may the Holy One be, beyond all song and psalm, beyond all tributes which man can utter. And let us say: Amen.

Morning service

Ashrei

אַשְׁרֵי יוֹשְׁבֵי בֵיתֶךָ, עוֹד יְהַלְלוּךָ סֶּלָה.

אַשְׁרֵי הָעָם שֶׁכָּכָה לּוֹ, אַשְׁרֵי הָעָם שֶׁיְיָ אֱלֹהָיו.

תְּהִלָּה לְדָוִד.

אֲרוֹמִמְךָ אֱלוֹהַי הַמֶּלֶךְ וַאֲבָרְכָה שִׁמְךָ לְעוֹלָם וָעֶד.

בְּכָל־יוֹם אֲבָרְכֶךָ וַאֲהַלְלָה שִׁמְךָ לְעוֹלָם וָעֶד.

גָּדוֹל יְיָ וּמְהֻלָּל מְאֹד וְלִגְדֻלָּתוֹ אֵין חֵקֶר.

דּוֹר לְדוֹר יְשַׁבַּח מַעֲשֶׂיךָ וּגְבוּרֹתֶיךָ יַגִּידוּ.

הֲדַר כְּבוֹד הוֹדֶךָ וְדִבְרֵי נִפְלְאֹתֶיךָ אָשִׂיחָה.

וֶעֱזוּז נוֹרְאוֹתֶיךָ יֹאמֵרוּ וּגְדוּלָּתְךָ אֲסַפְּרֶנָּה.

זֵכֶר רַב טוּבְךָ יַבִּיעוּ וְצִדְקָתְךָ יְרַנֵּנוּ.

חַנּוּן וְרַחוּם יְיָ, אֶרֶךְ אַפַּיִם וּגְדָל־חָסֶד.

טוֹב יְיָ לַכֹּל וְרַחֲמָיו עַל כָּל־מַעֲשָׂיו.

יוֹדוּךָ יְיָ כָּל־מַעֲשֶׂיךָ וַחֲסִידֶיךָ יְבָרְכוּכָה.

Ashrei

Blessed are they who dwell in Your house; they shall praise You forever.

Blessed the people who are so favored; blessed the people whose God is the Lord.

David sang: I glorify You, my God, my King;
I praise You throughout all time.

> *Every day do I praise You, exalting Your glory forever.*

Great is the Lord, and praiseworthy;
His greatness exceeds definition.

> *One generation lauds Your works to another,*
> *Declaring Your mighty deeds.*

They tell of Your wonders, and of Your glorious splendor.

> *They speak of Your greatness, and of Your awesome power.*

They recall Your goodness; they sing of Your faithfulness.

> *Gracious and compassionate is the Lord;*
> *Patient, and abounding in love.*

To all the Lord is good; His compassion embraces all.

> *All of Your creatures shall praise You;*
> *The faithful shall repeatedly bless You.*

Morning service

כְּבוֹד מַלְכוּתְךָ יֹאמֵרוּ וּגְבוּרָתְךָ יְדַבֵּרוּ.

לְהוֹדִיעַ לִבְנֵי הָאָדָם גְּבוּרֹתָיו וּכְבוֹד הֲדַר מַלְכוּתוֹ.

מַלְכוּתְךָ מַלְכוּת כָּל־עֹלָמִים וּמֶמְשַׁלְתְּךָ בְּכָל־דּוֹר וָדֹר.

סוֹמֵךְ יְיָ לְכָל־הַנֹּפְלִים וְזוֹקֵף לְכָל־הַכְּפוּפִים.

עֵינֵי כֹל אֵלֶיךָ יְשַׂבֵּרוּ וְאַתָּה נוֹתֵן לָהֶם אֶת־אָכְלָם בְּעִתּוֹ.

פּוֹתֵחַ אֶת־יָדֶךָ וּמַשְׂבִּיעַ לְכָל־חַי־רָצוֹן.

צַדִּיק יְיָ בְּכָל־דְּרָכָיו וְחָסִיד בְּכָל־מַעֲשָׂיו.

קָרוֹב יְיָ לְכָל־קֹרְאָיו, לְכֹל אֲשֶׁר יִקְרָאֻהוּ בֶאֱמֶת.

רְצוֹן יְרֵאָיו יַעֲשֶׂה וְאֶת־שַׁוְעָתָם יִשְׁמַע וְיוֹשִׁיעֵם.

שׁוֹמֵר יְיָ אֶת־כָּל־אֹהֲבָיו וְאֵת כָּל־הָרְשָׁעִים יַשְׁמִיד.

\תְּהִלַּת יְיָ יְדַבֶּר־פִּי וִיבָרֵךְ כָּל־בָּשָׂר שֵׁם קָדְשׁוֹ לְעוֹלָם וָעֶד.

וַאֲנַחְנוּ נְבָרֵךְ יָהּ מֵעַתָּה וְעַד עוֹלָם. הַלְלוּיָהּ.

They shall describe Your glorious kingdom, declaring Your power;

And men will know of Your might, the splendor of Your dominion.

Your kingdom is an everlasting kingdom;

Your dominion endures for all generations.

The Lord supports all who stumble,

He raises all who are bowed down.

All eyes look hopefully to You, to receive their food in due time.

You open Your hand, and all the living feast upon Your favor.

In all His paths the Lord is faithful,
In all His deeds He is loving.

To all who call the Lord is near,
To all who call upon Him in truth.

He fulfills the desire of those who revere Him;
He hears their cry and delivers them.

All who love the Lord He preserves,
but all the wicked He destroys.

My mouth shall praise the Lord.

Let all flesh praise His name throughout all time.

We shall praise the Lord now and always. Halleluyah!

The bracketed words are omitted in a House of Mourning.

וּבָא לְצִיּוֹן גּוֹאֵל וּלְשָׁבֵי פֶשַׁע בְּיַעֲקֹב, נְאֻם יְיָ. [וַאֲנִי זֹאת בְּרִיתִי אוֹתָם אָמַר יְיָ, רוּחִי אֲשֶׁר עָלֶיךָ וּדְבָרַי אֲשֶׁר שַׂמְתִּי בְּפִיךָ, לֹא יָמוּשׁוּ מִפִּיךָ וּמִפִּי זַרְעֲךָ וּמִפִּי זֶרַע זַרְעֲךָ, אָמַר יְיָ, מֵעַתָּה וְעַד עוֹלָם] וְאַתָּה קָדוֹשׁ, יוֹשֵׁב תְּהִלּוֹת יִשְׂרָאֵל. וְקָרָא זֶה אֶל זֶה וְאָמַר: קָדוֹשׁ קָדוֹשׁ קָדוֹשׁ יְיָ צְבָאוֹת, מְלֹא כָל־הָאָרֶץ כְּבוֹדוֹ. וּמְקַבְּלִין דֵּן מִן דֵּן וְאָמְרִין, קַדִּישׁ בִּשְׁמֵי מְרוֹמָא עִלָּאָה בֵּית שְׁכִינְתֵּהּ, קַדִּישׁ עַל אַרְעָא עוֹבַד גְּבוּרְתֵּהּ, קַדִּישׁ לְעָלַם וּלְעָלְמֵי עָלְמַיָּא. יְיָ צְבָאוֹת מַלְיָא כָל־אַרְעָה זִיו יְקָרֵהּ.

וַתִּשָּׂאֵנִי רוּחַ וָאֶשְׁמַע אַחֲרַי קוֹל רַעַשׁ גָּדוֹל: בָּרוּךְ כְּבוֹד יְיָ מִמְּקוֹמוֹ. וּנְטָלַתְנִי רוּחָא וְשִׁמְעֵת בַּתְרַי קָל זִיעַ סַגִּיא דִמְשַׁבְּחִין וְאָמְרִין: בְּרִיךְ יְקָרָא דִי יְיָ מֵאֲתַר בֵּית שְׁכִינְתֵּהּ. יְיָ יִמְלֹךְ לְעֹלָם וָעֶד. יְיָ מַלְכוּתֵהּ קָאֵם לְעָלַם וּלְעָלְמֵי עָלְמַיָּא.

יְיָ אֱלֹהֵי אַבְרָהָם יִצְחָק וְיִשְׂרָאֵל אֲבֹתֵינוּ שָׁמְרָה־זֹאת לְעוֹלָם לְיֵצֶר מַחְשְׁבוֹת לְבַב עַמֶּךָ, וְהָכֵן לְבָבָם אֵלֶיךָ. וְהוּא רַחוּם יְכַפֵּר עָוֹן וְלֹא יַשְׁחִית, וְהִרְבָּה לְהָשִׁיב אַפּוֹ, וְלֹא יָעִיר כָּל־חֲמָתוֹ. כִּי אַתָּה אֲדֹנָי טוֹב וְסַלָּח, וְרַב חֶסֶד לְכָל־קֹרְאֶיךָ. צִדְקָתְךָ צֶדֶק לְעוֹלָם וְתוֹרָתְךָ אֱמֶת. תִּתֵּן אֱמֶת לְיַעֲקֹב חֶסֶד לְאַבְרָהָם, אֲשֶׁר נִשְׁבַּעְתָּ לַאֲבֹתֵינוּ מִימֵי קֶדֶם. בָּרוּךְ אֲדֹנָי יוֹם יוֹם, יַעֲמָס־לָנוּ הָאֵל יְשׁוּעָתֵנוּ, סֶלָה. יְיָ צְבָאוֹת עִמָּנוּ, מִשְׂגָּב לָנוּ אֱלֹהֵי יַעֲקֹב, סֶלָה. יְיָ צְבָאוֹת, אַשְׁרֵי אָדָם בֹּטֵחַ בָּךְ. יְיָ הוֹשִׁיעָה, הַמֶּלֶךְ יַעֲנֵנוּ בְיוֹם קָרְאֵנוּ.

The Lord has assured a redeemer for Zion, for those in the House of Jacob who turn from sin. [The Lord has said, "This is My covenant with them: My spirit shall remain with you and with your descendants. My word shall be upon your lips now and forever."] For You, O Lord, are holy, enthroned upon the praises of the people Israel. The angels on high called one to another: "Holy, holy, holy Lord of hosts; His glory fills the whole world." They receive sanction from one another, saying "The Lord of hosts is holy in the highest heavens, holy on the earth and holy forever, throughout all time; the radiance of His glory fills the whole world."

Then a wind lifted me up and I heard the sound of a great rushing behind me, saying, "Praised be the Lord's glory from His place." Then a wind lifted me up and I heard the sound of a great rushing behind me, the sound of those who utter praise, saying, "Praised be the Lord's glory from the place of His Presence." The Lord shall reign throughout all time. The Lord's sovereignty endures forever, throughout all time.

Lord our God and God of our fathers, impress this forever upon Your people, directing our heart toward You: God is merciful, granting atonement for sin. You do not destroy; You avert punishment. Again and again You suppress Your wrath. The Lord is kind and forgiving, loving all who call to Him. Your righteousness is everlasting, Your Torah is truth. You will be faithful to Jacob, merciful to Abraham, fulfilling the promise You made to our fathers. Praised is the Lord who daily bears our burden; He is the God of our deliverance. Lord of hosts, blessed is the one who trusts in You. O Lord, help us; answer us, O King, when we call.

Morning service

בָּרוּךְ הוּא אֱלֹהֵינוּ שֶׁבְּרָאָנוּ לִכְבוֹדוֹ וְהִבְדִּילָנוּ מִן הַתּוֹעִים וְנָתַן לָנוּ תּוֹרַת אֱמֶת וְחַיֵּי עוֹלָם נָטַע בְּתוֹכֵנוּ. הוּא יִפְתַּח לִבֵּנוּ בְּתוֹרָתוֹ וְיָשֵׂם בְּלִבֵּנוּ אַהֲבָתוֹ וְיִרְאָתוֹ וְלַעֲשׂוֹת רְצוֹנוֹ וּלְעָבְדוֹ בְּלֵבָב שָׁלֵם לְמַעַן לֹא נִיגַע לָרִיק וְלֹא נֵלֵד לַבֶּהָלָה. יְהִי רָצוֹן מִלְּפָנֶיךָ יְיָ אֱלֹהֵינוּ וֵאלֹהֵי אֲבוֹתֵינוּ שֶׁנִּשְׁמֹר חֻקֶּיךָ בָּעוֹלָם הַזֶּה וְנִזְכֶּה וְנִחְיֶה וְנִרְאֶה וְנִירַשׁ טוֹבָה וּבְרָכָה לִשְׁנֵי יְמוֹת הַמָּשִׁיחַ וּלְחַיֵּי הָעוֹלָם הַבָּא. לְמַעַן יְזַמֶּרְךָ כָבוֹד וְלֹא יִדֹּם, יְיָ אֱלֹהַי לְעוֹלָם אוֹדֶךָ. בָּרוּךְ הַגֶּבֶר אֲשֶׁר יִבְטַח בַּיְיָ, וְהָיָה יְיָ מִבְטַחוֹ. בִּטְחוּ בַיְיָ עֲדֵי עַד, כִּי בְּיָהּ יְיָ צוּר עוֹלָמִים. וְיִבְטְחוּ בְךָ יוֹדְעֵי שְׁמֶךָ, כִּי לֹא עָזַבְתָּ דֹּרְשֶׁיךָ יְיָ. יְיָ חָפֵץ לְמַעַן צִדְקוֹ, יַגְדִּיל תּוֹרָה וְיַאְדִּיר.

On Rosh Ḥodesh, continue on page 193.

Praised is our God who created us for His glory, setting us apart from those who go astray by giving us His Torah, planting within us life eternal. May He open our hearts to His Torah, inspiring us to love and revere Him, wholeheartedly to serve Him. Thus shall we not labor in vain, nor shall our children suffer confusion. Lord our God and God of our fathers, may we fulfill Your precepts in this world, and be worthy of attaining happiness and blessing in the Messianic era and in the world to come. I shall never be silent, Lord my God; I shall always sing of Your glory. Praised is the one who trusts in the Lord. Trust in the Lord for ever and ever; the Lord God is an unfailing stronghold. Those who love Him trust in Him; He never forsakes those who seek Him. The Lord, through His righteousness, exalts the Torah with greatness and glory.

On Rosh Ḥodesh, continue on page 193.

Kaddish Shalem

Reader:

יִתְגַּדַּל וְיִתְקַדַּשׁ שְׁמֵהּ רַבָּא בְּעָלְמָא דִּי בְרָא כִרְעוּתֵהּ, וְיַמְלִיךְ מַלְכוּתֵהּ בְּחַיֵּיכוֹן וּבְיוֹמֵיכוֹן וּבְחַיֵּי דְכָל־בֵּית יִשְׂרָאֵל בַּעֲגָלָא וּבִזְמַן קָרִיב, וְאִמְרוּ אָמֵן.

Congregation and Reader:

יְהֵא שְׁמֵהּ רַבָּא מְבָרַךְ לְעָלַם וּלְעָלְמֵי עָלְמַיָּא.

Reader:

יִתְבָּרַךְ וְיִשְׁתַּבַּח וְיִתְפָּאַר וְיִתְרוֹמַם וְיִתְנַשֵּׂא וְיִתְהַדָּר וְיִתְעַלֶּה וְיִתְהַלָּל שְׁמֵהּ דְּקֻדְשָׁא בְּרִיךְ הוּא, לְעֵלָּא (לְעֵלָּא) מִן כָּל־בִּרְכָתָא וְשִׁירָתָא תֻּשְׁבְּחָתָא וְנֶחֱמָתָא דַּאֲמִירָן בְּעָלְמָא, וְאִמְרוּ אָמֵן.

Omit these two lines in a House of Mourning:

תִּתְקַבֵּל צְלוֹתְהוֹן וּבָעוּתְהוֹן דְּכָל־יִשְׂרָאֵל קֳדָם אֲבוּהוֹן דִּי בִשְׁמַיָּא, וְאִמְרוּ אָמֵן.

יְהֵא שְׁלָמָא רַבָּא מִן שְׁמַיָּא וְחַיִּים עָלֵינוּ וְעַל כָּל־יִשְׂרָאֵל, וְאִמְרוּ אָמֵן.

עוֹשֶׂה שָׁלוֹם בִּמְרוֹמָיו הוּא יַעֲשֶׂה שָׁלוֹם עָלֵינוּ וְעַל כָּל־יִשְׂרָאֵל, וְאִמְרוּ אָמֵן.

Morning service

92

Kaddish Shalem

Reader:

Hallowed and enhanced may He be throughout the world of His own creation. May He cause His sovereignty soon to be accepted, during our life and the life of all Israel. And let us say: Amen.

Congregation and Reader:

Ye-hei shmei raba meva-rakh l'alam ul'almei 'almaya.

May He be praised throughout all time.

Reader:

Glorified and celebrated, lauded and praised, acclaimed and honored, extolled and exalted may the Holy One be, beyond all song and psalm, beyond all tributes which man can utter. And let us say: Amen.

Omit these two lines in a House of Mourning:
May the prayers and pleas of the whole House of Israel be accepted by our Father in Heaven. And let us say: Amen.

Let there be abundant peace from Heaven, with life's goodness for us and for all the people Israel. And let us say: Amen.

He who brings peace to His universe will bring peace to us and to all the people Israel. And let us say: Amen.

אָמַר רַבִּי אֶלְעָזָר, אָמַר רַבִּי חֲנִינָא: תַּלְמִידֵי חֲכָמִים מַרְבִּים שָׁלוֹם בָּעוֹלָם, שֶׁנֶּאֱמַר: וְכָל־בָּנַיִךְ לִמּוּדֵי יְיָ, וְרַב שְׁלוֹם בָּנָיִךְ. אַל תִּקְרָא בָּנַיִךְ, אֶלָּא בּוֹנָיִךְ. שָׁלוֹם רַב לְאֹהֲבֵי תוֹרָתֶךָ, וְאֵין לָמוֹ מִכְשׁוֹל. יְהִי שָׁלוֹם בְּחֵילֵךְ, שַׁלְוָה בְּאַרְמְנוֹתָיִךְ. לְמַעַן אַחַי וְרֵעָי, אֲדַבְּרָה־נָּא שָׁלוֹם בָּךְ. לְמַעַן בֵּית יְיָ אֱלֹהֵינוּ, אֲבַקְשָׁה טוֹב לָךְ. יְיָ עֹז לְעַמּוֹ יִתֵּן, יְיָ יְבָרֵךְ אֶת־עַמּוֹ בַשָּׁלוֹם.

With the words of Aleinu we call upon all people to
join in acknowledging and serving the King of
kings. We acknowledge His sovereignty whenever
we reject idolatry, every claim to absolute devotion
made by any earthly power. When all people pledge
their supreme loyalty to the Holy One, the world
will be at one with itself and peace will prosper
everywhere. All that is savage and brutal will
vanish. Then righteousness and justice will be a
reality on earth. No one shall hurt or destroy in all
My holy mountain, says the Lord, for the
knowledge of the Lord shall fill the earth as the
waters fill the sea.

Rabbi Elazar taught in the name of Rabbi Ḥanina: Disciples of the Sages increase peace in the world, as it was said by the prophet Isaiah: "When all of your children are taught of the Lord, great will be the peace of your children" (Isaiah 54:13). The second mention of "your children" *(banayikh)* means all who have true understanding *(bonayikh)*, like disciples of the Sages; they too are taught of the Lord, serving and blessed with peace. And thus it is written in the Book of Psalms: "Those who love Your Torah have great peace; nothing makes them stumble" (Psalms 119:165). And it is also written: "May there be peace within your walls, security within your gates. For the sake of my brethren and companions I say: May peace reside within you. For the sake of the House of the Lord I seek your welfare" (Psalms 122:7-9). "May the Lord grant His people dignity; may the Lord bless His people with peace" (Psalms 29:11).

> *With the words of* Aleinu *we call upon all people to join in acknowledging and serving the King of kings. We acknowledge His sovereignty whenever we reject idolatry, every claim to absolute devotion made by any earthly power. When all people pledge their supreme loyalty to the Holy One, the world will be at one with itself and peace will prosper everywhere. All that is savage and brutal will vanish. Then righteousness and justice will be a reality on earth. No one shall hurt or destroy in all My holy mountain, says the Lord, for the knowledge of the Lord shall fill the earth as the waters fill the sea.*

עָלֵינוּ לְשַׁבֵּחַ לַאֲדוֹן הַכֹּל, לָתֵת גְּדֻלָּה לְיוֹצֵר בְּרֵאשִׁית, שֶׁלֹּא עָשָׂנוּ
כְּגוֹיֵי הָאֲרָצוֹת וְלֹא שָׂמָנוּ כְּמִשְׁפְּחוֹת הָאֲדָמָה, שֶׁלֹּא שָׂם חֶלְקֵנוּ כָּהֶם
וְגוֹרָלֵנוּ כְּכָל־הֲמוֹנָם. וַאֲנַחְנוּ כּוֹרְעִים וּמִשְׁתַּחֲוִים וּמוֹדִים לִפְנֵי מֶלֶךְ
מַלְכֵי הַמְּלָכִים הַקָּדוֹשׁ בָּרוּךְ הוּא, שֶׁהוּא נוֹטֶה שָׁמַיִם וְיוֹסֵד אָרֶץ
וּמוֹשַׁב יְקָרוֹ בַּשָּׁמַיִם מִמַּעַל וּשְׁכִינַת עֻזּוֹ בְּגָבְהֵי מְרוֹמִים. הוּא אֱלֹהֵינוּ
אֵין עוֹד. אֱמֶת מַלְכֵּנוּ אֶפֶס זוּלָתוֹ, כַּכָּתוּב בְּתוֹרָתוֹ: וְיָדַעְתָּ הַיּוֹם
וַהֲשֵׁבֹתָ אֶל לְבָבֶךָ כִּי יְיָ הוּא הָאֱלֹהִים בַּשָּׁמַיִם מִמַּעַל וְעַל הָאָרֶץ
מִתָּחַת, אֵין עוֹד.

עַל כֵּן נְקַוֶּה לְךָ יְיָ אֱלֹהֵינוּ לִרְאוֹת מְהֵרָה בְּתִפְאֶרֶת עֻזֶּךָ, לְהַעֲבִיר
גִּלּוּלִים מִן הָאָרֶץ וְהָאֱלִילִים כָּרוֹת יִכָּרֵתוּן, לְתַקֵּן עוֹלָם בְּמַלְכוּת
שַׁדַּי וְכָל־בְּנֵי בָשָׂר יִקְרְאוּ בִשְׁמֶךָ, לְהַפְנוֹת אֵלֶיךָ כָּל־רִשְׁעֵי־אָרֶץ.
יַכִּירוּ וְיֵדְעוּ כָּל־יוֹשְׁבֵי תֵבֵל כִּי לְךָ תִכְרַע כָּל־בֶּרֶךְ תִּשָּׁבַע כָּל־
לָשׁוֹן. לְפָנֶיךָ יְיָ אֱלֹהֵינוּ יִכְרְעוּ וְיִפֹּלוּ וְלִכְבוֹד שִׁמְךָ יְקָר יִתֵּנוּ,
וִיקַבְּלוּ כֻלָּם אֶת־עֹל מַלְכוּתֶךָ וְתִמְלֹךְ עֲלֵיהֶם מְהֵרָה לְעוֹלָם וָעֶד,
כִּי הַמַּלְכוּת שֶׁלְּךָ הִיא וּלְעוֹלְמֵי עַד תִּמְלֹךְ בְּכָבוֹד, כַּכָּתוּב
בְּתוֹרָתֶךָ: יְיָ יִמְלֹךְ לְעֹלָם וָעֶד:\וְנֶאֱמַר: וְהָיָה יְיָ לְמֶלֶךְ עַל כָּל־
הָאָרֶץ, בַּיּוֹם הַהוּא יִהְיֶה יְיָ אֶחָד וּשְׁמוֹ אֶחָד.

Aleinu

We rise to our duty to praise the Lord of all the world, to acclaim the Creator. He made our lot unlike that of other people, assigning us a unique destiny. We bend the knee and bow, proclaiming Him as King of kings, the Holy One praised be He, who stretched forth the heavens and established the earth. He is God, our King. There is no other.

*Va'anaḥnu kor'im u-mish-taḥavim u-modim
lifnei melekh malkhei ha-melakhim ha-kadosh barukh hu.*

And so we hope in You, Lord our God, soon to see Your splendor, sweeping idolatry away so that false gods will be utterly destroyed, perfecting earth by Your kingship so that all mankind will invoke Your name, bringing all the earth's wicked back to You, repentant. Then all who live will know that to You every knee must bend, every tongue pledge loyalty. To You, Lord, may all men bow in worship, may they give honor to Your glory. May everyone accept the rule of Your kingship. Reign over all, soon and for all time. Sovereignty is Yours in glory, now and forever. Thus is it written in Your Torah: The Lord reigns for ever and ever. Such is the assurance of Your prophet Zechariah: The Lord shall be acknowledged King of all the earth. On that day the Lord shall be One and His name One.

*Ve-ne'emar ve-haya Adonai le-melekh al kol ha'aretz,
bayom ha-hu yiyeh Adonai eḥad u-she-mo eḥad.*

Morning service

Mourner's Kaddish

In recalling our dead, of blessed memory, we
confront our loss with faith by rising to praise
God's name in public assembly, praying that all
men recognize His kingship soon. For when His
sovereignty is felt in the world, peace, blessing and
song fill the world, as well as great consolation.

Mourners and those observing Yahrzeit rise.

יִתְגַּדַּל וְיִתְקַדַּשׁ שְׁמֵהּ רַבָּא בְּעָלְמָא דִּי בְרָא כִרְעוּתֵהּ, וְיַמְלִיךְ מַלְכוּתֵהּ בְּחַיֵּיכוֹן וּבְיוֹמֵיכוֹן וּבְחַיֵּי דְכָל־בֵּית יִשְׂרָאֵל בַּעֲגָלָא וּבִזְמַן קָרִיב, וְאִמְרוּ אָמֵן.

Congregation and mourner:

יְהֵא שְׁמֵהּ רַבָּא מְבָרַךְ לְעָלַם וּלְעָלְמֵי עָלְמַיָּא.

Mourner:

יִתְבָּרַךְ וְיִשְׁתַּבַּח וְיִתְפָּאַר וְיִתְרוֹמַם וְיִתְנַשֵּׂא וְיִתְהַדָּר וְיִתְעַלֶּה וְיִתְהַלָּל שְׁמֵהּ דְּקֻדְשָׁא בְּרִיךְ הוּא, לְעֵלָּא (לְעֵלָּא) מִן כָּל־ בִּרְכָתָא וְשִׁירָתָא תֻּשְׁבְּחָתָא וְנֶחֱמָתָא דַּאֲמִירָן בְּעָלְמָא, וְאִמְרוּ אָמֵן.

יְהֵא שְׁלָמָא רַבָּא מִן שְׁמַיָּא וְחַיִּים עָלֵינוּ וְעַל כָּל־יִשְׂרָאֵל, וְאִמְרוּ אָמֵן.

עוֹשֶׂה שָׁלוֹם בִּמְרוֹמָיו הוּא יַעֲשֶׂה שָׁלוֹם עָלֵינוּ וְעַל כָּל־יִשְׂרָאֵל, וְאִמְרוּ אָמֵן.

Mourner's Kaddish

In recalling our dead, of blessed memory, we confront our loss with faith by rising to praise God's name in public assembly, praying that all men recognize His kingship soon. For when His sovereignty is felt in the world, peace, blessing and song fill the world, as well as great consolation.

Mourners and those observing Yahrzeit rise.

Yit-gadal ve-yit-kadash shmei raba, b'alma divra khir'utei ve-yamlikh mal-khutei be-hayei-khon uve'yomei-khon uve-hayei di-khol beit yisrael ba-agala u-vizman kariv v'imru amen.

Congregation and Mourner:

Ye-hei shmei raba meva-rakh l'alam ul'almei 'al-maya.

Mourner:

Yit-barakh ve-yish-tabah ve-yitpa'ar ve-yitromam ve-yitnasei ve-yit-hadar ve-yit'aleh ve-yit-halal shmei di-kudsha brikh hu, l'eila [l'eila] min kol bir-khata ve-shirata tush-be-hata ve-nehe-mata da-amiran b'alma, v'imru amen.

Ye-hei shlama raba min shmaya ve-hayim aleinu v'al kol yisrael v'imru amen.

Oseh shalom bimromav hu ya'aseh shalom aleinu v'al kol yisrael v'imru amen.

For a translation of the Mourner's Kaddish, see the following page.

Mourner's Kaddish

Mourners and those observing Yahrzeit rise.

Hallowed and enhanced may He be throughout the world of His own creation. May He cause His sovereignty soon to be accepted, during our life and the life of all Israel. And let us say: Amen.

Congregation and mourner:

May He be praised throughout all time.

Mourner:

Glorified and celebrated, lauded and praised, acclaimed and honored, extolled and exalted may the Holy One be, far beyond all song and psalm, beyond all tributes which man can utter. And let us say: Amen.

Let there be abundant peace from Heaven, with life's goodness for us and for all the people Israel. And let us say: Amen.

He who brings peace to His universe will bring peace to us and to all the people Israel. And let us say: Amen.

יְיָ רֹעִי לֹא אֶחְסָר. בִּנְאוֹת דֶּשֶׁא יַרְבִּיצֵנִי, עַל מֵי מְנֻחוֹת יְנַהֲלֵנִי. נַפְשִׁי
יְשׁוֹבֵב, יַנְחֵנִי בְמַעְגְּלֵי־צֶדֶק לְמַעַן שְׁמוֹ. גַּם כִּי אֵלֵךְ בְּגֵיא צַלְמָוֶת
לֹא אִירָא רָע כִּי אַתָּה עִמָּדִי, שִׁבְטְךָ וּמִשְׁעַנְתֶּךָ הֵמָּה יְנַחֲמֻנִי. תַּעֲרֹךְ
לְפָנַי שֻׁלְחָן נֶגֶד צֹרְרָי, דִּשַּׁנְתָּ בַשֶּׁמֶן רֹאשִׁי, כּוֹסִי רְוָיָה. אַךְ טוֹב
וָחֶסֶד יִרְדְּפוּנִי כָּל־יְמֵי חַיָּי, וְשַׁבְתִּי בְּבֵית יְיָ לְאֹרֶךְ יָמִים.

The Lord is my shepherd, I shall not want.

He gives me repose in green meadows.

He leads me beside the still waters; He revives my spirit.

He guides me on the right path, for that is His nature.

Though I walk in the valley of the shadow of death,
I fear no harm, for You are with me.

Your staff and Your rod comfort me.

You prepare a banquet for me in the presence of my foes.

You anoint my head with oil; my cup overflows.

Surely goodness and kindness shall be my portion
all the days of my life.

And I shall dwell in the House of the Lord forever.

The Daily Psalms

❧

*The Mourner's Kaddish may be repeated after recitation of
one of these daily psalms plus the appropriate psalm
or psalms which follow on pages 112 through 122.*

הַיּוֹם יוֹם רִאשׁוֹן בַּשַּׁבָּת,

שֶׁבּוֹ הָיוּ הַלְוִיִּם אוֹמְרִים בְּבֵית הַמִּקְדָּשׁ:

לְדָוִד מִזְמוֹר. לַיְיָ הָאָרֶץ וּמְלוֹאָהּ, תֵּבֵל וְיֹשְׁבֵי בָהּ. כִּי הוּא עַל
יַמִּים יְסָדָהּ, וְעַל נְהָרוֹת יְכוֹנְנֶהָ. מִי יַעֲלֶה בְהַר יְיָ, וּמִי יָקוּם
בִּמְקוֹם קָדְשׁוֹ. נְקִי כַפַּיִם וּבַר לֵבָב, אֲשֶׁר לֹא נָשָׂא לַשָּׁוְא נַפְשִׁי,
וְלֹא נִשְׁבַּע לְמִרְמָה. יִשָּׂא בְרָכָה מֵאֵת יְיָ, וּצְדָקָה מֵאֱלֹהֵי יִשְׁעוֹ.
זֶה דּוֹר דֹּרְשָׁיו, מְבַקְשֵׁי פָנֶיךָ יַעֲקֹב, סֶלָה. שְׂאוּ שְׁעָרִים רָאשֵׁיכֶם
וְהִנָּשְׂאוּ פִּתְחֵי עוֹלָם, וְיָבוֹא מֶלֶךְ הַכָּבוֹד. מִי זֶה מֶלֶךְ הַכָּבוֹד,
יְיָ עִזּוּז וְגִבּוֹר, יְיָ גִּבּוֹר מִלְחָמָה.\שְׂאוּ שְׁעָרִים רָאשֵׁיכֶם וּשְׂאוּ
פִּתְחֵי עוֹלָם, וְיָבֹא מֶלֶךְ הַכָּבוֹד. מִי הוּא זֶה מֶלֶךְ הַכָּבוֹד, יְיָ
צְבָאוֹת, הוּא מֶלֶךְ הַכָּבוֹד, סֶלָה.

Morning service

102

The Daily Psalms

The Mourner's Kaddish may be repeated after recitation of one of these daily psalms plus the appropriate psalm or psalms which follow on pages 113 through 123.

THE PSALM FOR SUNDAY

On Sunday the Levites would recite this Psalm in the Temple:

A Psalm of David. The earth is the Lord's, and all that it holds, the world and its inhabitants. He founded it upon the seas, He set it firm upon flowing waters. Who deserves to enter God's sanctuary? Who merits a place in His Presence? He who has clean hands and a pure heart, who has not used God's name in vain oaths, who has not sworn deceitfully. He shall receive a blessing from the Lord, a just reward from the God of his deliverance. Such are the people who seek Him, who, like Jacob, long for His Presence. Lift high your lintels, O you gates; open wide, you ancient doors! Welcome the glorious King! Who is the glorious King? The Lord, with dignity and power; the Lord, triumphant in battle. Lift high your lintels, O you gates; open wide, you ancient doors! Welcome the glorious King! Who is the glorious King? The Lord of hosts; He is the glorious King.

Psalm 24

Morning service

הַיּוֹם יוֹם שֵׁנִי בַּשַּׁבָּת,
שֶׁבּוֹ הָיוּ הַלְוִיִּים אוֹמְרִים בְּבֵית הַמִּקְדָּשׁ:

שִׁיר מִזְמוֹר לִבְנֵי־קֹרַח. גָּדוֹל יְיָ וּמְהֻלָּל מְאֹד, בְּעִיר אֱלֹהֵינוּ הַר קָדְשׁוֹ. יְפֵה נוֹף מְשׂוֹשׂ כָּל־הָאָרֶץ, הַר צִיּוֹן יַרְכְּתֵי צָפוֹן, קִרְיַת מֶלֶךְ רָב. אֱלֹהִים בְּאַרְמְנוֹתֶיהָ נוֹדַע לְמִשְׂגָּב. כִּי הִנֵּה הַמְּלָכִים נוֹעֲדוּ, עָבְרוּ יַחְדָּו. הֵמָּה רָאוּ כֵּן תָּמָהוּ, נִבְהֲלוּ נֶחְפָּזוּ. רְעָדָה אֲחָזָתַם שָׁם, חִיל כַּיּוֹלֵדָה. בְּרוּחַ קָדִים תְּשַׁבֵּר אֳנִיּוֹת תַּרְשִׁישׁ. כַּאֲשֶׁר שָׁמַעְנוּ כֵּן רָאִינוּ בְּעִיר יְיָ צְבָאוֹת בְּעִיר אֱלֹהֵינוּ, אֱלֹהִים יְכוֹנְנֶהָ עַד עוֹלָם, סֶלָה. דִּמִּינוּ אֱלֹהִים חַסְדֶּךָ בְּקֶרֶב הֵיכָלֶךָ. כְּשִׁמְךָ אֱלֹהִים כֵּן תְּהִלָּתְךָ עַל קַצְוֵי־אֶרֶץ, צֶדֶק מָלְאָה יְמִינֶךָ. יִשְׂמַח הַר צִיּוֹן, תָּגֵלְנָה בְּנוֹת יְהוּדָה, לְמַעַן מִשְׁפָּטֶיךָ. סֹבּוּ צִיּוֹן וְהַקִּיפוּהָ, סִפְרוּ מִגְדָּלֶיהָ. שִׁיתוּ לִבְּכֶם לְחֵילָה, פַּסְּגוּ אַרְמְנוֹתֶיהָ, לְמַעַן תְּסַפְּרוּ לְדוֹר אַחֲרוֹן.\כִּי זֶה אֱלֹהִים אֱלֹהֵינוּ עוֹלָם וָעֶד, הוּא יְנַהֲגֵנוּ עַל מוּת.

הַיּוֹם יוֹם שְׁלִישִׁי בַּשַּׁבָּת,
שֶׁבּוֹ הָיוּ הַלְוִיִּים אוֹמְרִים בְּבֵית הַמִּקְדָּשׁ:

מִזְמוֹר לְאָסָף. אֱלֹהִים נִצָּב בַּעֲדַת אֵל, בְּקֶרֶב אֱלֹהִים יִשְׁפֹּט. עַד מָתַי תִּשְׁפְּטוּ־עָוֶל, וּפְנֵי רְשָׁעִים תִּשְׂאוּ, סֶלָה. שִׁפְטוּ־דַל וְיָתוֹם, עָנִי וָרָשׁ הַצְדִּיקוּ. פַּלְּטוּ־דַל וְאֶבְיוֹן, מִיַּד רְשָׁעִים הַצִּילוּ. לֹא יָדְעוּ וְלֹא יָבִינוּ, בַּחֲשֵׁכָה יִתְהַלָּכוּ, יִמּוֹטוּ כָּל־מוֹסְדֵי אָרֶץ.

On Monday the Levites would recite this Psalm in the Temple:

A Psalm sung by the Korahites. Great is the Lord, and highly praised in the city of our God, on His holy mountain. Splendid and high on the north is Mount Zion, joy of all the earth, the city of the great king. Through her citadels God has revealed His power. The kings who conspired against her retreated. They saw her and were stunned, confused. Panic overwhelmed them; they fled in terror. They were seized with trembling like a woman in labor, like the fleet from Tarshish wrecked by the east wind. What we heard from our fathers we now have witnessed in the city of the Lord of hosts, in the city of our God. May God preserve it forever. In Your temple, God, we meditate upon Your kindness. Your glory, like Your name, is known to the ends of the earth. Justice is at Your command. Let Zion be glad, and let the cities of Judah rejoice because of the justice of Your decrees. Walk all about Zion, encircle her. Count her towers, examine her ramparts and citadels. Then tell their story to later generations, tell of our God who will guide us forever.

Psalm 48

THE PSALM FOR TUESDAY

On Tuesday the Levites would recite this Psalm in the Temple:

A Psalm of Asaph. God rises in the assembly of the mighty; He pronounces judgment over the rulers. "How long will you pervert justice? How long will you show favor to the wicked? Uphold the poor and the orphan; let the afflicted

אֲנִי אָמַרְתִּי אֱלֹהִים אַתֶּם, וּבְנֵי עֶלְיוֹן כֻּלְּכֶם. אָכֵן כְּאָדָם תְּמוּתוּן, וּכְאַחַד הַשָּׂרִים תִּפֹּלוּ. \קוּמָה אֱלֹהִים, שָׁפְטָה הָאָרֶץ, כִּי אַתָּה תִנְחַל בְּכָל־הַגּוֹיִם.

הַיּוֹם יוֹם רְבִיעִי בַּשַּׁבָּת,
שֶׁבּוֹ הָיוּ הַלְוִיִּם אוֹמְרִים בְּבֵית הַמִּקְדָּשׁ:

אֵל נְקָמוֹת יְיָ, אֵל נְקָמוֹת הוֹפִיעַ. הִנָּשֵׂא שֹׁפֵט הָאָרֶץ, הָשֵׁב גְּמוּל עַל גֵּאִים. עַד מָתַי רְשָׁעִים יְיָ, עַד מָתַי רְשָׁעִים יַעֲלֹזוּ. יַבִּיעוּ יְדַבְּרוּ עָתָק, יִתְאַמְּרוּ כָּל־פֹּעֲלֵי אָוֶן. עַמְּךָ יְיָ יְדַכְּאוּ, וְנַחֲלָתְךָ יְעַנּוּ. אַלְמָנָה וְגֵר יַהֲרֹגוּ, וִיתוֹמִים יְרַצֵּחוּ. וַיֹּאמְרוּ לֹא יִרְאֶה יָּהּ, וְלֹא יָבִין אֱלֹהֵי יַעֲקֹב. בִּינוּ בֹּעֲרִים בָּעָם, וּכְסִילִים מָתַי תַּשְׂכִּילוּ. הֲנֹטַע אֹזֶן הֲלֹא יִשְׁמָע, אִם יֹצֵר עַיִן הֲלֹא יַבִּיט. הֲיֹסֵר גּוֹיִם הֲלֹא יוֹכִיחַ, הַמְלַמֵּד אָדָם דָּעַת. יְיָ יוֹדֵעַ מַחְשְׁבוֹת אָדָם, כִּי הֵמָּה הָבֶל. אַשְׁרֵי הַגֶּבֶר אֲשֶׁר תְּיַסְּרֶנּוּ יָּהּ, וּמִתּוֹרָתְךָ תְלַמְּדֶנּוּ. לְהַשְׁקִיט לוֹ מִימֵי רָע, עַד יִכָּרֶה לָרָשָׁע שָׁחַת. כִּי לֹא יִטֹּשׁ יְיָ עַמּוֹ, וְנַחֲלָתוֹ לֹא יַעֲזֹב. כִּי עַד צֶדֶק יָשׁוּב מִשְׁפָּט, וְאַחֲרָיו כָּל־יִשְׁרֵי־לֵב. מִי יָקוּם לִי עִם מְרֵעִים, מִי יִתְיַצֵּב לִי עִם פֹּעֲלֵי אָוֶן. לוּלֵי יְיָ עֶזְרָתָה לִי, כִּמְעַט שָׁכְנָה דוּמָה נַפְשִׁי. אִם אָמַרְתִּי מָטָה רַגְלִי, חַסְדְּךָ יְיָ יִסְעָדֵנִי. בְּרֹב שַׂרְעַפַּי בְּקִרְבִּי, תַּנְחוּמֶיךָ יְשַׁעַשְׁעוּ נַפְשִׁי. הַיְחָבְרְךָ כִּסֵּא הַוּוֹת, יֹצֵר עָמָל עֲלֵי־חֹק. יָגוֹדּוּ

and the destitute have justice. Rescue the wretched and the needy, save them from the grip of the wicked." But the rulers do not understand justice; they wander about in darkness while the earth is shaken to its foundations. "I had thought you were superior beings, extraordinary and godlike, but you will die as mortals do, perish like all earthly princes." Arise, O God, and judge the earth, for Your dominion is over all nations.

Psalm 82

On Wednesday the Levites would recite this Psalm in the Temple:

Lord God of vengeance, appear. Judge of the earth, arise to punish the arrogant. How long, Lord, how long shall the wicked exult? How long shall the wicked speak insolently, ceaselessly acting arrogantly? They crush Your people, Lord, they afflict Your heritage. They slay the widow and the stranger, they murder the fatherless, thinking, "The Lord does not see it, the God of Jacob pays no heed." Understand, brutish people. Fools, when will you learn? Surely He who implants the ear can hear. Surely He who forms the eye can see. Surely He who instructs nations will reprove them. Surely He who gives men knowledge will punish them. The Lord knows man's schemes, how futile they are. Happy is the man disciplined by the Lord, happy is he whom the Lord has taught Torah. He will find relief from trouble, until a pit is dug for the wicked. The Lord will not abandon His people, He will not forsake His heritage. Justice shall be restored to the righteous; all the upright in heart shall rally to it. Who

עַל נֶפֶשׁ צַדִּיק, וְדָם נָקִי יַרְשִׁיעוּ. וַיְהִי יְיָ לִי לְמִשְׂגָּב, וֵאלֹהַי לְצוּר מַחְסִי. וַיָּשֶׁב עֲלֵיהֶם אֶת־אוֹנָם, וּבְרָעָתָם יַצְמִיתֵם, יַצְמִיתֵם יְיָ אֱלֹהֵינוּ.

\לְכוּ נְרַנְּנָה לַיְיָ, נָרִיעָה לְצוּר יִשְׁעֵנוּ. נְקַדְּמָה פָנָיו בְּתוֹדָה, בִּזְמִרוֹת נָרִיעַ לוֹ. כִּי אֵל גָּדוֹל יְיָ, וּמֶלֶךְ גָּדוֹל עַל כָּל־אֱלֹהִים.

הַיּוֹם יוֹם חֲמִישִׁי בַּשַּׁבָּת,
שֶׁבּוֹ הָיוּ הַלְוִיִּם אוֹמְרִים בְּבֵית הַמִּקְדָּשׁ:

לַמְנַצֵּחַ עַל הַגִּתִּית לְאָסָף. הַרְנִינוּ לֵאלֹהִים עוּזֵּנוּ, הָרִיעוּ לֵאלֹהֵי יַעֲקֹב. שְׂאוּ זִמְרָה וּתְנוּ־תֹף, כִּנּוֹר נָעִים עִם נָבֶל. תִּקְעוּ בַחֹדֶשׁ שׁוֹפָר, בַּכֶּסֶה לְיוֹם חַגֵּנוּ. כִּי חֹק לְיִשְׂרָאֵל הוּא, מִשְׁפָּט לֵאלֹהֵי יַעֲקֹב. עֵדוּת בִּיהוֹסֵף שָׂמוֹ בְּצֵאתוֹ עַל אֶרֶץ מִצְרָיִם, שְׂפַת לֹא יָדַעְתִּי אֶשְׁמָע. הֲסִירוֹתִי מִסֵּבֶל שִׁכְמוֹ, כַּפָּיו מִדּוּד תַּעֲבֹרְנָה. בַּצָּרָה קָרָאתָ וָאֲחַלְּצֶךָּ, אֶעֶנְךָ בְּסֵתֶר רָעַם, אֶבְחָנְךָ עַל מֵי מְרִיבָה, סֶלָה. שְׁמַע עַמִּי וְאָעִידָה בָּךְ, יִשְׂרָאֵל אִם תִּשְׁמַע לִי. לֹא יִהְיֶה בְךָ אֵל זָר, וְלֹא תִשְׁתַּחֲוֶה לְאֵל נֵכָר. אָנֹכִי יְיָ אֱלֹהֶיךָ הַמַּעַלְךָ מֵאֶרֶץ מִצְרָיִם, הַרְחֶב־פִּיךָ וַאֲמַלְאֵהוּ. וְלֹא שָׁמַע עַמִּי לְקוֹלִי, וְיִשְׂרָאֵל לֹא אָבָה לִי. וָאֲשַׁלְּחֵהוּ בִּשְׁרִירוּת לִבָּם, יֵלְכוּ

will stand up for me against evildoers? Who will take my part against the ungodly? Were it not for God's help I would be in my grave. When my foot slips, the Lord's faithfulness supports me. When worry crowds upon me, He comforts my soul. Shall they who sit on thrones of wickedness, administering injustice by perverting the law, have You as an ally? They organize attacks against honest men, they condemn the innocent to death. The Lord is my sure Refuge; my God is my sheltering Rock. He will repay them for their wickedness, He will destroy them with their own evil. The Lord our God will surely destroy them.

Psalm 94

Come, let us sing to the Lord; let us acclaim our Rock and Deliverer. Let us approach Him with thanksgiving, let us acclaim Him with joyful psalms. For the Lord is a great God, a King, greater than all gods.

Psalm 95:1-3

THE PSALM FOR THURSDAY

On Thursday the Levites would recite this Psalm in the Temple:

For the leader, with instrumental accompaniment, a Psalm of Asaph. Sing with joy to God, our strength; shout with gladness to the God of Jacob. Strike up the melody, sound the timbrel, play sweet tones on harp and lyre. Sound the shofar on the New Moon, on the full moon for our festive day. It is a law for the people Israel, a ruling of the God of Jacob. He ordained it as a decree for Joseph when He rose against the land of Egypt; then I heard a language I had never known. I removed the burden from your back, I freed your hands from

Morning service

109

בְּמוֹעֲצוֹתֵיהֶם. לוּ עַמִּי שֹׁמֵעַ לִי, יִשְׂרָאֵל בִּדְרָכַי יְהַלֵּכוּ. כִּמְעַט
אוֹיְבֵיהֶם אַכְנִיעַ, וְעַל צָרֵיהֶם אָשִׁיב יָדִי.\מְשַׂנְאֵי יְיָ יְכַחֲשׁוּ־לוֹ,
וִיהִי עִתָּם לְעוֹלָם. וַיַּאֲכִילֵהוּ מֵחֵלֶב חִטָּה, וּמִצּוּר דְּבַשׁ אַשְׂבִּיעֶךָ.

הַיּוֹם יוֹם שִׁשִּׁי בַּשַּׁבָּת,

שֶׁבּוֹ הָיוּ הַלְוִיִּם אוֹמְרִים בְּבֵית הַמִּקְדָּשׁ:

יְיָ מָלָךְ גֵּאוּת לָבֵשׁ, לָבֵשׁ יְיָ, עֹז הִתְאַזָּר, אַף תִּכּוֹן תֵּבֵל בַּל
תִּמּוֹט. נָכוֹן כִּסְאֲךָ מֵאָז, מֵעוֹלָם אָתָּה. נָשְׂאוּ נְהָרוֹת יְיָ, נָשְׂאוּ
נְהָרוֹת קוֹלָם, יִשְׂאוּ נְהָרוֹת דָּכְיָם. מִקֹּלוֹת מַיִם רַבִּים אַדִּירִים
מִשְׁבְּרֵי־יָם, אַדִּיר בַּמָּרוֹם יְיָ.\עֵדֹתֶיךָ נֶאֶמְנוּ מְאֹד, לְבֵיתְךָ נַאֲוָה
קֹדֶשׁ יְיָ לְאֹרֶךְ יָמִים.

the heavy load. I rescued you when you called in distress, I answered you from out of clouds and thunder, I tested your loyalty at the waters of Meribah. Hear this warning, My people; Israel, if you would only listen. Let there be no strange god among you, never bow to an alien god. I, the Lord, am your God who brought you out of the land of Egypt; open your mouth wide and I will fill it. But My people did not heed My plea, Israel would have none of Me. So I let them follow their willful ways, I let them follow their own devices. If only My people would listen to Me, if Israel would walk in My ways, then would I quickly subdue their foes and strike out at their oppressors. Enemies of the Lord will be humbled; their doom shall be eternal. But you would I feed with richest wheat, I would satisfy you with honey from the rock.

Psalm 81

THE PSALM FOR FRIDAY

On Friday the Levites would recite this Psalm in the Temple:

The Lord is King, crowned with splendor. The Lord reigns, robed in strength. He set the earth on a sure foundation. He created a world that stands firm. His kingdom stands from earliest time. He is eternal. The rivers may rise and rage, the waters may pound and roar, the floods may spread and storm. Above the waves of the raging sea, awesome is the Lord our God. Your decrees, O Lord, never fail. Holiness describes Your house for eternity.

Psalm 93

We live in the light of God's compassion.

לְדָוִד. יְיָ אוֹרִי וְיִשְׁעִי מִמִּי אִירָא, יְיָ מָעוֹז חַיַּי מִמִּי אֶפְחָד.
בִּקְרֹב עָלַי מְרֵעִים לֶאֱכֹל אֶת־בְּשָׂרִי, צָרַי וְאֹיְבַי לִי הֵמָּה כָּשְׁלוּ
וְנָפָלוּ. אִם תַּחֲנֶה עָלַי מַחֲנֶה לֹא יִירָא לִבִּי, אִם תָּקוּם עָלַי
מִלְחָמָה בְּזֹאת אֲנִי בוֹטֵחַ. אַחַת שָׁאַלְתִּי מֵאֵת יְיָ אוֹתָהּ אֲבַקֵּשׁ,
שִׁבְתִּי בְּבֵית יְיָ כָּל־יְמֵי חַיַּי, לַחֲזוֹת בְּנֹעַם יְיָ וּלְבַקֵּר בְּהֵיכָלוֹ.
כִּי יִצְפְּנֵנִי בְּסֻכֹּה בְּיוֹם רָעָה, יַסְתִּרֵנִי בְּסֵתֶר אָהֳלוֹ בְּצוּר יְרוֹמְמֵנִי.
וְעַתָּה יָרוּם רֹאשִׁי עַל אֹיְבַי סְבִיבוֹתַי, וְאֶזְבְּחָה בְאָהֳלוֹ זִבְחֵי
תְרוּעָה, אָשִׁירָה וַאֲזַמְּרָה לַיְיָ. שְׁמַע יְיָ קוֹלִי אֶקְרָא, וְחָנֵּנִי וַעֲנֵנִי.
לְךָ אָמַר לִבִּי בַּקְּשׁוּ פָנָי, אֶת־פָּנֶיךָ יְיָ אֲבַקֵּשׁ. אַל תַּסְתֵּר פָּנֶיךָ
מִמֶּנִּי אַל תַּט בְּאַף עַבְדֶּךָ, עֶזְרָתִי הָיִיתָ, אַל תִּטְּשֵׁנִי וְאַל תַּעַזְבֵנִי
אֱלֹהֵי יִשְׁעִי. כִּי אָבִי וְאִמִּי עֲזָבוּנִי, וַיְיָ יַאַסְפֵנִי. הוֹרֵנִי יְיָ דַּרְכֶּךָ
וּנְחֵנִי בְּאֹרַח מִישׁוֹר לְמַעַן שׁוֹרְרָי. אַל תִּתְּנֵנִי בְּנֶפֶשׁ צָרָי, כִּי קָמוּ
בִי עֵדֵי שֶׁקֶר וִיפֵחַ חָמָס.\לוּלֵא הֶאֱמַנְתִּי לִרְאוֹת בְּטוּב יְיָ בְּאֶרֶץ
חַיִּים. קַוֵּה אֶל יְיָ, חֲזַק וְיַאֲמֵץ לִבֶּךָ וְקַוֵּה אֶל יְיָ.

The Mourner's Kaddish is found on page 98.

ON ROSH ḤODESH

בָּרְכִי נַפְשִׁי אֶת־יְיָ. יְיָ אֱלֹהַי גָּדַלְתָּ מְּאֹד, הוֹד וְהָדָר לָבָשְׁתָּ.
עֹטֶה אוֹר כַּשַּׂלְמָה, נוֹטֶה שָׁמַיִם כַּיְרִיעָה. הַמְקָרֶה בַמַּיִם
עֲלִיּוֹתָיו, הַשָּׂם עָבִים רְכוּבוֹ, הַמְהַלֵּךְ עַל כַּנְפֵי־רוּחַ. עֹשֶׂה
מַלְאָכָיו רוּחוֹת, מְשָׁרְתָיו אֵשׁ לֹהֵט. יָסַד אֶרֶץ עַל מְכוֹנֶיהָ, בַּל

Morning service

We live in the light of God's compassion.

A Psalm of David. The Lord is my light and my help. Whom shall I fear? The Lord is the strength of my life. Whom shall I dread? When evildoers draw near to devour me, when foes threaten, they stumble and fall. Though armies be arrayed against me, I have no fear. Though wars threaten, I remain steadfast in my faith.

One thing I ask of the Lord, for this I yearn: To dwell in the House of the Lord all the days of my life, to pray in His sanctuary, to behold the Lord's beauty. He will hide me in His shrine, safe from peril. He will shelter me, and put me beyond the reach of disaster. He will raise my head high above my enemies about me. I will bring Him offerings with shouts of joy. I will sing, I will chant praise to the Lord.

O Lord, hear my voice when I call; be gracious, and answer me. "It is You that I seek," says my heart. It is Your Presence that I crave, O Lord. Hide not Your Presence from me, reject not Your servant. You are my help, do not desert me. Forsake me not, God of my deliverance. Though my father and mother forsake me, the Lord will gather me in, and care for me. Teach me Your way, O Lord. Guide me on the right path, to confound those who mock me. Deceivers have risen against me, men who breathe out violence. Abandon me not to the will of my foes. Mine is the faith that I surely will see the Lord's goodness in the land of the living. Hope in the Lord and be strong. Hope in the Lord and take courage.

Psalm 27

The Mourner's Kaddish is found on page 99.

Morning service

תִּמּוֹט עוֹלָם וָעֶד. תְּהוֹם כַּלְּבוּשׁ כִּסִּיתוֹ, עַל הָרִים יַעַמְדוּ מָיִם. מִן גַּעֲרָתְךָ יְנוּסוּן, מִן קוֹל רַעַמְךָ יֵחָפֵזוּן. יַעֲלוּ הָרִים יֵרְדוּ בְקָעוֹת, אֶל מְקוֹם זֶה יָסַדְתָּ לָהֶם. גְּבוּל שַׂמְתָּ בַּל יַעֲבֹרוּן, בַּל יְשׁוּבוּן לְכַסּוֹת הָאָרֶץ. הַמְשַׁלֵּחַ מַעְיָנִים בַּנְּחָלִים, בֵּין הָרִים יְהַלֵּכוּן. יַשְׁקוּ כָּל־חַיְתוֹ שָׂדָי, יִשְׁבְּרוּ פְרָאִים צְמָאָם. עֲלֵיהֶם עוֹף הַשָּׁמַיִם יִשְׁכּוֹן, מִבֵּין עֳפָאיִם יִתְּנוּ קוֹל. מַשְׁקֶה הָרִים מֵעֲלִיּוֹתָיו, מִפְּרִי מַעֲשֶׂיךָ תִּשְׂבַּע הָאָרֶץ.

מַצְמִיחַ חָצִיר לַבְּהֵמָה וְעֵשֶׂב לַעֲבוֹדַת הָאָדָם, לְהוֹצִיא לֶחֶם מִן הָאָרֶץ. וְיַיִן יְשַׂמַּח לְבַב אֱנוֹשׁ לְהַצְהִיל פָּנִים מִשָּׁמֶן, וְלֶחֶם לְבַב אֱנוֹשׁ יִסְעָד. יִשְׂבְּעוּ עֲצֵי יְיָ, אַרְזֵי לְבָנוֹן אֲשֶׁר נָטָע. אֲשֶׁר שָׁם צִפֳּרִים יְקַנֵּנוּ, חֲסִידָה בְּרוֹשִׁים בֵּיתָהּ. הָרִים הַגְּבֹהִים לַיְּעֵלִים, סְלָעִים מַחְסֶה לַשְׁפַנִּים. עָשָׂה יָרֵחַ לְמוֹעֲדִים, שֶׁמֶשׁ יָדַע מְבוֹאוֹ. תָּשֶׁת חֹשֶׁךְ וִיהִי לָיְלָה, בּוֹ תִרְמֹשׂ כָּל־חַיְתוֹ־יָעַר. הַכְּפִירִים שֹׁאֲגִים לַטָּרֶף וּלְבַקֵּשׁ מֵאֵל אָכְלָם. תִּזְרַח הַשֶּׁמֶשׁ יֵאָסֵפוּן וְאֶל מְעוֹנֹתָם יִרְבָּצוּן. יֵצֵא אָדָם לְפָעֳלוֹ וְלַעֲבֹדָתוֹ עֲדֵי עָרֶב.

מָה רַבּוּ מַעֲשֶׂיךָ יְיָ, כֻּלָּם בְּחָכְמָה עָשִׂיתָ, מָלְאָה הָאָרֶץ קִנְיָנֶךָ. זֶה הַיָּם גָּדוֹל וּרְחַב יָדַיִם, שָׁם רֶמֶשׂ וְאֵין מִסְפָּר, חַיּוֹת קְטַנּוֹת עִם גְּדֹלוֹת. שָׁם אֳנִיּוֹת יְהַלֵּכוּן, לִוְיָתָן זֶה יָצַרְתָּ לְשַׂחֶק בּוֹ. כֻּלָּם אֵלֶיךָ יְשַׂבֵּרוּן לָתֵת אָכְלָם בְּעִתּוֹ. תִּתֵּן לָהֶם יִלְקֹטוּן, תִּפְתַּח יָדְךָ יִשְׂבְּעוּן טוֹב. תַּסְתִּיר פָּנֶיךָ יִבָּהֵלוּן, תֹּסֵף רוּחָם יִגְוָעוּן וְאֶל עֲפָרָם יְשׁוּבוּן. תְּשַׁלַּח רוּחֲךָ יִבָּרֵאוּן, וּתְחַדֵּשׁ פְּנֵי

Praise the Lord, my soul. O Lord, my God, You are great indeed, clothed in grandeur and glory, wrapped in light as in a garment, unfolding the heavens as a curtain. On waters You lay the beams of Your chambers; You take the clouds for Your chariot, riding the wings of the wind. You make the winds Your messengers, fire and flame Your servants. You set the earth on its foundation, so that is should never be shaken, drawing the deep over it, till the waters rose over the mountains. At Your rebuke they fled, rushing away at the sound of Your thunder, climbing mountains, pouring into valleys to places You had established for them. You set bounds which they may not pass, so that never again shall they cover the earth. . . .

You cause grass to grow for cattle, and plants for people to cultivate, bringing forth bread from the earth, wine to gladden the human heart, and bread to sustain human life. . . . You made the moon to measure the seasons; the sun knows its time for setting. You bring on darkness and it is night, when all the beasts of the forests stir. . . .

How varied are Your works, O Lord; in wisdom have You made them all. The earth is filled with Your creatures. . . . All of them look to You to give them their food at the proper time. What You give them they gather; when You open Your hand they eat their fill. When You hide Your face they feel panic; when You take their breath they perish and return to their dust. With Your breath You restore them; they are created anew, and You renew the face of the earth. The glory of the Lord endures forever; may He rejoice in His works. At His glance the earth begins to quake, at His touch the mountains begin to smoke. I will sing to the Lord while I live; I will

Morning service

115

אֲדָמָה. יְהִי כְבוֹד יְיָ לְעוֹלָם, יִשְׂמַח יְיָ בְּמַעֲשָׂיו. הַמַּבִּיט לָאָרֶץ וַתִּרְעָד, יִגַּע בֶּהָרִים וְיֶעֱשָׁנוּ. אָשִׁירָה לַיְיָ בְּחַיָּי, אֲזַמְּרָה לֵאלֹהַי בְּעוֹדִי. \ יֶעֱרַב עָלָיו שִׂיחִי, אָנֹכִי אֶשְׂמַח בַּיְיָ. יִתַּמּוּ חַטָּאִים מִן הָאָרֶץ וּרְשָׁעִים עוֹד אֵינָם, בָּרְכִי נַפְשִׁי אֶת־יְיָ, הַלְלוּיָהּ.

The Mourner's Kaddish is found on page 98.

ON ROSH ḤODESH

לְדָוִד. בָּרְכִי נַפְשִׁי אֶת־יְיָ, וְכָל־קְרָבַי אֶת־שֵׁם קָדְשׁוֹ. בָּרְכִי נַפְשִׁי אֶת־יְיָ, וְאַל־תִּשְׁכְּחִי כָּל־גְּמוּלָיו.

הַסֹּלֵחַ לְכָל־עֲוֺנֵכִי, הָרֹפֵא לְכָל־תַּחֲלוּאָיְכִי. הַגּוֹאֵל מִשַּׁחַת חַיָּיְכִי, הַמְעַטְּרֵכִי חֶסֶד וְרַחֲמִים.

הַמַּשְׂבִּיעַ בַּטּוֹב עֶדְיֵךְ, תִּתְחַדֵּשׁ כַּנֶּשֶׁר נְעוּרָיְכִי.

עֹשֵׂה צְדָקוֹת יְיָ, וּמִשְׁפָּטִים לְכָל־עֲשׁוּקִים.

יוֹדִיעַ דְּרָכָיו לְמֹשֶׁה, לִבְנֵי יִשְׂרָאֵל עֲלִילוֹתָיו.

רַחוּם וְחַנּוּן יְיָ, אֶרֶךְ אַפַּיִם וְרַב חָסֶד.

לֹא לָנֶצַח יָרִיב, וְלֹא לְעוֹלָם יִטּוֹר.

לֹא כַחֲטָאֵינוּ עָשָׂה לָנוּ, וְלֹא כַעֲוֺנוֹתֵינוּ גָּמַל עָלֵינוּ.

כִּי כִגְבֹהַּ שָׁמַיִם עַל הָאָרֶץ, גָּבַר חַסְדּוֹ עַל יְרֵאָיו.

כִּרְחֹק מִזְרָח מִמַּעֲרָב, הִרְחִיק מִמֶּנּוּ אֶת־פְּשָׁעֵינוּ.

Morning service

praise God while I have breath. May my prayer be pleasing to Him; I will rejoice in the Lord. Let sins disappear from the earth, and the wicked will be no more. Praise the Lord, my soul. Halleluyah.

Adapted from Psalm 104.

The Mourner's Kaddish is found on page 99.

The Mourner's Kaddish is found on page 99.

ON ROSH ḤODESH

A Psalm of David.
My soul, my heart, and every inward part:
Praise God! Forget not all His kindness.
> *He pardons all sin; He heals all sickness.*
> *He redeems life from the grave,*
> *He crowns us with love and with compassion.*

He satisfies us with goodness,
renewing life as eagles renew their plumage,
> *The righteous Lord brings justice for the oppressed.*

He showed His ways to Moses, His deeds to Israel.
> *The Lord is gracious and compassionate,*
> *patient and abounding in kindness.*

He does not quarrel endlessly,
nor does He bear a grudge forever.
> *He does not discipline us as we deserve,*
> *nor punish us according to our sins.*

His love for those who revere Him is greater
than the distance between heaven and earth.
> *As far removed as east from west*
> *does He remove our sins from us.*

As tender as a father with his children,
the Lord is merciful with His worshipers.
> *He knows how we are fashioned,*
> *He remembers that we are dust.*

Morning service

117

כְּרַחֵם אָב עַל בָּנִים, רִחַם יְיָ עַל יְרֵאָיו.

כִּי הוּא יָדַע יִצְרֵנוּ, זָכוּר כִּי עָפָר אֲנָחְנוּ.

אֱנוֹשׁ כֶּחָצִיר יָמָיו, כְּצִיץ הַשָּׂדֶה כֵּן יָצִיץ.

כִּי רוּחַ עָבְרָה בּוֹ וְאֵינֶנּוּ, וְלֹא יַכִּירֶנּוּ עוֹד מְקוֹמוֹ.

וְחֶסֶד יְיָ מֵעוֹלָם וְעַד עוֹלָם עַל יְרֵאָיו, וְצִדְקָתוֹ לִבְנֵי בָנִים,
לְשֹׁמְרֵי בְרִיתוֹ וּלְזֹכְרֵי פִקֻּדָיו לַעֲשׂוֹתָם.

יְיָ בַּשָּׁמַיִם הֵכִין כִּסְאוֹ, וּמַלְכוּתוֹ בַּכֹּל מָשָׁלָה.

בָּרְכוּ יְיָ מַלְאָכָיו גִּבֹּרֵי כֹחַ, עֹשֵׂי דְבָרוֹ
לִשְׁמֹעַ בְּקוֹל דְּבָרוֹ.

בָּרְכוּ יְיָ כָּל־צְבָאָיו, מְשָׁרְתָיו עֹשֵׂי רְצוֹנוֹ.
בָּרְכוּ יְיָ כָּל־מַעֲשָׂיו בְּכָל־מְקֹמוֹת מֶמְשַׁלְתּוֹ.
בָּרְכִי נַפְשִׁי אֶת־יְיָ. הַלְלוּיָהּ.

The Mourner's Kaddish is found on page 98.

A PSALM FOR A HOUSE OF MOURNING

Aware of our mortality, we must embrace enduring values.

לַמְנַצֵּחַ לִבְנֵי־קֹרַח מִזְמוֹר. שִׁמְעוּ־זֹאת כָּל־הָעַמִּים, הַאֲזִינוּ כָּל־
יֹשְׁבֵי חָלֶד. גַּם בְּנֵי אָדָם גַּם בְּנֵי־אִישׁ, יַחַד עָשִׁיר וְאֶבְיוֹן. פִּי
יְדַבֵּר חָכְמוֹת, וְהָגוּת לִבִּי תְבוּנוֹת. אַטֶּה לְמָשָׁל אָזְנִי, אֶפְתַּח
בְּכִנּוֹר חִידָתִי. לָמָּה אִירָא בִּימֵי רָע, עֲוֹן עֲקֵבַי יְסוּבֵּנִי. הַבֹּטְחִים
עַל חֵילָם, וּבְרֹב עָשְׁרָם יִתְהַלָּלוּ. אָח לֹא פָדֹה יִפְדֶּה אִישׁ, לֹא

Morning service

118

The days of man are as grass.
He flourishes as a flower in the field.
> *The wind passes over it and it is gone,*
> *and no one can recognize where it grew.*

But the Lord's love for His worshipers,
His righteousness to children's children,
remain, age after age, if they keep His covenant.
> *The Lord is enthroned in the heavens;*
> *His dominion embraces all.*

Praise the Lord, all creatures throughout His dominion.
> *Let all my being praise the Lord. Halleluyah!*

Psalm 103

The Mourner's Kaddish is found on page 99.

A PSALM FOR A HOUSE OF MOURNING

Aware of our mortality, we must embrace enduring values.

Hear this, all you nations; listen well, all who dwell on earth, the mighty as well as the lowly, the rich as well as the poor. My mouth will utter wisdom, the probings of a discerning heart. I will turn my attention now to teaching, present my lesson to the music of a harp.

Why should I be afraid in days of evil, even when surrounded by treacherous foes, men who put their trust in riches, who glory in their great wealth? Man cannot save a brother from death; there is no bribing God to recall His decree. The most costly ransom cannot save a life. There is no way to evade death forever.

Shall man live eternally? Shall he never see the grave? Wise men too must die, even as the foolish and the senseless, leaving their possessions to others. Their home eternal is the grave, though they were famous on the earth. For all the

יִתֵּן לֵאלֹהִים כָּפְרוֹ. וְיֵקַר פִּדְיוֹן נַפְשָׁם, וְחָדַל לְעוֹלָם. וִיחִי־
עוֹד לָנֶצַח, לֹא יִרְאֶה הַשָּׁחַת. כִּי יִרְאֶה חֲכָמִים יָמוּתוּ, יַחַד
כְּסִיל וָבַעַר יֹאבֵדוּ, וְעָזְבוּ לַאֲחֵרִים חֵילָם. קִרְבָּם בָּתֵּימוֹ לְעוֹלָם,
מִשְׁכְּנֹתָם לְדוֹר וָדֹר, קָרְאוּ בִשְׁמוֹתָם עֲלֵי אֲדָמוֹת. וְאָדָם בִּיקָר
בַּל יָלִין, נִמְשַׁל כַּבְּהֵמוֹת נִדְמוּ. זֶה דַרְכָּם כֵּסֶל לָמוֹ, וְאַחֲרֵיהֶם
בְּפִיהֶם יִרְצוּ, סֶלָה. כַּצֹּאן לִשְׁאוֹל שַׁתּוּ מָוֶת יִרְעֵם וַיִּרְדּוּ־בָם
יְשָׁרִים לַבֹּקֶר וְצוּרָם לְבַלּוֹת שְׁאוֹל מִזְּבֻל לוֹ. אַךְ אֱלֹהִים
יִפְדֶּה נַפְשִׁי מִיַּד שְׁאוֹל, כִּי יִקָּחֵנִי, סֶלָה. אַל תִּירָא כִּי יַעֲשִׁר
אִישׁ, כִּי יִרְבֶּה כְּבוֹד בֵּיתוֹ. כִּי לֹא בְמוֹתוֹ יִקַּח הַכֹּל, לֹא יֵרֵד
אַחֲרָיו כְּבוֹדוֹ.\כִּי נַפְשׁוֹ בְּחַיָּיו יְבָרֵךְ, וְיוֹדֻךָ כִּי תֵיטִיב לָךְ.
תָּבוֹא עַד דּוֹר אֲבוֹתָיו, עַד נֵצַח לֹא יִרְאוּ־אוֹר. אָדָם בִּיקָר וְלֹא
יָבִין, נִמְשַׁל כַּבְּהֵמוֹת נִדְמוּ.

The Mourner's Kaddish is found on page 98.

A PSALM FOR A HOUSE OF MOURNING

לַמְנַצֵּחַ מַשְׂכִּיל לִבְנֵי־קֹרַח.

כְּאַיָּל תַּעֲרֹג עַל אֲפִיקֵי־מָיִם
כֵּן נַפְשִׁי תַעֲרֹג אֵלֶיךָ אֱלֹהִים.

צָמְאָה נַפְשִׁי לֵאלֹהִים, לְאֵל חָי,
מָתַי אָבוֹא וְאֵרָאֶה פְּנֵי אֱלֹהִים.

הָיְתָה לִּי דִמְעָתִי לֶחֶם יוֹמָם וָלָיְלָה
בֶּאֱמֹר אֵלַי כָּל־הַיּוֹם, אַיֵּה אֱלֹהֶיךָ.

Morning service

glory that they cherish, men die, even as the beasts that perish. Such is the fate of the foolishly self-satisfied, those who delight in their own speech. Like sheep are they marked for death, like sheep are they herded to their graves. Straight down into their tombs they go, where they remain to waste away. But God will ransom me from death; when He takes me, He will save my soul.

Envy not a man his riches, nor be jealous of his growing possessions. For in death he will take nothing with him, his wealth will not follow him to the grave. He may flatter himself in his lifetime because men praise him for his good fortune. Yet he must join his ancestors who will never again see the light of day. For all the glory that they cherish, men die, even as the beasts that perish.

Psalm 49

The Mourner's Kaddish is found on page 99.

A PSALM FOR A HOUSE OF MOURNING

As a deer longs for flowing streams
I long for You, O God.
>*My soul thirsts for God, the living God.*
>*When shall I sense God's Presence?*

Day and night, tears are my nourishment,
taunted all day with, "Where is your God?"
>*My soul in secret sorrow melts with grief,*
>*recalling our procession to the house of God,*
>*a festive throng, chanting songs of praise.*

How downcast my soul in despair.
>*Still I have hope in God;*
>*I will yet praise Him for His saving Presence.*

Morning service

אֵלֶּה אֶזְכְּרָה וְאֶשְׁפְּכָה עָלַי נַפְשִׁי
כִּי אֶעֱבֹר בַּסָּךְ אֶדַּדֵּם עַד בֵּית אֱלֹהִים
בְּקוֹל רִנָּה וְתוֹדָה הָמוֹן חוֹגֵג.

מַה תִּשְׁתּוֹחֲחִי נַפְשִׁי וַתֶּהֱמִי עָלַי,
הוֹחִלִי לֵאלֹהִים כִּי עוֹד אוֹדֶנּוּ יְשׁוּעוֹת פָּנָיו.

אֱלֹהַי עָלַי נַפְשִׁי תִשְׁתּוֹחָח,
עַל כֵּן אֶזְכָּרְךָ מֵאֶרֶץ יַרְדֵּן, וְחֶרְמוֹנִים מֵהַר מִצְעָר.

תְּהוֹם אֶל תְּהוֹם קוֹרֵא לְקוֹל צִנּוֹרֶיךָ,
כָּל־מִשְׁבָּרֶיךָ וְגַלֶּיךָ עָלַי עָבָרוּ.

יוֹמָם יְצַוֶּה יְיָ חַסְדּוֹ
וּבַלַּיְלָה שִׁירֹה עִמִּי תְּפִלָּה לְאֵל חַיָּי.

אוֹמְרָה לְאֵל סַלְעִי, לָמָה שְׁכַחְתָּנִי,
לָמָּה קֹדֵר אֵלֵךְ בְּלַחַץ אוֹיֵב.

בְּרֶצַח בְּעַצְמוֹתַי חֵרְפוּנִי צוֹרְרָי
בְּאָמְרָם אֵלַי כָּל־הַיּוֹם, אַיֵּה אֱלֹהֶיךָ.

מַה תִּשְׁתּוֹחֲחִי נַפְשִׁי וּמַה תֶּהֱמִי עָלַי.
הוֹחִילִי לֵאלֹהִים כִּי עוֹד אוֹדֶנּוּ יְשׁוּעֹת פָּנַי וֵאלֹהָי.

The Mourner's Kaddish is found on page 98.

With my spirit brought low I remember the past,
Your miracles at Mount Sinai and the Jordan.
>
> *Deep calls to deep in the roar of Your torrents;*
> *all of Your breakers and billows overwhelm me.*

May the Lord show me His love by day;
then at night will I sing, praying to God of my life.
>
> *To God, my Rock, I cry: Why have You forgotten me?*
> *Why must I walk in darkness, oppressed by evil?*

When evil men taunt me murderously it is agony,
when all day long I hear, "Where is your God?"
>
> *How downcast my soul in despair.*
> *Still I hope in God; I will yet praise Him,*
> *my ever-present help, my God.*

Psalm 42

The Mourner's Kaddish is found on page 99.

Morning service

Afternoon service

מִנְחָה

Ashrei

࿆

אַשְׁרֵי יוֹשְׁבֵי בֵיתֶךָ, עוֹד יְהַלְלוּךָ סֶּלָה.
אַשְׁרֵי הָעָם שֶׁכָּכָה לוֹ, אַשְׁרֵי הָעָם שֶׁיְיָ אֱלֹהָיו.

תְּהִלָּה לְדָוִד.

אֲרוֹמִמְךָ אֱלוֹהַי הַמֶּלֶךְ וַאֲבָרְכָה שִׁמְךָ לְעוֹלָם וָעֶד.
בְּכָל־יוֹם אֲבָרְכֶךָ וַאֲהַלְלָה שִׁמְךָ לְעוֹלָם וָעֶד.
גָּדוֹל יְיָ וּמְהֻלָּל מְאֹד וְלִגְדֻלָּתוֹ אֵין חֵקֶר.
דּוֹר לְדוֹר יְשַׁבַּח מַעֲשֶׂיךָ וּגְבוּרֹתֶיךָ יַגִּידוּ.
הֲדַר כְּבוֹד הוֹדֶךָ וְדִבְרֵי נִפְלְאֹתֶיךָ אָשִׂיחָה.
וֶעֱזוּז נוֹרְאֹתֶיךָ יֹאמֵרוּ וּגְדוּלָּתְךָ אֲסַפְּרֶנָּה.
זֵכֶר רַב טוּבְךָ יַבִּיעוּ וְצִדְקָתְךָ יְרַנֵּנוּ.
חַנּוּן וְרַחוּם יְיָ, אֶרֶךְ אַפַּיִם וּגְדָל־חָסֶד.
טוֹב יְיָ לַכֹּל וְרַחֲמָיו עַל כָּל־מַעֲשָׂיו.
יוֹדוּךָ יְיָ כָּל־מַעֲשֶׂיךָ וַחֲסִידֶיךָ יְבָרְכוּכָה.
כְּבוֹד מַלְכוּתְךָ יֹאמֵרוּ וּגְבוּרָתְךָ יְדַבֵּרוּ.
לְהוֹדִיעַ לִבְנֵי הָאָדָם גְּבוּרֹתָיו וּכְבוֹד הֲדַר מַלְכוּתוֹ.
מַלְכוּתְךָ מַלְכוּת כָּל־עֹלָמִים וּמֶמְשַׁלְתְּךָ בְּכָל־דּוֹר וָדֹר.
סוֹמֵךְ יְיָ לְכָל־הַנֹּפְלִים וְזוֹקֵף לְכָל־הַכְּפוּפִים.

Ashrei

Blessed are they who dwell in Your house; they shall praise You forever.

Blessed the people who are so favored; blessed the people whose God is the Lord.

David sang: I glorify You, my God, my King;
I praise You throughout all time.

> Every day do I praise You, exalting Your glory forever.

Great is the Lord, and praiseworthy;
His greatness exceeds definition.

> One generation lauds Your works to another,
> Declaring Your mighty deeds.

They tell of Your wonders, and of Your glorious splendor.

> They speak of Your greatness, and of Your awesome power.

They recall Your goodness; they sing of Your faithfulness.

> Gracious and compassionate is the Lord;
> Patient, and abounding in love.

To all the Lord is good; His compassion embraces all.

> All of Your creatures shall praise You;
> The faithful shall repeatedly bless You.

They shall describe Your glorious kingdom, declaring Your power;

> And men will know of Your might, the splendor of Your dominion.

Your kingdom is an everlasting kingdom;

> Your dominion endures for all generations.

The Lord supports all who stumble,

> He raises all who are bowed down.

עֵינֵי כֹל אֵלֶיךָ יְשַׂבֵּרוּ וְאַתָּה נוֹתֵן לָהֶם אֶת־אָכְלָם בְּעִתּוֹ.
פּוֹתֵחַ אֶת־יָדֶךָ וּמַשְׂבִּיעַ לְכָל־חַי רָצוֹן.
צַדִּיק יְיָ בְּכָל־דְּרָכָיו וְחָסִיד בְּכָל־מַעֲשָׂיו.
קָרוֹב יְיָ לְכָל־קֹרְאָיו, לְכֹל אֲשֶׁר יִקְרָאֻהוּ בֶאֱמֶת.
רְצוֹן יְרֵאָיו יַעֲשֶׂה וְאֶת־שַׁוְעָתָם יִשְׁמַע וְיוֹשִׁיעֵם.
שׁוֹמֵר יְיָ אֶת־כָּל־אֹהֲבָיו וְאֵת כָּל־הָרְשָׁעִים יַשְׁמִיד.
\תְּהִלַּת יְיָ יְדַבֶּר־פִּי וִיבָרֵךְ כָּל־בָּשָׂר שֵׁם קָדְשׁוֹ לְעוֹלָם וָעֶד.
וַאֲנַחְנוּ נְבָרֵךְ יָהּ מֵעַתָּה וְעַד עוֹלָם. הַלְלוּיָהּ.

Ḥatzi Kaddish

Reader:

יִתְגַּדַּל וְיִתְקַדַּשׁ שְׁמֵהּ רַבָּא בְּעָלְמָא דִּי בְרָא כִרְעוּתֵהּ, וְיַמְלִיךְ מַלְכוּתֵהּ בְּחַיֵּיכוֹן וּבְיוֹמֵיכוֹן וּבְחַיֵּי דְכָל־בֵּית יִשְׂרָאֵל בַּעֲגָלָא וּבִזְמַן קָרִיב, וְאִמְרוּ אָמֵן.

Congregation and Reader:

יְהֵא שְׁמֵהּ רַבָּא מְבָרַךְ לְעָלַם וּלְעָלְמֵי עָלְמַיָּא.

Reader:

יִתְבָּרַךְ וְיִשְׁתַּבַּח וְיִתְפָּאַר וְיִתְרוֹמַם וְיִתְנַשֵּׂא וְיִתְהַדָּר וְיִתְעַלֶּה וְיִתְהַלָּל שְׁמֵהּ דְּקֻדְשָׁא בְּרִיךְ הוּא, לְעֵלָּא (לְעֵלָּא) מִן כָּל־בִּרְכָתָא וְשִׁירָתָא תֻּשְׁבְּחָתָא וְנֶחֱמָתָא דַּאֲמִירָן בְּעָלְמָא, וְאִמְרוּ אָמֵן.

Afternoon service

All eyes look hopefully to You, to receive their food in due
time.

> *You open Your hand, and all the living feast upon Your*
> *favor.*

In all His paths the Lord is faithful,
In all His deeds He is loving.

> *To all who call the Lord is near,*
> *To all who call upon Him in truth.*

He fulfills the desire of those who revere Him;
He hears their cry and delivers them.

> *All who love the Lord He preserves,*
> *but all the wicked He destroys.*

My mouth shall praise the Lord.

> *Let all flesh praise His name throughout all time.*

We shall praise the Lord now and always. Halleluyah!

Hatzi Kaddish

Reader:

Hallowed and enhanced may He be throughout the world of
His own creation. May He cause His sovereignty soon to be
accepted, during our life and the life of all Israel. And let us
say: Amen.

Congregation and Reader:
Ye-hei shmei raba meva-rakh l'alam ul'almei 'almaya.

May He be praised throughout all time.

Reader:

Glorified and celebrated, lauded and praised, acclaimed and
honored, extolled and exalted may the Holy One be, far
beyond all song and psalm, beyond all tributes which man
can utter. And let us say: Amen.

Afternoon service

129

Amidah

We stand in silent prayer, which ends on page 142.

כִּי שֵׁם יְיָ אֶקְרָא הָבוּ גֹדֶל לֵאלֹהֵינוּ.
אֲדֹנָי שְׂפָתַי תִּפְתָּח וּפִי יַגִּיד תְּהִלָּתֶךָ.

בָּרוּךְ אַתָּה יְיָ אֱלֹהֵינוּ וֵאלֹהֵי אֲבוֹתֵינוּ, אֱלֹהֵי אַבְרָהָם אֱלֹהֵי יִצְחָק
וֵאלֹהֵי יַעֲקֹב, הָאֵל הַגָּדוֹל הַגִּבּוֹר וְהַנּוֹרָא אֵל עֶלְיוֹן גּוֹמֵל חֲסָדִים
טוֹבִים וְקוֹנֵה הַכֹּל, וְזוֹכֵר חַסְדֵי אָבוֹת וּמֵבִיא גוֹאֵל לִבְנֵי בְנֵיהֶם
לְמַעַן שְׁמוֹ בְּאַהֲבָה.

From Rosh Hashanah through Yom Kippur:

זָכְרֵנוּ לְחַיִּים מֶלֶךְ חָפֵץ בְּחַיִּים,
וְכָתְבֵנוּ בְּסֵפֶר הַחַיִּים לְמַעַנְךָ אֱלֹהִים חַיִּים.

מֶלֶךְ עוֹזֵר וּמוֹשִׁיעַ וּמָגֵן. בָּרוּךְ אַתָּה יְיָ מָגֵן אַבְרָהָם.

אַתָּה גִּבּוֹר לְעוֹלָם אֲדֹנָי מְחַיֵּה מֵתִים אַתָּה רַב לְהוֹשִׁיעַ.

From Shmini Atzeret to Pesaḥ:

מַשִּׁיב הָרוּחַ וּמוֹרִיד הַגָּשֶׁם.

מְכַלְכֵּל חַיִּים בְּחֶסֶד מְחַיֵּה מֵתִים בְּרַחֲמִים רַבִּים, סוֹמֵךְ נוֹפְלִים
וְרוֹפֵא חוֹלִים וּמַתִּיר אֲסוּרִים וּמְקַיֵּם אֱמוּנָתוֹ לִישֵׁנֵי עָפָר. מִי כָמוֹךָ
בַּעַל גְּבוּרוֹת וּמִי דוֹמֶה לָּךְ, מֶלֶךְ מֵמִית וּמְחַיֶּה וּמַצְמִיחַ יְשׁוּעָה.

Afternoon service

Amidah

We stand in silent prayer, which ends on page 143.

When I call upon the Lord, give glory to our God. Open my mouth, O Lord, and my lips will proclaim Your praise.

Praised are You, Lord our God and God of our fathers, God of Abraham, of Isaac and of Jacob, great, mighty, awesome, exalted God, bestowing lovingkindness and creating all things. You remember the pious deeds of our fathers, and will send a redeemer to their children's children because of Your love and for the sake of Your glory.

From Rosh Hashanah through Yom Kippur:

Remember us that we may live, O King who delights in life. Inscribe us in the Book of Life, for Your sake, living God.

You are the King who helps and saves and shields. Praised are You, Lord, Shield of Abraham.

Your might, O Lord, is boundless. You give life to the dead; great is Your saving power.

From Shmini Atzeret to Pesaḥ:

You cause the wind to blow and the rain to fall.

Your lovingkindness sustains the living, Your great mercies give life to the dead. You support the falling, heal the ailing, free the fettered. You keep Your faith with those who sleep in dust. Whose power can compare with Yours? You are the master of life and death and deliverance.

Afternoon service

131

From Rosh Hashanah through Yom Kippur:

מִי כָמְוֹךָ אַב הָרַחֲמִים, זוֹכֵר יְצוּרָיו לְחַיִּים בְּרַחֲמִים.

וְנֶאֱמָן אַתָּה לְהַחֲיוֹת מֵתִים. בָּרוּךְ אַתָּה יְיָ מְחַיֵּה הַמֵּתִים.

The Silent Amidah continues on page 134.

Kedushah

When the Reader chants the Amidah aloud,
Kedushah is added. The congregation chants the
indented portions aloud.

נְקַדֵּשׁ אֶת־שִׁמְךָ בָּעוֹלָם כְּשֵׁם שֶׁמַּקְדִּישִׁים אוֹתוֹ בִּשְׁמֵי מָרוֹם כַּכָּתוּב
עַל יַד נְבִיאֶךָ, וְקָרָא זֶה אֶל זֶה וְאָמַר:

קָדוֹשׁ קָדוֹשׁ קָדוֹשׁ יְיָ צְבָאוֹת, מְלֹא כָל־הָאָרֶץ כְּבוֹדוֹ.

לְעֻמָּתָם בָּרוּךְ יֹאמֵרוּ:

בָּרוּךְ כְּבוֹד יְיָ מִמְּקוֹמוֹ.

וּבְדִבְרֵי קָדְשְׁךָ כָּתוּב לֵאמֹר:

יִמְלֹךְ יְיָ לְעוֹלָם אֱלֹהַיִךְ צִיּוֹן לְדֹר וָדֹר, הַלְלוּיָהּ.

לְדוֹר וָדוֹר נַגִּיד גָּדְלֶךָ, וּלְנֵצַח נְצָחִים קְדֻשָּׁתְךָ נַקְדִּישׁ, וְשִׁבְחֲךָ
אֱלֹהֵינוּ מִפִּינוּ לֹא יָמוּשׁ לְעוֹלָם וָעֶד כִּי אֵל מֶלֶךְ גָּדוֹל וְקָדוֹשׁ אָתָּה.

From Rosh Hashanah through Yom Kippur:

Whose mercy can compare with Yours, merciful Father?
In mercy You remember Your creatures with life.

Faithful are You in giving life to the dead. Praised are You,
Lord, Master of life and death.

The Silent Amidah continues on page 135.

Kedushah

*When the Reader chants the Amidah aloud,
Kedushah is added. The congregation chants
the indented portions aloud.*

We proclaim Your holiness on earth as it is proclaimed in the
heavens above. We sing the words of heavenly voices as
recorded in Your prophet's vision:
> *Ka-dosh ka-dosh ka-dosh Ado-nai tz'va-ot, m'lo khol ha-
> aretz k'vodo.*
> Holy, holy, holy Lord of hosts. The whole world is filled
> with His glory.

Heavenly voices respond with praise:
> *Barukh k'vod Ado-nai mi-m'komo.*
> Praised is the Lord's glory throughout the universe.

And in Your holy psalms it is written:
> *Yim-lokh Ado-nai l'olam Elo-ha-yikh tzi-yon ledor va-dor
> ha-le-lu-yah.*
> The Lord shall reign through all generations; your God,
> Zion, shall reign forever. Halleluyah.

We declare Your greatness through all generations, hallow
Your holiness to all eternity. Your praise will never leave our
lips, for You are God and King, great and holy.

From Rosh Hashanah through Yom Kippur:

בָּרוּךְ אַתָּה יְיָ הַמֶּלֶךְ הַקָּדוֹשׁ.

בָּרוּךְ אַתָּה יְיָ הָאֵל הַקָּדוֹשׁ.

The Silent Amidah continues here:

אַתָּה קָדוֹשׁ וְשִׁמְךָ קָדוֹשׁ וּקְדוֹשִׁים בְּכָל־יוֹם יְהַלְלוּךָ סֶּלָה.

From Rosh Hashanah through Yom Kippur:

בָּרוּךְ אַתָּה יְיָ הַמֶּלֶךְ הַקָּדוֹשׁ.

בָּרוּךְ אַתָּה יְיָ הָאֵל הַקָּדוֹשׁ.

אַתָּה חוֹנֵן לְאָדָם דַּעַת וּמְלַמֵּד לֶאֱנוֹשׁ בִּינָה. חָנֵּנוּ מֵאִתְּךָ דֵּעָה בִּינָה וְהַשְׂכֵּל. בָּרוּךְ אַתָּה יְיָ חוֹנֵן הַדָּעַת.

הֲשִׁיבֵנוּ אָבִינוּ לְתוֹרָתֶךָ וְקָרְבֵנוּ מַלְכֵּנוּ לַעֲבוֹדָתֶךָ, וְהַחֲזִירֵנוּ בִּתְשׁוּבָה שְׁלֵמָה לְפָנֶיךָ. בָּרוּךְ אַתָּה יְיָ הָרוֹצֶה בִּתְשׁוּבָה.

סְלַח לָנוּ אָבִינוּ כִּי חָטָאנוּ, מְחַל לָנוּ מַלְכֵּנוּ כִּי פָשָׁעְנוּ, כִּי מוֹחֵל וְסוֹלֵחַ אָתָּה. בָּרוּךְ אַתָּה יְיָ חַנּוּן הַמַּרְבֶּה לִסְלֹחַ.

רְאֵה נָא בְעָנְיֵנוּ וְרִיבָה רִיבֵנוּ וּגְאָלֵנוּ מְהֵרָה לְמַעַן שְׁמֶךָ, כִּי גוֹאֵל חָזָק אָתָּה. בָּרוּךְ אַתָּה יְיָ גּוֹאֵל יִשְׂרָאֵל.

On Fast Days, Reader only continues on page 212.

רְפָאֵנוּ יְיָ וְנֵרָפֵא, הוֹשִׁיעֵנוּ וְנִוָּשֵׁעָה, כִּי תְהִלָּתֵנוּ אָתָּה. וְהַעֲלֵה רְפוּאָה שְׁלֵמָה לְכָל־מַכּוֹתֵינוּ, כִּי אֵל מֶלֶךְ רוֹפֵא נֶאֱמָן וְרַחֲמָן אָתָּה. בָּרוּךְ אַתָּה יְיָ רוֹפֵא חוֹלֵי עַמּוֹ יִשְׂרָאֵל.

Afternoon service

From Rosh Hashanah through Yom Kippur:
Praised are You, Lord and holy King.

Praised are You, Lord and holy God.

The Silent Amidah continues here:

Holy are you and holy is Your name. Holy are those who praise you daily.

From Rosh Hashanah through Yom Kippur:
Praised are You, Lord and holy King.

Praised are You, Lord and holy God.

You graciously endow man with intelligence, You teach him wisdom and understanding. Grant us knowledge, discernment and wisdom. Praised are You, Lord, for the gift of knowledge.

Our Father, bring us back to Your Torah. Our King, draw us near to Your service. Lead us back to You, truly repentant. Praised are You, Lord who welcomes repentance.

Forgive us, our Father, for we have sinned; pardon us, our King, for we have transgressed, for You forgive and pardon. Praised are You, gracious and forgiving Lord.

Behold our affliction and deliver us. Redeem us soon for the sake of Your name, for You are the mighty Redeemer. Praised are You, Lord, Redeemer of the people Israel.

On Fast Days, Reader only continues on page 213.

Heal us, O Lord, and we shall be healed. Help us and save us, for You are our glory. Grant perfect healing for all our afflictions, faithful and merciful God of healing. Praised are You, Lord, Healer of His people.

Afternoon service

135

בָּרֵךְ עָלֵינוּ יְיָ אֱלֹהֵינוּ אֶת־הַשָּׁנָה הַזֹּאת וְאֶת־כָּל־מִינֵי תְבוּאָתָהּ לְטוֹבָה

Summer (From Pesaḥ to December fourth):

וְתֵן בְּרָכָה עַל פְּנֵי הָאֲדָמָה

Winter (From December fourth to Pesaḥ):

וְתֵן טַל וּמָטָר לִבְרָכָה עַל פְּנֵי הָאֲדָמָה

וְשַׂבְּעֵנוּ מִטּוּבֶךְ וּבָרֵךְ שְׁנָתֵנוּ כַּשָּׁנִים הַטּוֹבוֹת. בָּרוּךְ אַתָּה יְיָ מְבָרֵךְ הַשָּׁנִים.

תְּקַע בְּשׁוֹפָר גָּדוֹל לְחֵרוּתֵנוּ וְשָׂא נֵס לְקַבֵּץ גָּלְיוֹתֵינוּ וְקַבְּצֵנוּ יַחַד מֵאַרְבַּע כַּנְפוֹת הָאָרֶץ. בָּרוּךְ אַתָּה יְיָ מְקַבֵּץ נִדְחֵי עַמּוֹ יִשְׂרָאֵל.

הָשִׁיבָה שׁוֹפְטֵינוּ כְּבָרִאשׁוֹנָה וְיוֹעֲצֵינוּ כְּבַתְּחִלָּה, וְהָסֵר מִמֶּנּוּ יָגוֹן וַאֲנָחָה, וּמְלֹךְ עָלֵינוּ אַתָּה יְיָ לְבַדְּךָ בְּחֶסֶד וּבְרַחֲמִים וְצַדְּקֵנוּ בַּמִּשְׁפָּט.

From Rosh Hashanah through Yom Kippur:

בָּרוּךְ אַתָּה יְיָ הַמֶּלֶךְ הַמִּשְׁפָּט.
בָּרוּךְ אַתָּה יְיָ מֶלֶךְ אוֹהֵב צְדָקָה וּמִשְׁפָּט.

וְלַמַּלְשִׁינִים אַל תְּהִי תִקְוָה וְכָל־הָרִשְׁעָה כְּרֶגַע תֹּאבֵד. וְכָל־אוֹיְבֶיךָ מְהֵרָה יִכָּרֵתוּ וּמַלְכוּת זָדוֹן מְהֵרָה תְעַקֵּר וּתְשַׁבֵּר וּתְמַגֵּר וְתַכְנִיעַ בִּמְהֵרָה בְיָמֵינוּ. בָּרוּךְ אַתָּה יְיָ שׁוֹבֵר אוֹיְבִים וּמַכְנִיעַ זֵדִים.

Afternoon service

Lord our God, make this a blessed year. May its varied produce bring us happiness.

Summer (Between Pesaḥ and December fourth):

Bring blessing upon the whole earth.

Winter (Between December fourth and Pesaḥ):

Bless the earth with dew and rain.

Bless the year with Your abounding goodness. Praised are You, Lord who blesses the years.

Sound the great shofar to herald our freedom, raise high the banner to gather all exiles. Gather the dispersed from the corners of the earth. Praised are You, Lord who gathers our exiles.

Restore our judges as in days of old, restore our counsellors as in former times. Remove from us sorrow and anguish. Reign alone over us with loving-kindness; with justice and mercy sustain our cause.

From Rosh Hashanah through Yom Kippur:

Praised are You, Lord, King of judgment.

Praised are You, Lord, King who loves justice.

Frustrate the hopes of those who malign us; let all evil very soon disappear. Let all Your enemies soon be destroyed. May You quickly uproot and crush the arrogant; may You subdue and humble them in our time. Praised are You, Lord who humbles the arrogant.

Afternoon service

עַל הַצַּדִּיקִים וְעַל הַחֲסִידִים וְעַל זִקְנֵי עַמְּךָ בֵּית יִשְׂרָאֵל וְעַל פְּלֵיטַת סוֹפְרֵיהֶם וְעַל גֵּרֵי הַצֶּדֶק וְעָלֵינוּ יֶהֱמוּ נָא רַחֲמֶיךָ יְיָ אֱלֹהֵינוּ, וְתֵן שָׂכָר טוֹב לְכָל הַבּוֹטְחִים בְּשִׁמְךָ בֶּאֱמֶת, וְשִׂים חֶלְקֵנוּ עִמָּהֶם לְעוֹלָם וְלֹא נֵבוֹשׁ כִּי בְךָ בָּטָחְנוּ. בָּרוּךְ אַתָּה יְיָ מִשְׁעָן וּמִבְטָח לַצַּדִּיקִים.

וְלִירוּשָׁלַיִם עִירְךָ בְּרַחֲמִים תָּשׁוּב וְתִשְׁכֹּן בְּתוֹכָהּ כַּאֲשֶׁר דִּבַּרְתָּ, וּבְנֵה אוֹתָהּ בְּקָרוֹב בְּיָמֵינוּ בִּנְיַן עוֹלָם וְכִסֵּא דָוִד מְהֵרָה לְתוֹכָהּ תָּכִין. בָּרוּךְ אַתָּה יְיָ בּוֹנֵה יְרוּשָׁלָיִם.

On Tisha B'av turn to page 210.

אֶת־צֶמַח דָּוִד עַבְדְּךָ מְהֵרָה תַצְמִיחַ וְקַרְנוֹ תָּרוּם בִּישׁוּעָתֶךָ, כִּי לִישׁוּעָתְךָ קִוִּינוּ כָּל־הַיּוֹם. בָּרוּךְ אַתָּה יְיָ מַצְמִיחַ קֶרֶן יְשׁוּעָה.

שְׁמַע קוֹלֵנוּ יְיָ אֱלֹהֵינוּ, חוּס וְרַחֵם עָלֵינוּ, וְקַבֵּל בְּרַחֲמִים וּבְרָצוֹן אֶת־תְּפִלָּתֵנוּ, כִּי אֵל שׁוֹמֵעַ תְּפִלּוֹת וְתַחֲנוּנִים אָתָּה. וּמִלְּפָנֶיךָ מַלְכֵּנוּ רֵיקָם אַל תְּשִׁיבֵנוּ.

On Fast Days, individuals turn to page 212.

כִּי אַתָּה שׁוֹמֵעַ תְּפִלַּת עַמְּךָ יִשְׂרָאֵל בְּרַחֲמִים. בָּרוּךְ אַתָּה יְיָ שׁוֹמֵעַ תְּפִלָּה.

רְצֵה יְיָ אֱלֹהֵינוּ בְּעַמְּךָ יִשְׂרָאֵל וּבִתְפִלָּתָם וְהָשֵׁב אֶת־הָעֲבוֹדָה לִדְבִיר בֵּיתֶךָ וּתְפִלָּתָם בְּאַהֲבָה תְקַבֵּל בְּרָצוֹן וּתְהִי לְרָצוֹן תָּמִיד עֲבוֹדַת יִשְׂרָאֵל עַמֶּךָ.

Afternoon service

Let Your tender mercies be stirred for the righteous, the pious and the leaders of the House of Israel, toward devoted scholars and faithful proselytes. Be merciful to us of the House of Israel. Reward all who trust in You, cast our lot with those who are faithful to You. May we never come to despair, for our trust is in You. Praised are You, Lord who sustains the righteous.

Have mercy, Lord, and return to Jerusalem, Your city. May Your Presence dwell there as You promised. Rebuild it now, in our days and for all time. Re-establish there the majesty of David, Your servant. Praised are You, Lord who rebuilds Jerusalem.

On Tisha B'av turn to page 211.

Bring to flower the shoot of Your servant David. Hasten the advent of Messianic redemption. Each and every day we hope for Your deliverance. Praised are You, Lord who assures our deliverance.

Lord our God, hear our voice. Have compassion upon us, pity us, accept our prayer with loving favor. You listen to entreaty and prayer. Do not turn us away unanswered, our King, for You mercifully heed Your people's supplication. Praised are You, Lord who hears prayer.

On Fast Days, individuals turn to page 213.

For You mercifully heed Your people's supplication. Praised are You, Lord who hears prayer.

Accept the prayer of Your people Israel as lovingly as it is offered. Restore worship to Your sanctuary. May the worship of Your people Israel always be acceptable to You.

Afternoon service

אֱלֹהֵינוּ וֵאלֹהֵי אֲבוֹתֵינוּ, יַעֲלֶה וְיָבוֹא וְיַגִּיעַ וְיֵרָאֶה וְיֵרָצֶה וְיִשָּׁמַע וְיִפָּקֵד וְיִזָּכֵר זִכְרוֹנֵנוּ וּפִקְדוֹנֵנוּ, וְזִכְרוֹן אֲבוֹתֵינוּ וְזִכְרוֹן מָשִׁיחַ בֶּן־דָּוִד עַבְדֶּךָ וְזִכְרוֹן יְרוּשָׁלַיִם עִיר קָדְשֶׁךָ, וְזִכְרוֹן כָּל־עַמְּךָ בֵּית יִשְׂרָאֵל לְפָנֶיךָ, לִפְלֵיטָה וּלְטוֹבָה וּלְחֵן וּלְחֶסֶד וּלְרַחֲמִים וּלְחַיִּים וּלְשָׁלוֹם בְּיוֹם רֹאשׁ הַחֹדֶשׁ הַזֶּה. זָכְרֵנוּ יְיָ אֱלֹהֵינוּ בּוֹ לְטוֹבָה, וּפָקְדֵנוּ בוֹ לִבְרָכָה, וְהוֹשִׁיעֵנוּ בוֹ לְחַיִּים. וּבִדְבַר יְשׁוּעָה וְרַחֲמִים חוּס וְחָנֵּנוּ וְרַחֵם עָלֵינוּ וְהוֹשִׁיעֵנוּ כִּי אֵלֶיךָ עֵינֵינוּ, כִּי אֵל מֶלֶךְ חַנּוּן וְרַחוּם אָתָּה.

וְתֶחֱזֶינָה עֵינֵינוּ בְּשׁוּבְךָ לְצִיּוֹן בְּרַחֲמִים. בָּרוּךְ אַתָּה יְיָ הַמַּחֲזִיר שְׁכִינָתוֹ לְצִיּוֹן.

During repetition of Amidah, read this paragraph silently while Reader chants the next paragraph.

מוֹדִים אֲנַחְנוּ לָךְ שָׁאַתָּה הוּא יְיָ אֱלֹהֵינוּ וֵאלֹהֵי אֲבוֹתֵינוּ אֱלֹהֵי כָל־בָּשָׂר יוֹצְרֵנוּ יוֹצֵר בְּרֵאשִׁית. בְּרָכוֹת וְהוֹדָאוֹת לְשִׁמְךָ הַגָּדוֹל וְהַקָּדוֹשׁ עַל שֶׁהֶחֱיִיתָנוּ וְקִיַּמְתָּנוּ. כֵּן תְּחַיֵּנוּ וּתְקַיְּמֵנוּ וְתֶאֱסֹף גָּלֻיּוֹתֵינוּ לְחַצְרוֹת קָדְשֶׁךָ לִשְׁמֹר חֻקֶּיךָ וְלַעֲשׂוֹת רְצוֹנֶךָ וּלְעָבְדְּךָ בְּלֵבָב שָׁלֵם עַל שֶׁאֲנַחְנוּ מוֹדִים לָךְ. בָּרוּךְ אֵל הַהוֹדָאוֹת.

מוֹדִים אֲנַחְנוּ לָךְ שָׁאַתָּה הוּא יְיָ אֱלֹהֵינוּ וֵאלֹהֵי אֲבוֹתֵינוּ לְעוֹלָם וָעֶד, צוּר חַיֵּינוּ מָגֵן יִשְׁעֵנוּ אַתָּה הוּא. לְדוֹר וָדוֹר נוֹדֶה לְךָ וּנְסַפֵּר תְּהִלָּתֶךָ עַל חַיֵּינוּ הַמְּסוּרִים בְּיָדֶךָ וְעַל נִשְׁמוֹתֵינוּ הַפְּקוּדוֹת לָךְ וְעַל נִסֶּיךָ שֶׁבְּכָל־יוֹם עִמָּנוּ וְעַל נִפְלְאוֹתֶיךָ וְטוֹבוֹתֶיךָ שֶׁבְּכָל־עֵת עֶרֶב וָבֹקֶר וְצָהֳרָיִם. הַטּוֹב כִּי לֹא כָלוּ רַחֲמֶיךָ וְהַמְרַחֵם כִּי לֹא תַמּוּ חֲסָדֶיךָ מֵעוֹלָם קִוִּינוּ לָךְ.

Afternoon service

Our God and God of our fathers, on this Rosh Hodesh remember our fathers and be gracious to us. Consider the people standing before You praying for the days of Messiah and for Jerusalem Your holy city. Grant us life, well-being, lovingkindness and peace. Bless us, Lord our God, with all that is good. Remember Your promise of mercy and redemption. Be merciful to us and save us, for we place our hope in You, gracious and merciful God and King.

May we bear witness to Your merciful return to Zion. Praised are You, Lord who restores His Presence to Zion.

During repetition of Amidah, read this paragraph silently, while Reader chants the next paragraph.

We proclaim that You are the Lord our God and God of our fathers, Creator of all who created us, God of all flesh. We praise You and thank You for granting us life and for sustaining us. May You continue to do so, and may You gather our exiles, that we may all fulfill Your commandments and serve You wholeheartedly, doing Your will. For this shall we thank You. Praised be God to whom thanksgiving is due.

We proclaim that You are the Lord our God and God of our fathers throughout all time. You are the Rock of our lives, the Shield of our salvation. We thank You and praise You through all generations, for our lives are in Your hand, our souls are in Your charge. We thank You for Your miracles which daily attend us, for Your wondrous kindness, morning, noon and night. Your mercy and love are boundless. We have always placed our hope in You.

Afternoon service

On Ḥanukkah, turn to page 204.

On Purim, turn to page 206.

On Israel's Independence Day, turn to page 208.

וְעַל כֻּלָּם יִתְבָּרַךְ וְיִתְרוֹמַם שִׁמְךָ מַלְכֵּנוּ תָּמִיד לְעוֹלָם וָעֶד.

From Rosh Hashanah through Yom Kippur:

וּכְתֹב לְחַיִּים טוֹבִים כָּל־בְּנֵי בְרִיתֶךָ.

וְכֹל הַחַיִּים יוֹדוּךָ סֶּלָה וִיהַלְלוּ אֶת־שִׁמְךָ בֶּאֱמֶת הָאֵל יְשׁוּעָתֵנוּ וְעֶזְרָתֵנוּ סֶלָה. בָּרוּךְ אַתָּה יְיָ הַטּוֹב שִׁמְךָ וּלְךָ נָאֶה לְהוֹדוֹת.

שָׁלוֹם רַב עַל יִשְׂרָאֵל עַמְּךָ וְעַל כָּל־יוֹשְׁבֵי תֵבֵל תָּשִׂים לְעוֹלָם כִּי אַתָּה הוּא מֶלֶךְ אָדוֹן לְכָל־הַשָּׁלוֹם. וְטוֹב בְּעֵינֶיךָ לְבָרֵךְ אֶת־עַמְּךָ יִשְׂרָאֵל בְּכָל־עֵת וּבְכָל־שָׁעָה בִּשְׁלוֹמֶךָ.

From Rosh Hashanah through Yom Kippur:

בְּסֵפֶר חַיִּים בְּרָכָה וְשָׁלוֹם וּפַרְנָסָה טוֹבָה נִזָּכֵר וְנִכָּתֵב לְפָנֶיךָ אֲנַחְנוּ וְכָל־עַמְּךָ בֵּית יִשְׂרָאֵל לְחַיִּים טוֹבִים וּלְשָׁלוֹם. בָּרוּךְ אַתָּה יְיָ עוֹשֵׂה הַשָּׁלוֹם.

בָּרוּךְ אַתָּה יְיָ הַמְבָרֵךְ אֶת־עַמּוֹ יִשְׂרָאֵל בַּשָּׁלוֹם.

At the conclusion of the Amidah, personal prayers
may be added, before or instead of the following.

אֱלֹהַי, נְצֹר לְשׁוֹנִי מֵרָע וּשְׂפָתַי מִדַּבֵּר מִרְמָה, וְלִמְקַלְלַי נַפְשִׁי תִדֹּם וְנַפְשִׁי כֶּעָפָר לַכֹּל תִּהְיֶה. פְּתַח לִבִּי בְּתוֹרָתֶךָ וּבְמִצְוֹתֶיךָ תִּרְדֹּף נַפְשִׁי. וְכֹל הַחוֹשְׁבִים עָלַי רָעָה, מְהֵרָה הָפֵר עֲצָתָם וְקַלְקֵל מַחֲשַׁבְתָּם. עֲשֵׂה לְמַעַן שְׁמֶךָ, עֲשֵׂה לְמַעַן יְמִינֶךָ, עֲשֵׂה לְמַעַן

Afternoon service

142

On Hanukkah, turn to page 205.
On Purim, turn to page 207.
On Israel's Independence Day, turn to page 209.

For all these blessings we shall ever praise and exalt You.

From Rosh Hashanah through Yom Kippur:

Inscribe all the people of Your covenant for a good life.

May every living creature thank You and praise You faithfully, our deliverance and our help. Praised are You, beneficent Lord to whom all praise is due.

Grant true and lasting peace to Your people Israel and to all who dwell on earth, for You are the King of supreme peace. May it please You to bless Your people Israel at all times with Your gift of peace.

From Rosh Hashanah through Yom Kippur:

May we and the entire House of Israel be remembered and recorded in the Book of life, blessing, sustenance and peace. Praised are You, Lord, Source of peace.

Praised are You, Lord who blesses His people Israel with peace.

At the conclusion of the Amidah, personal prayers
may be added, before or instead of the following.

My God, keep my tongue from telling evil, my lips from speaking lies. Help me ignore those who slander me. Let me be humble before all. Open my heart to Your Torah, so that I may pursue Your commandments. Frustrate the designs of those who plot evil against me. Make nothing of their

Afternoon service

143

קָדְשֶׁךָ, עֲשֵׂה לְמַעַן תּוֹרָתֶךָ, לְמַעַן יֵחָלְצוּן יְדִידֶיךָ הוֹשִׁיעָה יְמִינְךָ
וַעֲנֵנִי. יִהְיוּ לְרָצוֹן אִמְרֵי־פִי וְהֶגְיוֹן לִבִּי לְפָנֶיךָ, יְיָ צוּרִי וְגֹאֲלִי.
עוֹשֶׂה שָׁלוֹם בִּמְרוֹמָיו הוּא יַעֲשֶׂה שָׁלוֹם עָלֵינוּ וְעַל כָּל־יִשְׂרָאֵל,
וְאִמְרוּ אָמֵן.

Kaddish Shalem
Reader:

יִתְגַּדַּל וְיִתְקַדַּשׁ שְׁמֵהּ רַבָּא בְּעָלְמָא דִּי בְרָא כִרְעוּתֵהּ, וְיַמְלִיךְ
מַלְכוּתֵהּ בְּחַיֵּיכוֹן וּבְיוֹמֵיכוֹן וּבְחַיֵּי דְכָל־בֵּית יִשְׂרָאֵל בַּעֲגָלָא
וּבִזְמַן קָרִיב, וְאִמְרוּ אָמֵן.

Congregation and Reader:

יְהֵא שְׁמֵהּ רַבָּא מְבָרַךְ לְעָלַם וּלְעָלְמֵי עָלְמַיָּא.

Reader:

יִתְבָּרַךְ וְיִשְׁתַּבַּח וְיִתְפָּאַר וְיִתְרוֹמַם וְיִתְנַשֵּׂא וְיִתְהַדָּר וְיִתְעַלֶּה
וְיִתְהַלָּל שְׁמֵהּ דְּקֻדְשָׁא בְּרִיךְ הוּא, לְעֵלָּא (לְעֵלָּא) מִן כָּל־
בִּרְכָתָא וְשִׁירָתָא תֻּשְׁבְּחָתָא וְנֶחֱמָתָא דַּאֲמִירָן בְּעָלְמָא, וְאִמְרוּ אָמֵן.

Omit these two lines in a House of Mourning:

תִּתְקַבֵּל צְלוֹתְהוֹן וּבָעוּתְהוֹן דְּכָל־יִשְׂרָאֵל קֳדָם אֲבוּהוֹן דִּי בִשְׁמַיָּא,
וְאִמְרוּ אָמֵן.

יְהֵא שְׁלָמָא רַבָּא מִן שְׁמַיָּא וְחַיִּים עָלֵינוּ וְעַל כָּל־יִשְׂרָאֵל, וְאִמְרוּ
אָמֵן.

עוֹשֶׂה שָׁלוֹם בִּמְרוֹמָיו הוּא יַעֲשֶׂה שָׁלוֹם עָלֵינוּ וְעַל כָּל־יִשְׂרָאֵל,
וְאִמְרוּ אָמֵן.

Afternoon service

144

schemes. Do so for the sake of Your power, Your holiness and Your Torah. Answer my prayer for the deliverance of Your people. May the words of my mouth and the meditations of my heart be acceptable to You, my Rock and my Redeemer. He who brings peace to His universe will bring peace to us, to the people Israel and to all mankind. Amen.

Kaddish Shalem

Reader:

Hallowed and enhanced may He be throughout the world of His own creation. May He cause His sovereignty soon to be accepted, during our life and the life of all Israel. And let us say: Amen.

Congregation and Reader:

Ye-hei shmei raba meva-rakh l'alam ul'almei 'almaya.

May He be praised throughout all time.

Reader:

Glorified and celebrated, lauded and praised, acclaimed and honored, extolled and exalted may the Holy One be, beyond all song and psalm, beyond all tributes which man can utter. And let us say: Amen.

Omit these two lines in a House of Mourning:

May the prayers and pleas of the whole House of Israel be accepted by our Father in Heaven. And let us say: Amen.

Let there be abundant peace from Heaven, with life's goodness for us and for all the people Israel. And let us say: Amen.

He who brings peace to His universe will bring peace to us and to all the people Israel. And let us say: Amen.

Afternoon service

עָלֵינוּ לְשַׁבֵּחַ לַאֲדוֹן הַכֹּל, לָתֵת גְּדֻלָּה לְיוֹצֵר בְּרֵאשִׁית, שֶׁלֹּא עָשָׂנוּ
כְּגוֹיֵי הָאֲרָצוֹת וְלֹא שָׂמָנוּ כְּמִשְׁפְּחוֹת הָאֲדָמָה, שֶׁלֹּא שָׂם חֶלְקֵנוּ כָּהֶם
וְגוֹרָלֵנוּ כְּכָל־הֲמוֹנָם. וַאֲנַחְנוּ כּוֹרְעִים וּמִשְׁתַּחֲוִים וּמוֹדִים לִפְנֵי מֶלֶךְ
מַלְכֵי הַמְּלָכִים הַקָּדוֹשׁ בָּרוּךְ הוּא, שֶׁהוּא נוֹטֶה שָׁמַיִם וְיוֹסֵד אָרֶץ
וּמוֹשַׁב יְקָרוֹ בַּשָּׁמַיִם מִמַּעַל וּשְׁכִינַת עֻזּוֹ בְּגָבְהֵי מְרוֹמִים. הוּא אֱלֹהֵינוּ
אֵין עוֹד. אֱמֶת מַלְכֵּנוּ אֶפֶס זוּלָתוֹ, כַּכָּתוּב בְּתוֹרָתוֹ: וְיָדַעְתָּ הַיּוֹם
וַהֲשֵׁבֹתָ אֶל לְבָבֶךָ כִּי יְיָ הוּא הָאֱלֹהִים בַּשָּׁמַיִם מִמַּעַל וְעַל הָאָרֶץ
מִתָּחַת, אֵין עוֹד.

עַל כֵּן נְקַוֶּה לְךָ יְיָ אֱלֹהֵינוּ לִרְאוֹת מְהֵרָה בְּתִפְאֶרֶת עֻזֶּךָ, לְהַעֲבִיר
גִּלּוּלִים מִן הָאָרֶץ וְהָאֱלִילִים כָּרוֹת יִכָּרֵתוּן, לְתַקֵּן עוֹלָם בְּמַלְכוּת
שַׁדַּי וְכָל־בְּנֵי בָשָׂר יִקְרְאוּ בִשְׁמֶךָ, לְהַפְנוֹת אֵלֶיךָ כָּל־רִשְׁעֵי־אָרֶץ.
יַכִּירוּ וְיֵדְעוּ כָּל־יוֹשְׁבֵי תֵבֵל כִּי לְךָ תִּכְרַע כָּל־בֶּרֶךְ תִּשָּׁבַע כָּל־
לָשׁוֹן. לְפָנֶיךָ יְיָ אֱלֹהֵינוּ יִכְרְעוּ וְיִפֹּלוּ וְלִכְבוֹד שִׁמְךָ יְקָר יִתֵּנוּ,
וִיקַבְּלוּ כֻלָּם אֶת־עֹל מַלְכוּתֶךָ וְתִמְלֹךְ עֲלֵיהֶם מְהֵרָה לְעוֹלָם וָעֶד,
כִּי הַמַּלְכוּת שֶׁלְּךָ הִיא וּלְעוֹלְמֵי עַד תִּמְלֹךְ בְּכָבוֹד, כַּכָּתוּב
בְּתוֹרָתֶךָ: יְיָ יִמְלֹךְ לְעֹלָם וָעֶד.\וְנֶאֱמַר: וְהָיָה יְיָ לְמֶלֶךְ עַל כָּל־
הָאָרֶץ, בַּיּוֹם הַהוּא יִהְיֶה יְיָ אֶחָד וּשְׁמוֹ אֶחָד.

Afternoon service

146

Aleinu

We rise to our duty to praise the Lord of all the world, to acclaim the Creator. He made our lot unlike that of other people, assigning us a unique destiny. We bend the knee and bow, proclaiming Him as King of kings, the Holy One praised be He, who stretched forth the heavens and established the earth. He is God, our King. There is no other.

*Va'anaḥnu kor'im u-mish-taḥavim u-modim
lifnei melekh malkhei ha-melakhim ha-kadosh barukh hu.*

And so we hope in You, Lord our God, soon to see Your splendor, sweeping idolatry away so that false gods will be utterly destroyed, perfecting earth by Your kingship so that all mankind will invoke Your name, bringing all the earth's wicked back to You, repentant. Then all who live will know that to You every knee must bend, every tongue pledge loyalty. To You, Lord, may all men bow in worship, may they give honor to Your glory. May everyone accept the rule of Your kingship. Reign over all, soon and for all time. Sovereignty is Yours in glory, now and forever. Thus is it written in Your Torah: The Lord reigns for ever and ever. Such is the assurance of Your prophet Zechariah: The Lord shall be acknowledged King of all the earth. On that day the Lord shall be One and His name One.

Ve-ne'emar ve-haya Adonai le-melekh 'al kol ha-aretz, bayom ha-hu yiyeh Adonai eḥad u-she-mo eḥad.

Afternoon service

147

Mourner's Kaddish

*In recalling our dead, of blessed memory, we
confront our loss with faith by rising to praise
God's name in public assembly, praying that all
men recognize His kingship soon. For when His
sovereignty is felt in the world, peace, blessing and
song fill the world, as well as great consolation.*

Mourners and those observing Yahrzeit rise.

יִתְגַּדַּל וְיִתְקַדַּשׁ שְׁמֵהּ רַבָּא בְּעָלְמָא דִּי בְרָא כִרְעוּתֵהּ, וְיַמְלִיךְ
מַלְכוּתֵהּ בְּחַיֵּיכוֹן וּבְיוֹמֵיכוֹן וּבְחַיֵּי דְכָל־בֵּית יִשְׂרָאֵל בַּעֲגָלָא
וּבִזְמַן קָרִיב, וְאִמְרוּ אָמֵן.

Congregation and mourner:

יְהֵא שְׁמֵהּ רַבָּא מְבָרַךְ לְעָלַם וּלְעָלְמֵי עָלְמַיָּא.

Mourner:

יִתְבָּרַךְ וְיִשְׁתַּבַּח וְיִתְפָּאַר וְיִתְרוֹמַם וְיִתְנַשֵּׂא וְיִתְהַדָּר וְיִתְעַלֶּה
וְיִתְהַלָּל שְׁמֵהּ דְּקֻדְשָׁא בְּרִיךְ הוּא, לְעֵלָּא (לְעֵלָּא) מִן כָּל־
בִּרְכָתָא וְשִׁירָתָא תֻּשְׁבְּחָתָא וְנֶחֱמָתָא דַּאֲמִירָן בְּעָלְמָא, וְאִמְרוּ אָמֵן.

יְהֵא שְׁלָמָא רַבָּא מִן שְׁמַיָּא וְחַיִּים עָלֵינוּ וְעַל כָּל־יִשְׂרָאֵל,
וְאִמְרוּ אָמֵן.

עוֹשֶׂה שָׁלוֹם בִּמְרוֹמָיו הוּא יַעֲשֶׂה שָׁלוֹם עָלֵינוּ וְעַל כָּל־יִשְׂרָאֵל,
וְאִמְרוּ אָמֵן.

Mourner's Kaddish

In recalling our dead, of blessed memory, we con-
front our loss with faith by rising to praise God's
name in public assembly, praying that all men rec-
ognize His kingship soon. For when His
sovereignty is felt in the world, peace, blessing and
song fill the world, as well as great consolation.

Mourners and those observing Yahrzeit rise.

Yit-gadal ve-yit-kadash shmei raba, b'alma divra khir'utei ve-
yamlikh mal-khutei be-ḥayei-khon uve'yomei-khon uve-ḥayei
di-khol beit yisrael ba-agala u-vizman kariv v'imru amen.

Congregation and Mourner:

Ye-hei shmei raba meva-rakh l'alam ul'almei 'al-maya.

Mourner:

Yit-barakh ve-yish-tabaḥ ve-yitpa'ar ve-yitromam ve-yitnasei
ve-yit-hadar ve-yit'aleh ve-yit-halal shmei di-kudsha brikh hu,
l'eila [l'eila] min kol bir-khata ve-shirata tush-be-ḥata ve-
neḥe-mata da-amiran b'alma, v'imru amen.

Ye-hei shlama raba min shmaya ve-ḥayim aleinu v'al kol yisrael
v'imru amen.

Oseh shalom bimromav hu ya'aseh shalom aleinu v'al kol yisrael
v'imru amen.

For a translation of the Mourner's Kaddish, see page 100.

Evening service

עַרְבִית ‏‏🙠🙠

וְהוּא רַחוּם, יְכַפֵּר עָוֹן וְלֹא יַשְׁחִית, וְהִרְבָּה לְהָשִׁיב אַפּוֹ, וְלֹא יָעִיר כָּל־חֲמָתוֹ. יְיָ הוֹשִׁיעָה, הַמֶּלֶךְ יַעֲנֵנוּ בְיוֹם קָרְאֵנוּ.

Barkhu

We rise.

Reader:

בָּרְכוּ אֶת־יְיָ הַמְבֹרָךְ.

Congregation and Reader:

בָּרוּךְ יְיָ הַמְבֹרָךְ לְעוֹלָם וָעֶד.

We are seated.

בָּרוּךְ אַתָּה יְיָ אֱלֹהֵינוּ מֶלֶךְ הָעוֹלָם אֲשֶׁר בִּדְבָרוֹ מַעֲרִיב עֲרָבִים. בְּחָכְמָה פּוֹתֵחַ שְׁעָרִים וּבִתְבוּנָה מְשַׁנֶּה עִתִּים וּמַחֲלִיף אֶת־הַזְּמַנִּים וּמְסַדֵּר אֶת־הַכּוֹכָבִים בְּמִשְׁמְרוֹתֵיהֶם בָּרָקִיעַ כִּרְצוֹנוֹ. בּוֹרֵא יוֹם וָלָיְלָה, גּוֹלֵל אוֹר מִפְּנֵי חֹשֶׁךְ וְחֹשֶׁךְ מִפְּנֵי אוֹר, וּמַעֲבִיר יוֹם וּמֵבִיא לָיְלָה וּמַבְדִּיל בֵּין יוֹם וּבֵין לָיְלָה, יְיָ צְבָאוֹת שְׁמוֹ.\אֵל חַי וְקַיָּם, תָּמִיד יִמְלֹךְ עָלֵינוּ לְעוֹלָם וָעֶד. בָּרוּךְ אַתָּה יְיָ הַמַּעֲרִיב עֲרָבִים.

God is merciful. He pardons sin and does not destroy. He restrains His wrath; He is generous and forgiving. O Lord, help us: Answer us, O King, when we call.

Barkhu
ᕲᕲ

We rise.

Reader:

PRAISE THE LORD, SOURCE OF BLESSING.

Congregation and Reader:

Barukh Adonai ha-mevorakh l'olam va'ed.

PRAISED BE THE LORD, SOURCE OF BLESSING, THROUGHOUT ALL TIME.

We are seated.

Praised are You, Lord our God, King of the universe whose word brings the evening dusk. You open the gates of dawn with wisdom, change the day's divisions with understanding, set the succession of seasons, and arrange the stars in the sky according to Your will. Lord of the heavenly hosts, You create day and night, rolling light away from darkness and darkness away from light. Eternal God, Your rule shall embrace us forever. Praised are You, Lord, for each evening's dusk.

Evening service

אַהֲבַת עוֹלָם בֵּית יִשְׂרָאֵל עַמְּךָ אָהָבְתָּ. תּוֹרָה וּמִצְוֹת חֻקִּים
וּמִשְׁפָּטִים אוֹתָנוּ לִמַּדְתָּ. עַל כֵּן יְיָ אֱלֹהֵינוּ בְּשָׁכְבֵנוּ וּבְקוּמֵנוּ נָשִׂיחַ
בְּחֻקֶּיךָ, וְנִשְׂמַח בְּדִבְרֵי תוֹרָתֶךָ וּבְמִצְוֹתֶיךָ לְעוֹלָם וָעֶד. כִּי הֵם חַיֵּינוּ
וְאֹרֶךְ יָמֵינוּ וּבָהֶם נֶהְגֶּה יוֹמָם וָלָיְלָה.\וְאַהֲבָתְךָ אַל תָּסִיר מִמֶּנּוּ
לְעוֹלָמִים. בָּרוּךְ אַתָּה יְיָ אוֹהֵב עַמּוֹ יִשְׂרָאֵל.

K'riat Sh'ma

≈

If there is no minyan, add:

אֵל מֶלֶךְ נֶאֱמָן

שְׁמַע יִשְׂרָאֵל יְהֹוָה אֱלֹהֵינוּ יְהֹוָה | אֶחָד:

Silently:

בָּרוּךְ שֵׁם כְּבוֹד מַלְכוּתוֹ לְעוֹלָם וָעֶד.

וְאָהַבְתָּ אֵת יְהֹוָה אֱלֹהֶיךָ בְּכָל־לְבָבְךָ וּבְכָל־נַפְשְׁךָ וּבְכָל־
מְאֹדֶךָ: וְהָיוּ הַדְּבָרִים הָאֵלֶּה אֲשֶׁר אָנֹכִי מְצַוְּךָ הַיּוֹם עַל־לְבָבֶךָ:
וְשִׁנַּנְתָּם לְבָנֶיךָ וְדִבַּרְתָּ בָּם בְּשִׁבְתְּךָ בְּבֵיתֶךָ וּבְלֶכְתְּךָ בַדֶּרֶךְ
וּבְשָׁכְבְּךָ וּבְקוּמֶךָ: וּקְשַׁרְתָּם לְאוֹת עַל־יָדֶךָ וְהָיוּ לְטֹטָפֹת בֵּין
עֵינֶיךָ: וּכְתַבְתָּם עַל־מְזֻזוֹת בֵּיתֶךָ וּבִשְׁעָרֶיךָ:

Evening service

154

With constancy You have loved Your people Israel, teaching us Torah and *mitzvot*, statutes and laws. Therefore, Lord our God, when we lie down to sleep and when we rise, we shall think of Your laws and speak of them, rejoicing in Your Torah and *mitzvot* always. For they are our life and the length of our days; we will meditate on them day and night. Never take away Your love from us. Praised are You, Lord who loves His people Israel.

K'riat Sh'ma

If there is no minyan, add:
God is a faithful King.

HEAR, O ISRAEL: THE LORD OUR GOD, THE LORD IS ONE.

Silently:
Praised be His glorious sovereignty throughout all time.

Love the Lord your God with all your heart, with all your soul, with all your might. And these words which I command you this day shall you take to heart. You shall diligently teach them to your children. You shall repeat them at home and away, morning and night. You shall bind them as a sign upon your hand, they shall be a reminder above your eyes, and you shall inscribe them upon the doorposts of your homes and upon your gates.

Deuteronomy 6:4–9

Evening service

155

וְהָיָה אִם־שָׁמֹעַ תִּשְׁמְעוּ אֶל־מִצְוֺתַי אֲשֶׁר אָנֹכִי מְצַוֶּה אֶתְכֶם
הַיּוֹם לְאַהֲבָה אֶת־יְהֹוָה אֱלֹהֵיכֶם וּלְעָבְדוֹ בְּכָל־לְבַבְכֶם וּבְכָל־
נַפְשְׁכֶם: וְנָתַתִּי מְטַר־אַרְצְכֶם בְּעִתּוֹ יוֹרֶה וּמַלְקוֹשׁ וְאָסַפְתָּ דְגָנֶךָ
וְתִירֹשְׁךָ וְיִצְהָרֶךָ: וְנָתַתִּי עֵשֶׂב בְּשָׂדְךָ לִבְהֶמְתֶּךָ וְאָכַלְתָּ וְשָׂבָעְתָּ:
הִשָּׁמְרוּ לָכֶם פֶּן־יִפְתֶּה לְבַבְכֶם וְסַרְתֶּם וַעֲבַדְתֶּם אֱלֹהִים אֲחֵרִים
וְהִשְׁתַּחֲוִיתֶם לָהֶם: וְחָרָה אַף־יְהֹוָה בָּכֶם וְעָצַר אֶת־הַשָּׁמַיִם
וְלֹא־יִהְיֶה מָטָר וְהָאֲדָמָה לֹא תִתֵּן אֶת־יְבוּלָהּ וַאֲבַדְתֶּם מְהֵרָה
מֵעַל הָאָרֶץ הַטֹּבָה אֲשֶׁר יְהֹוָה נֹתֵן לָכֶם: וְשַׂמְתֶּם אֶת־דְּבָרַי אֵלֶּה
עַל־לְבַבְכֶם וְעַל־נַפְשְׁכֶם וּקְשַׁרְתֶּם אֹתָם לְאוֹת עַל־יֶדְכֶם וְהָיוּ
לְטוֹטָפֹת בֵּין עֵינֵיכֶם: וְלִמַּדְתֶּם אֹתָם אֶת־בְּנֵיכֶם לְדַבֵּר בָּם
בְּשִׁבְתְּךָ בְּבֵיתֶךָ וּבְלֶכְתְּךָ בַדֶּרֶךְ וּבְשָׁכְבְּךָ וּבְקוּמֶךָ: וּכְתַבְתָּם
עַל־מְזוּזוֹת בֵּיתֶךָ וּבִשְׁעָרֶיךָ: לְמַעַן יִרְבּוּ יְמֵיכֶם וִימֵי בְנֵיכֶם עַל
הָאֲדָמָה אֲשֶׁר נִשְׁבַּע יְהֹוָה לַאֲבֹתֵיכֶם לָתֵת לָהֶם כִּימֵי הַשָּׁמַיִם
עַל־הָאָרֶץ:

וַיֹּאמֶר יְהֹוָה אֶל־מֹשֶׁה לֵּאמֹר: דַּבֵּר אֶל־בְּנֵי יִשְׂרָאֵל וְאָמַרְתָּ
אֲלֵהֶם וְעָשׂוּ לָהֶם צִיצִת עַל־כַּנְפֵי בִגְדֵיהֶם לְדֹרֹתָם וְנָתְנוּ עַל־
צִיצִת הַכָּנָף פְּתִיל תְּכֵלֶת: וְהָיָה לָכֶם לְצִיצִת וּרְאִיתֶם אֹתוֹ
וּזְכַרְתֶּם אֶת־כָּל־מִצְוֺת יְהֹוָה וַעֲשִׂיתֶם אֹתָם וְלֹא תָתוּרוּ אַחֲרֵי
לְבַבְכֶם וְאַחֲרֵי עֵינֵיכֶם אֲשֶׁר־אַתֶּם זֹנִים אַחֲרֵיהֶם: לְמַעַן תִּזְכְּרוּ

If you will earnestly heed the commandments I give you this day, to love the Lord your God and to serve Him with all your heart and all your soul, then I will favor your land with rain at the proper season—rain in autumn and rain in spring—and you will have an ample harvest of grain and wine and oil. I will assure abundance in the fields for your cattle. You will eat to contentment. Take care lest you be tempted to forsake God and turn to false gods in worship. For then the wrath of the Lord will be directed against you. He will close the heavens and hold back the rain; the earth will not yield its produce. You will soon disappear from the good land which the Lord gives you.

Therefore, impress these words of Mine upon your heart. Bind them as a sign upon your hand, and let them be a reminder above your eyes. Teach them to your children. Repeat them at home and away, morning and night. Inscribe them upon the doorposts of your homes and upon your gates. Then your days and the days of your children will endure as the days of the heavens over the earth, on the land which the Lord swore to give to your fathers.

Deuteronomy 11:13–21

The Lord said to Moses: Instruct the people Israel that in every generation they shall put fringes on the corners of their garments, and bind a thread of blue to the fringe of each corner. Looking upon these fringes you will be reminded of all the commandments of the Lord and fulfill them, and not be seduced by your heart or led astray by your eyes. Then you will remember and observe all My commandments and

וַעֲשִׂיתֶם אֶת־כָּל־מִצְוֹתָי וִהְיִיתֶם קְדֹשִׁים לֵאלֹהֵיכֶם: אֲנִי יְהֹוָה אֱלֹהֵיכֶם אֲשֶׁר הוֹצֵאתִי אֶתְכֶם מֵאֶרֶץ מִצְרַיִם לִהְיוֹת לָכֶם לֵאלֹהִים אֲנִי יְהֹוָה אֱלֹהֵיכֶם:

יְיָ אֱלֹהֵיכֶם אֱמֶת.

אֱמֶת וֶאֱמוּנָה כָּל־זֹאת וְקַיָּם עָלֵינוּ כִּי הוּא יְיָ אֱלֹהֵינוּ וְאֵין זוּלָתוֹ וַאֲנַחְנוּ יִשְׂרָאֵל עַמּוֹ. הַפּוֹדֵנוּ מִיַּד מְלָכִים, מַלְכֵּנוּ הַגּוֹאֲלֵנוּ מִכַּף כָּל־הֶעָרִיצִים, הָאֵל הַנִּפְרָע לָנוּ מִצָּרֵינוּ וְהַמְשַׁלֵּם גְּמוּל לְכָל־אוֹיְבֵי נַפְשֵׁנוּ, הָעוֹשֶׂה גְדוֹלוֹת עַד אֵין חֵקֶר וְנִפְלָאוֹת עַד אֵין מִסְפָּר, הַשָּׂם נַפְשֵׁנוּ בַּחַיִּים וְלֹא נָתַן לַמּוֹט רַגְלֵנוּ, הַמַּדְרִיכֵנוּ עַל בָּמוֹת אוֹיְבֵינוּ וַיָּרֶם קַרְנֵנוּ עַל כָּל־שׂוֹנְאֵינוּ, הָעוֹשֶׂה לָנוּ נִסִּים וּנְקָמָה בְּפַרְעֹה אוֹתוֹת וּמוֹפְתִים בְּאַדְמַת בְּנֵי חָם, הַמַּכֶּה בְעֶבְרָתוֹ כָּל־בְּכוֹרֵי מִצְרַיִם וַיּוֹצֵא אֶת־עַמּוֹ יִשְׂרָאֵל מִתּוֹכָם לְחֵרוּת עוֹלָם, הַמַּעֲבִיר בָּנָיו בֵּין גִּזְרֵי יַם סוּף, אֶת־רוֹדְפֵיהֶם וְאֶת־שׂוֹנְאֵיהֶם בִּתְהוֹמוֹת טִבַּע, וְרָאוּ בָנָיו גְּבוּרָתוֹ שִׁבְּחוּ וְהוֹדוּ לִשְׁמוֹ.\וּמַלְכוּתוֹ בְּרָצוֹן קִבְּלוּ עֲלֵיהֶם. מֹשֶׁה וּבְנֵי יִשְׂרָאֵל לְךָ עָנוּ שִׁירָה בְּשִׂמְחָה רַבָּה, וְאָמְרוּ כֻלָּם:

מִי־כָמֹכָה בָּאֵלִם יְיָ,
מִי כָּמֹכָה נֶאְדָּר בַּקֹּדֶשׁ,
נוֹרָא תְהִלֹּת, עֹשֵׂה פֶלֶא.

be holy before your God. I am the Lord your God who brought you out of the land of Egypt to be your God. I, the Lord, am your God.

Numbers 15:37-41

The Lord your God is faithful.

We affirm the truth that He is our God, that there is no other, and that we are His people Israel. He redeems us from the power of kings, delivers us from the hand of all tyrants. He brings judgment upon our oppressors, retribution upon all our mortal enemies. He performs wonders beyond understanding, marvelous things beyond all reckoning. He has maintained us among the living. He has not allowed our steps to falter. He guided us to triumph over mighty foes, exalted our strength over all our enemies. He vindicated us with miracles before Pharaoh, with signs and wonders in the land of Egypt. In wrath He smote all of Egypt's firstborn, bringing His people to lasting freedom. He led His children through divided waters as their pursuers sank in the sea.

When His children beheld His might they sang in praise of Him, gladly accepting His sovereignty. Moses and the people Israel sang with great joy this song to the Lord:

Mi khamokha, ba-eilim Adonai, mi kamokha nedar bakodesh nora te-hilot oseh feleh.

Who is like You, Lord, among all that is worshipped?
Who is like You, majestic in holiness,
awesome in splendor, working wonders?

Evening service

159

מַלְכוּתְךָ רָאוּ בָנֶיךָ בּוֹקֵעַ יָם לִפְנֵי מֹשֶׁה, זֶה אֵלִי עָנוּ וְאָמְרוּ: יְיָ יִמְלֹךְ לְעֹלָם וָעֶד.

וְנֶאֱמַר: כִּי פָדָה יְיָ אֶת־יַעֲקֹב, וּגְאָלוֹ מִיַּד חָזָק מִמֶּנּוּ. בָּרוּךְ אַתָּה יְיָ גָּאַל יִשְׂרָאֵל.

הַשְׁכִּיבֵנוּ, יְיָ אֱלֹהֵינוּ, לְשָׁלוֹם וְהַעֲמִידֵנוּ מַלְכֵּנוּ לְחַיִּים, וּפְרֹשׂ עָלֵינוּ סֻכַּת שְׁלוֹמֶךָ וְתַקְּנֵנוּ בְּעֵצָה טוֹבָה מִלְּפָנֶיךָ וְהוֹשִׁיעֵנוּ לְמַעַן שְׁמֶךָ. וְהָגֵן בַּעֲדֵנוּ וְהָסֵר מֵעָלֵינוּ אוֹיֵב דֶּבֶר וְחֶרֶב וְרָעָב וְיָגוֹן, וְהָסֵר שָׂטָן מִלְּפָנֵינוּ וּמֵאַחֲרֵינוּ. וּבְצֵל כְּנָפֶיךָ תַּסְתִּירֵנוּ כִּי אֵל שׁוֹמְרֵנוּ וּמַצִּילֵנוּ אָתָּה, כִּי אֵל מֶלֶךְ חַנּוּן וְרַחוּם אָתָּה. וּשְׁמֹר צֵאתֵנוּ וּבוֹאֵנוּ לְחַיִּים וּלְשָׁלוֹם מֵעַתָּה וְעַד עוֹלָם. בָּרוּךְ אַתָּה יְיָ שׁוֹמֵר עַמּוֹ יִשְׂרָאֵל לָעַד.

בָּרוּךְ יְיָ לְעוֹלָם, אָמֵן וְאָמֵן. בָּרוּךְ יְיָ מִצִּיּוֹן, שֹׁכֵן יְרוּשָׁלָיִם, הַלְלוּיָהּ. בָּרוּךְ יְיָ אֱלֹהִים, אֱלֹהֵי יִשְׂרָאֵל, עֹשֵׂה נִפְלָאוֹת לְבַדּוֹ. וּבָרוּךְ שֵׁם כְּבוֹדוֹ לְעוֹלָם, וְיִמָּלֵא כְבוֹדוֹ אֶת־כָּל־הָאָרֶץ, אָמֵן וְאָמֵן. יְהִי כְבוֹד יְיָ לְעוֹלָם, יִשְׂמַח יְיָ בְּמַעֲשָׂיו. יְהִי שֵׁם יְיָ מְבֹרָךְ מֵעַתָּה וְעַד עוֹלָם. כִּי לֹא יִטֹּשׁ יְיָ אֶת־עַמּוֹ בַּעֲבוּר שְׁמוֹ הַגָּדוֹל, כִּי הוֹאִיל יְיָ לַעֲשׂוֹת אֶתְכֶם לוֹ לְעָם. וַיַּרְא

Your children beheld Your sovereignty as You divided the sea before Moses. "This is my God," they responded, declaring:

Adonai yimlokh l'olam va'ed.

"The Lord shall reign throughout all time."

And thus it is written: "The Lord has rescued Jacob; He redeemed him from those more powerful." Praised are You, Lord, Redeemer of the people Israel.

Help us, our Father, to lie down in peace; and awaken us to life again, our King. Spread over us Your shelter of peace, guide us with Your good counsel. Save us for the sake of Your mercy. Shield us from enemies and pestilence, from starvation, sword and sorrow. Remove the evil forces that surround us, shelter us in the shadow of Your wings. You, O God, guard us and deliver us. You are a gracious and merciful King. Guard our coming and our going, grant us life and peace, now and always. Praised are You, O Lord, eternal guardian of Your people Israel.

Praised is the Lord forever. Amen! Amen! Let praise of the Lord come forth from Zion; praise Him who dwells in Jerusalem. Halleluyah! Praised is the Lord, God of Israel. He alone works wondrous deeds. Praised is His glory forever. The glory of the Lord shall be forever; the Lord shall rejoice in His works. His glory fills the world. Amen! Praised is the glory of the Lord now and always. For the sake of His glory He will not abandon His people; the Lord desires to make you His own.

Evening service

161

כָּל־הָעָם וַיִּפְּלוּ עַל פְּנֵיהֶם, וַיֹּאמְרוּ: יְיָ הוּא הָאֱלֹהִים, יְיָ הוּא הָאֱלֹהִים. וְהָיָה יְיָ לְמֶלֶךְ עַל כָּל־הָאָרֶץ, בַּיּוֹם הַהוּא יִהְיֶה יְיָ אֶחָד וּשְׁמוֹ אֶחָד. יְהִי חַסְדְּךָ יְיָ עָלֵינוּ, כַּאֲשֶׁר יִחַלְנוּ לָךְ. הוֹשִׁיעֵנוּ, אֱלֹהֵי יִשְׁעֵנוּ וְקַבְּצֵנוּ וְהַצִּילֵנוּ מִן הַגּוֹיִם, לְהֹדוֹת לְשֵׁם קָדְשֶׁךָ, לְהִשְׁתַּבֵּחַ בִּתְהִלָּתֶךָ. כָּל־גּוֹיִם אֲשֶׁר עָשִׂיתָ יָבוֹאוּ וְיִשְׁתַּחֲווּ לְפָנֶיךָ, אֲדֹנָי, וִיכַבְּדוּ לִשְׁמֶךָ. כִּי גָדוֹל אַתָּה וְעֹשֵׂה נִפְלָאוֹת, אַתָּה אֱלֹהִים לְבַדֶּךָ. וַאֲנַחְנוּ עַמְּךָ וְצֹאן מַרְעִיתֶךָ, נוֹדֶה לְךָ לְעוֹלָם, לְדוֹר וָדֹר נְסַפֵּר תְּהִלָּתֶךָ.

בָּרוּךְ יְיָ בַּיּוֹם, בָּרוּךְ יְיָ בַּלָּיְלָה, בָּרוּךְ יְיָ בְּשָׁכְבֵנוּ, בָּרוּךְ יְיָ בְּקוּמֵנוּ, כִּי בְיָדְךָ נַפְשׁוֹת הַחַיִּים וְהַמֵּתִים. אֲשֶׁר בְּיָדוֹ נֶפֶשׁ כָּל־חָי, וְרוּחַ כָּל־בְּשַׂר אִישׁ. בְּיָדְךָ אַפְקִיד רוּחִי, פָּדִיתָה אוֹתִי, יְיָ אֵל אֱמֶת. אֱלֹהֵינוּ שֶׁבַּשָּׁמַיִם, יַחֵד שִׁמְךָ וְקַיֵּם מַלְכוּתְךָ תָּמִיד וּמְלֹךְ עָלֵינוּ לְעוֹלָם וָעֶד.

יִרְאוּ עֵינֵינוּ וְיִשְׂמַח לִבֵּנוּ, וְתָגֵל נַפְשֵׁנוּ בִּישׁוּעָתְךָ בֶּאֱמֶת, בֶּאֱמֹר לְצִיּוֹן מָלַךְ אֱלֹהָיִךְ. יְיָ מֶלֶךְ, יְיָ מָלָךְ, יְיָ יִמְלֹךְ לְעוֹלָם וָעֶד. \כִּי הַמַּלְכוּת שֶׁלְּךָ הִיא וּלְעוֹלְמֵי עַד תִּמְלֹךְ בְּכָבוֹד, כִּי אֵין לָנוּ מֶלֶךְ אֶלָּא אָתָּה. בָּרוּךְ אַתָּה יְיָ הַמֶּלֶךְ בִּכְבוֹדוֹ תָּמִיד יִמְלֹךְ עָלֵינוּ לְעוֹלָם וָעֶד, וְעַל כָּל־מַעֲשָׂיו.

When the people saw the wonders wrought by God, they fell to the ground in worship, exclaiming: The Lord, He is God; the Lord, He is God. The Lord shall be King of all the earth; on that day the Lord shall be One and His name One. Let Your mercy be upon us, as our hope is in You. Help us, Lord our God, and deliver us. Gather us, and free us from oppression, that we may praise Your glory, that we may be exalted in praising You. All the nations You have created, Lord, will worship You and glorify You. Great are You, wondrous are Your deeds; You alone are God. We are Your people, the flock You shepherd. We will never cease thanking You, recounting Your praises to all generations.

Praised is the Lord by day and praised by night, praised when we lie down and praised when we rise up. In Your hands are the souls of the living and the dead, the life of every creature, the breath of all flesh. Into Your hand I entrust my spirit; You will redeem me, Lord God of truth. Our God in Heaven, assert the unity of Your rule; affirm Your sovereignty, and reign over us forever.

May our eyes behold, our hearts rejoice, and our souls be glad in our sure deliverance, when it shall be said to Zion: Your God is King. The Lord is King, the Lord was King, the Lord shall be King throughout all time. All sovereignty is Yours; unto all eternity only You reign in glory, only You are King. Praised are You, Lord and glorious King, eternal Ruler over us, and over all creation.

Ḥatzi Kaddish

Reader:

יִתְגַּדַּל וְיִתְקַדַּשׁ שְׁמֵהּ רַבָּא בְּעָלְמָא דִּי בְרָא כִרְעוּתֵהּ, וְיַמְלִיךְ
מַלְכוּתֵהּ בְּחַיֵּיכוֹן וּבְיוֹמֵיכוֹן וּבְחַיֵּי דְכָל־בֵּית יִשְׂרָאֵל בַּעֲגָלָא
וּבִזְמַן קָרִיב, וְאִמְרוּ אָמֵן.

Congregation and Reader:

יְהֵא שְׁמֵהּ רַבָּא מְבָרַךְ לְעָלַם וּלְעָלְמֵי עָלְמַיָּא.

Reader:

יִתְבָּרַךְ וְיִשְׁתַּבַּח וְיִתְפָּאַר וְיִתְרוֹמַם וְיִתְנַשֵּׂא וְיִתְהַדָּר וְיִתְעַלֶּה
וְיִתְהַלָּל שְׁמֵהּ דְּקֻדְשָׁא בְּרִיךְ הוּא, לְעֵלָּא (לְעֵלָּא) מִן כָּל־
בִּרְכָתָא וְשִׁירָתָא תֻּשְׁבְּחָתָא וְנֶחֱמָתָא דַּאֲמִירָן בְּעָלְמָא, וְאִמְרוּ אָמֵן.

Ḥatzi Kaddish

Reader:

Hallowed and enhanced may He be throughout the world of His own creation. May He cause His sovereignty soon to be accepted, during our life and the life of all Israel. And let us say: Amen.

Congregation and Reader:

Ye-hei shmei raba meva-rakh l'alam ul'almei 'almaya.
May He be praised throughout all time.

Reader:

Glorified and celebrated, lauded and praised, acclaimed and honored, extolled and exalted may the Holy One be, beyond all song and psalm, beyond all tributes which man can utter. And let us say: Amen.

Amidah

We stand in silent prayer, which ends on page 178.

אֲדֹנָי שְׂפָתַי תִּפְתָּח וּפִי יַגִּיד תְּהִלָּתֶךָ.

בָּרוּךְ אַתָּה יְיָ אֱלֹהֵינוּ וֵאלֹהֵי אֲבוֹתֵינוּ, אֱלֹהֵי אַבְרָהָם אֱלֹהֵי יִצְחָק
וֵאלֹהֵי יַעֲקֹב, הָאֵל הַגָּדוֹל הַגִּבּוֹר וְהַנּוֹרָא אֵל עֶלְיוֹן גּוֹמֵל חֲסָדִים
טוֹבִים וְקוֹנֵה הַכֹּל, וְזוֹכֵר חַסְדֵי אָבוֹת וּמֵבִיא גוֹאֵל לִבְנֵי בְנֵיהֶם
לְמַעַן שְׁמוֹ בְּאַהֲבָה.

From Rosh Hashanah through Yom Kippur:

זָכְרֵנוּ לְחַיִּים מֶלֶךְ חָפֵץ בַּחַיִּים,
וְכָתְבֵנוּ בְּסֵפֶר הַחַיִּים לְמַעַנְךָ אֱלֹהִים חַיִּים.

מֶלֶךְ עוֹזֵר וּמוֹשִׁיעַ וּמָגֵן. בָּרוּךְ אַתָּה יְיָ מָגֵן אַבְרָהָם.

אַתָּה גִּבּוֹר לְעוֹלָם אֲדֹנָי מְחַיֵּה מֵתִים אַתָּה רַב לְהוֹשִׁיעַ.

From Shmini Atzeret to Pesah:

מַשִּׁיב הָרוּחַ וּמוֹרִיד הַגָּשֶׁם.

מְכַלְכֵּל חַיִּים בְּחֶסֶד מְחַיֵּה מֵתִים בְּרַחֲמִים רַבִּים, סוֹמֵךְ נוֹפְלִים
וְרוֹפֵא חוֹלִים וּמַתִּיר אֲסוּרִים וּמְקַיֵּם אֱמוּנָתוֹ לִישֵׁנֵי עָפָר. מִי כָמוֹךָ
בַּעַל גְּבוּרוֹת וּמִי דּוֹמֶה לָךְ, מֶלֶךְ מֵמִית וּמְחַיֵּה וּמַצְמִיחַ יְשׁוּעָה.

Evening service

166

Amidah

We stand in silent prayer, which ends on page 179.

Open my mouth, O Lord, and my lips will proclaim Your praise.

Praised are You, Lord our God and God of our fathers, God of Abraham, of Isaac and of Jacob, great, mighty, awesome, exalted God, bestowing lovingkindness and creating all things. You remember the pious deeds of our fathers, and will send a redeemer to their children's children because of Your love and for the sake of Your glory.

From Rosh Hashanah through Yom Kippur:

Remember us that we may live, O King who delights in life. Inscribe us in the Book of Life, for Your sake, living God.

You are the King who helps and saves and shields. Praised are You, Lord, Shield of Abraham.

Your might, O Lord, is boundless. You give life to the dead; great is Your saving power.

From Shmini Atzeret to Pesaḥ:

You cause the wind to blow and the rain to fall.

Your lovingkindness sustains the living, Your great mercies give life to the dead. You support the falling, heal the ailing, free the fettered. You keep Your faith with those who sleep in dust. Whose power can compare with Yours? You are the master of life and death and deliverance.

Evening service

167

From Rosh Hashanah through Yom Kippur:

מִי כָמְוֹךָ אַב הָרַחֲמִים, זוֹכֵר יְצוּרָיו לְחַיִּים בְּרַחֲמִים.

וְנֶאֱמָן אַתָּה לְהַחֲיוֹת מֵתִים. בָּרוּךְ אַתָּה יְיָ מְחַיֵּה הַמֵּתִים.

אַתָּה קָדוֹשׁ וְשִׁמְךָ קָדוֹשׁ וּקְדוֹשִׁים בְּכָל־יוֹם יְהַלְלוּךָ סֶּלָה.

From Rosh Hashanah through Yom Kippur:

בָּרוּךְ אַתָּה יְיָ הַמֶּלֶךְ הַקָּדוֹשׁ.

בָּרוּךְ אַתָּה יְיָ הָאֵל הַקָּדוֹשׁ.

Following Shabbat or a Festival:

אַתָּה חוֹנֵן לְאָדָם דַּעַת וּמְלַמֵּד לֶאֱנוֹשׁ בִּינָה. אַתָּה חוֹנַנְתָּנוּ מַדַּע תּוֹרָתֶךָ וַתְּלַמְּדֵנוּ לַעֲשׂוֹת חֻקֵּי רְצוֹנֶךָ. וַתַּבְדֵּל, יְיָ אֱלֹהֵינוּ, בֵּין קְדֶשׁ לְחוֹל, בֵּין אוֹר לְחֹשֶׁךְ, בֵּין יִשְׂרָאֵל לָעַמִּים, בֵּין יוֹם הַשְּׁבִיעִי לְשֵׁשֶׁת יְמֵי הַמַּעֲשֶׂה. אָבִינוּ מַלְכֵּנוּ, הָחֵל עָלֵינוּ הַיָּמִים הַבָּאִים לִקְרָאתֵנוּ לְשָׁלוֹם, חֲשׂוּכִים מִכָּל־חֵטְא וּמְנֻקִּים מִכָּל־עָוֹן וּמְדֻבָּקִים בְּיִרְאָתֶךָ. וְחָנֵּנוּ מֵאִתְּךָ דֵּעָה בִּינָה וְהַשְׂכֵּל . בָּרוּךְ אַתָּה יְיָ חוֹנֵן הַדָּעַת.

Continue on following page, second paragraph.

Evening service

From Rosh Hashanah through Yom Kippur:

Whose mercy can compare with Yours, merciful Father? In mercy You remember Your creatures with life.

Faithful are You in giving life to the dead. Praised are You, Lord, Master of life and death.

Holy are You and holy is Your name. Holy are those who praise You daily.

From Rosh Hashanah through Yom Kippur:
Praised are You, Lord and holy King.

Praised are You, Lord and holy God.

Following Shabbat or a Festival:

You graciously endow man with intelligence, You teach him wisdom and understanding. You favored us with the knowledge of Torah, You instructed us to perform Your commandments. You set apart the sacred from the profane, even as You separated light from darkness, singled out Israel from among the nations, and distinguished Shabbat from all other days. Our Father, our King, may the coming days bring us peace. May they be free of sin and cleansed of wrongdoing; may they find us more closely attached to You. Grant us knowledge, discernment and wisdom. Praised are You, Lord, for the gift of knowledge.

Continue on following page, second paragraph.

Evening service

אַתָּה חוֹנֵן לְאָדָם דַּעַת וּמְלַמֵּד לֶאֱנוֹשׁ בִּינָה. חָנֵּנוּ מֵאִתְּךָ דֵּעָה בִּינָה וְהַשְׂכֵּל. בָּרוּךְ אַתָּה יְיָ חוֹנֵן הַדָּעַת.

הֲשִׁיבֵנוּ אָבִינוּ לְתוֹרָתֶךָ וְקָרְבֵנוּ מַלְכֵּנוּ לַעֲבוֹדָתֶךָ, וְהַחֲזִירֵנוּ בִּתְשׁוּבָה שְׁלֵמָה לְפָנֶיךָ. בָּרוּךְ אַתָּה יְיָ הָרוֹצֶה בִּתְשׁוּבָה.

סְלַח לָנוּ אָבִינוּ כִּי חָטָאנוּ, מְחַל לָנוּ מַלְכֵּנוּ כִּי פָשָׁעְנוּ, כִּי מוֹחֵל וְסוֹלֵחַ אָתָּה. בָּרוּךְ אַתָּה יְיָ חַנּוּן הַמַּרְבֶּה לִסְלֹחַ.

רְאֵה נָא בְעָנְיֵנוּ וְרִיבָה רִיבֵנוּ וּגְאָלֵנוּ מְהֵרָה לְמַעַן שְׁמֶךָ, כִּי גּוֹאֵל חָזָק אָתָּה. בָּרוּךְ אַתָּה יְיָ גּוֹאֵל יִשְׂרָאֵל.

רְפָאֵנוּ יְיָ וְנֵרָפֵא, הוֹשִׁיעֵנוּ וְנִוָּשֵׁעָה, כִּי תְהִלָּתֵנוּ אָתָּה. וְהַעֲלֵה רְפוּאָה שְׁלֵמָה לְכָל־מַכּוֹתֵינוּ, כִּי אֵל מֶלֶךְ רוֹפֵא נֶאֱמָן וְרַחֲמָן אָתָּה. בָּרוּךְ אַתָּה יְיָ רוֹפֵא חוֹלֵי עַמּוֹ יִשְׂרָאֵל.

בָּרֵךְ עָלֵינוּ יְיָ אֱלֹהֵינוּ אֶת־הַשָּׁנָה הַזֹּאת וְאֶת־כָּל־מִינֵי תְבוּאָתָה לְטוֹבָה

Summer (From Pesaḥ to December fourth):

וְתֵן בְּרָכָה עַל פְּנֵי הָאֲדָמָה

Winter (From December fourth to Pesaḥ):

וְתֵן טַל וּמָטָר לִבְרָכָה עַל פְּנֵי הָאֲדָמָה

Evening service

170

You graciously endow man with intelligence, You teach him wisdom and understanding. Grant us knowledge, discernment and wisdom. Praised are You, Lord, for the gift of knowledge.

Our Father, bring us back to Your Torah. Our King, draw us near to Your service. Lead us back to You, truly repentant. Praised are You, Lord who welcomes repentance.

Forgive us, our Father, for we have sinned; pardon us, our King, for we have transgressed, for You forgive and pardon. Praised are You, gracious and forgiving Lord.

Behold our affliction and deliver us. Redeem us soon for the sake of Your name, for You are the mighty Redeemer. Praised are You, Lord, Redeemer of the people Israel.

Heal us, O Lord, and we shall be healed. Help us and save us, for You are our glory. Grant perfect healing for all our afflictions, faithful and merciful God of healing. Praised are You, Lord, Healer of His people.

Lord our God, make this a blessed year. May its varied produce bring us happiness.

Summer (From Pesaḥ to December fourth):

Bring blessing upon the whole earth.

Winter (From December fourth to Pesaḥ):

Bless the earth with dew and rain.

וְשַׂבְּעֵנוּ מִטּוּבֶךְ וּבָרֵךְ שְׁנָתֵנוּ כַּשָּׁנִים הַטּוֹבוֹת. בָּרוּךְ אַתָּה יְיָ מְבָרֵךְ הַשָּׁנִים.

תְּקַע בְּשׁוֹפָר גָּדוֹל לְחֵרוּתֵנוּ וְשָׂא נֵס לְקַבֵּץ גָּלֻיּוֹתֵינוּ וְקַבְּצֵנוּ יַחַד מֵאַרְבַּע כַּנְפוֹת הָאָרֶץ. בָּרוּךְ אַתָּה יְיָ מְקַבֵּץ נִדְחֵי עַמּוֹ יִשְׂרָאֵל.

הָשִׁיבָה שׁוֹפְטֵינוּ כְּבָרִאשׁוֹנָה וְיוֹעֲצֵינוּ כְּבַתְּחִלָּה, וְהָסֵר מִמֶּנּוּ יָגוֹן וַאֲנָחָה, וּמְלֹךְ עָלֵינוּ אַתָּה יְיָ לְבַדְּךָ בְּחֶסֶד וּבְרַחֲמִים וְצַדְּקֵנוּ בַּמִּשְׁפָּט.

From Rosh Hashanah through Yom Kippur:

בָּרוּךְ אַתָּה יְיָ הַמֶּלֶךְ הַמִּשְׁפָּט.

בָּרוּךְ אַתָּה יְיָ מֶלֶךְ אוֹהֵב צְדָקָה וּמִשְׁפָּט.

וְלַמַּלְשִׁינִים אַל תְּהִי תִקְוָה וְכָל־הָרִשְׁעָה כְּרֶגַע תֹּאבֵד. וְכָל־אוֹיְבֶיךָ מְהֵרָה יִכָּרֵתוּ וּמַלְכוּת זָדוֹן מְהֵרָה תְעַקֵּר וּתְשַׁבֵּר וּתְמַגֵּר וְתַכְנִיעַ בִּמְהֵרָה בְיָמֵינוּ. בָּרוּךְ אַתָּה יְיָ שׁוֹבֵר אוֹיְבִים וּמַכְנִיעַ זֵדִים.

עַל הַצַּדִּיקִים וְעַל הַחֲסִידִים וְעַל זִקְנֵי עַמְּךָ בֵּית יִשְׂרָאֵל וְעַל פְּלֵיטַת סוֹפְרֵיהֶם וְעַל גֵּרֵי הַצֶּדֶק וְעָלֵינוּ יֶהֱמוּ נָא רַחֲמֶיךָ יְיָ אֱלֹהֵינוּ, וְתֵן שָׂכָר טוֹב לְכָל הַבּוֹטְחִים בְּשִׁמְךָ בֶּאֱמֶת, וְשִׂים

Bless the year with Your abounding goodness. Praised are You, Lord who blesses the years.

Sound the great shofar to herald our freedom, raise high the banner to gather all exiles. Gather the dispersed from the corners of the earth. Praised are You, Lord who gathers our exiles.

Restore our judges as in days of old, restore our counsellors as in former times. Remove from us sorrow and anguish. Reign alone over us with lovingkindness; with justice and mercy sustain our cause.

From Rosh Hashanah through Yom Kippur:

Praised are You, Lord, King of judgment.

Praised are You, Lord, King who loves justice.

Frustrate the hopes of those who malign us; let all evil very soon disappear. Let all Your enemies soon be destroyed. May You quickly uproot and crush the arrogant; may You subdue and humble them in our time. Praised are You, Lord who humbles the arrogant.

Let Your tender mercies be stirred for the righteous, the pious and the leaders of the House of Israel, toward devoted scholars and faithful proselytes. Be merciful to us of the House of Israel. Reward all who trust in You, cast our lot with those who are faithful to You. May we never come to

Evening service

חֶלְקֵנוּ עִמָּהֶם לְעוֹלָם וְלֹא נֵבוֹשׁ כִּי בְךָ בָּטָחְנוּ. בָּרוּךְ אַתָּה יְיָ מִשְׁעָן וּמִבְטָח לַצַּדִּיקִים.

וְלִירוּשָׁלַיִם עִירְךָ בְּרַחֲמִים תָּשׁוּב וְתִשְׁכֹּן בְּתוֹכָהּ כַּאֲשֶׁר דִּבַּרְתָּ, וּבְנֵה אוֹתָהּ בְּקָרוֹב בְּיָמֵינוּ בִּנְיַן עוֹלָם וְכִסֵּא דָוִד מְהֵרָה לְתוֹכָהּ תָּכִין. בָּרוּךְ אַתָּה יְיָ בּוֹנֵה יְרוּשָׁלָיִם.

אֶת־צֶמַח דָּוִד עַבְדְּךָ מְהֵרָה תַצְמִיחַ וְקַרְנוֹ תָּרוּם בִּישׁוּעָתֶךָ, כִּי לִישׁוּעָתְךָ קִוִּינוּ כָּל־הַיּוֹם. בָּרוּךְ אַתָּה יְיָ מַצְמִיחַ קֶרֶן יְשׁוּעָה.

שְׁמַע קוֹלֵנוּ יְיָ אֱלֹהֵינוּ, חוּס וְרַחֵם עָלֵינוּ, וְקַבֵּל בְּרַחֲמִים וּבְרָצוֹן אֶת־תְּפִלָּתֵנוּ, כִּי אֵל שׁוֹמֵעַ תְּפִלּוֹת וְתַחֲנוּנִים אָתָּה. וּמִלְּפָנֶיךָ מַלְכֵּנוּ רֵיקָם אַל תְּשִׁיבֵנוּ. כִּי אַתָּה שׁוֹמֵעַ תְּפִלַּת עַמְּךָ יִשְׂרָאֵל בְּרַחֲמִים. בָּרוּךְ אַתָּה יְיָ שׁוֹמֵעַ תְּפִלָּה.

רְצֵה יְיָ אֱלֹהֵינוּ בְּעַמְּךָ יִשְׂרָאֵל וּבִתְפִלָּתָם וְהָשֵׁב אֶת־הָעֲבוֹדָה לִדְבִיר בֵּיתֶךָ וּתְפִלָּתָם בְּאַהֲבָה תְקַבֵּל בְּרָצוֹן וּתְהִי לְרָצוֹן תָּמִיד עֲבוֹדַת יִשְׂרָאֵל עַמֶּךָ.

On Rosh Ḥodesh:

אֱלֹהֵינוּ וֵאלֹהֵי אֲבוֹתֵינוּ, יַעֲלֶה וְיָבוֹא וְיַגִּיעַ וְיֵרָאֶה וְיֵרָצֶה וְיִשָּׁמַע וְיִפָּקֵד וְיִזָּכֵר זִכְרוֹנֵנוּ וּפִקְדוֹנֵנוּ, וְזִכְרוֹן אֲבוֹתֵינוּ וְזִכְרוֹן מָשִׁיחַ בֶּן־דָּוִד עַבְדֶּךָ וְזִכְרוֹן יְרוּשָׁלַיִם עִיר קָדְשֶׁךָ, וְזִכְרוֹן כָּל־עַמְּךָ בֵּית יִשְׂרָאֵל לְפָנֶיךָ, לִפְלֵיטָה וּלְטוֹבָה וּלְחֵן וּלְחֶסֶד וּלְרַחֲמִים וּלְחַיִּים וּלְשָׁלוֹם בְּיוֹם רֹאשׁ הַחֹדֶשׁ הַזֶּה. זָכְרֵנוּ יְיָ אֱלֹהֵינוּ בּוֹ לְטוֹבָה, וּפָקְדֵנוּ בּוֹ לִבְרָכָה, וְהוֹשִׁיעֵנוּ בּוֹ לְחַיִּים. וּבִדְבַר יְשׁוּעָה וְרַחֲמִים חוּס וְחָנֵּנוּ וְרַחֵם עָלֵינוּ וְהוֹשִׁיעֵנוּ כִּי אֵלֶיךָ עֵינֵינוּ, כִּי אֵל מֶלֶךְ חַנּוּן וְרַחוּם אָתָּה.

Evening service

174

despair, for our trust is in You. Praised are You, Lord who sustains the righteous.

Have mercy, Lord, and return to Jerusalem, Your city. May Your Presence dwell there as You promised. Rebuild it now, in our days and for all time. Re-establish there the majesty of David, Your servant. Praised are You, Lord who rebuilds Jerusalem.

Bring to flower the shoot of Your servant David. Hasten the advent of Messianic redemption. Each and every day we hope for Your deliverance. Praised are You, Lord who assures our deliverance.

Lord our God, hear our voice. Have compassion upon us, pity us, accept our prayer with loving favor. You listen to entreaty and prayer. Do not turn us away unanswered, our King, for You mercifully heed Your people's supplication. Praised are You, Lord who hears prayer.

Accept the prayer of Your people Israel as lovingly as it is offered. Restore worship to Your sanctuary. May the worship of Your people Israel always be acceptable to You.

On Rosh Ḥodesh:

Our God and God of our fathers, on this Rosh Ḥodesh remember our fathers and be gracious to us. Consider the people standing before You praying for the days of Messiah and for Jerusalem Your holy city. Grant us life, well-being, lovingkindness and peace. Bless us, Lord our God, with all that is good. Remember Your promise of mercy and redemption. Be merciful to us and save us, for we place our hope in You, gracious and merciful God and King.

Evening service

וְתֶחֱזֶינָה עֵינֵינוּ בְּשׁוּבְךָ לְצִיּוֹן בְּרַחֲמִים. בָּרוּךְ אַתָּה יְיָ הַמַּחֲזִיר שְׁכִינָתוֹ לְצִיּוֹן.

מוֹדִים אֲנַחְנוּ לָךְ שָׁאַתָּה הוּא יְיָ אֱלֹהֵינוּ וֵאלֹהֵי אֲבוֹתֵינוּ לְעוֹלָם וָעֶד, צוּר חַיֵּינוּ מָגֵן יִשְׁעֵנוּ אַתָּה הוּא. לְדוֹר וָדוֹר נוֹדֶה לְךָ וּנְסַפֵּר תְּהִלָּתֶךָ עַל חַיֵּינוּ הַמְּסוּרִים בְּיָדֶךָ וְעַל נִשְׁמוֹתֵינוּ הַפְּקוּדוֹת לָךְ וְעַל נִסֶּיךָ שֶׁבְּכָל־יוֹם עִמָּנוּ וְעַל נִפְלְאוֹתֶיךָ וְטוֹבוֹתֶיךָ שֶׁבְּכָל־עֵת עֶרֶב וָבֹקֶר וְצָהֳרָיִם. הַטּוֹב כִּי לֹא כָלוּ רַחֲמֶיךָ וְהַמְרַחֵם כִּי לֹא תַמּוּ חֲסָדֶיךָ מֵעוֹלָם קִוִּינוּ לָךְ.

On Ḥanukkah turn to page 204.
On Purim turn to page 206.
On Israel's Independence Day, turn to page 208.

וְעַל כֻּלָּם יִתְבָּרַךְ וְיִתְרוֹמַם שִׁמְךָ מַלְכֵּנוּ תָּמִיד לְעוֹלָם וָעֶד.

From Rosh Hashanah through Yom Kippur:

וּכְתֹב לְחַיִּים טוֹבִים כָּל־בְּנֵי בְרִיתֶךָ.

וְכֹל הַחַיִּים יוֹדוּךָ סֶּלָה וִיהַלְלוּ אֶת־שִׁמְךָ בֶּאֱמֶת הָאֵל יְשׁוּעָתֵנוּ וְעֶזְרָתֵנוּ סֶלָה. בָּרוּךְ אַתָּה יְיָ הַטּוֹב שִׁמְךָ וּלְךָ נָאֶה לְהוֹדוֹת.

שָׁלוֹם רָב עַל יִשְׂרָאֵל עַמְּךָ וְעַל כָּל־יוֹשְׁבֵי תֵבֵל תָּשִׂים לְעוֹלָם כִּי אַתָּה הוּא מֶלֶךְ אָדוֹן לְכָל־הַשָּׁלוֹם. וְטוֹב בְּעֵינֶיךָ לְבָרֵךְ אֶת־עַמְּךָ יִשְׂרָאֵל בְּכָל־עֵת וּבְכָל־שָׁעָה בִּשְׁלוֹמֶךָ.

May we bear witness to Your merciful return to Zion. Praised are You, Lord who restores His Presence to Zion.

We proclaim that You are the Lord our God and God of our fathers throughout all time. You are the Rock of our lives, the Shield of our salvation. We thank You and praise You through all generations, for our lives are in Your hand, our souls are in Your charge. We thank You for Your miracles which daily attend us, for Your wondrous kindness, morning, noon and night. Your mercy and love are boundless. We have always placed our hope in You.

> On Ḥanukkah, turn to page 205.
> On Purim, turn to page 207.
> On Israel's Independence Day, turn to page 209.

For all these blessings we shall ever praise and exalt You.

> From Rosh Hashanah through Yom Kippur:

> Inscribe all the people of Your covenant for a good life.

May every living creature thank You and praise You faithfully, our deliverance and our help. Praised are You, beneficent Lord to whom all praise is due.

Grant true and lasting peace to Your people Israel and to all who dwell on earth, for You are the King of supreme peace. May it please You to bless Your people Israel at all times with Your gift of peace.

בְּסֵפֶר חַיִּים בְּרָכָה וְשָׁלוֹם וּפַרְנָסָה טוֹבָה נִזָּכֵר וְנִכָּתֵב לְפָנֶיךָ אֲנַחְנוּ וְכָל־עַמְּךָ
בֵּית יִשְׂרָאֵל לְחַיִּים טוֹבִים וּלְשָׁלוֹם. בָּרוּךְ אַתָּה יְיָ עוֹשֵׂה הַשָּׁלוֹם.

בָּרוּךְ אַתָּה יְיָ הַמְבָרֵךְ אֶת־עַמּוֹ יִשְׂרָאֵל בַּשָּׁלוֹם.

At the conclusion of the Amidah, personal
prayers may be added, before or instead
of the following.

אֱלֹהַי, נְצֹר לְשׁוֹנִי מֵרָע וּשְׂפָתַי מִדַּבֵּר מִרְמָה, וְלִמְקַלְלַי נַפְשִׁי תִדֹּם
וְנַפְשִׁי כֶּעָפָר לַכֹּל תִּהְיֶה. פְּתַח לִבִּי בְּתוֹרָתֶךָ וּבְמִצְוֹתֶיךָ תִּרְדֹּף
נַפְשִׁי. וְכָל הַחוֹשְׁבִים עָלַי רָעָה, מְהֵרָה הָפֵר עֲצָתָם וְקַלְקֵל
מַחֲשַׁבְתָּם. עֲשֵׂה לְמַעַן שְׁמֶךָ, עֲשֵׂה לְמַעַן יְמִינֶךָ, עֲשֵׂה לְמַעַן
קְדֻשָּׁתֶךָ, עֲשֵׂה לְמַעַן תּוֹרָתֶךָ, לְמַעַן יֵחָלְצוּן יְדִידֶיךָ הוֹשִׁיעָה יְמִינְךָ
וַעֲנֵנִי. יִהְיוּ לְרָצוֹן אִמְרֵי־פִי וְהֶגְיוֹן לִבִּי לְפָנֶיךָ, יְיָ צוּרִי וְגֹאֲלִי.
עוֹשֵׂה שָׁלוֹם בִּמְרוֹמָיו הוּא יַעֲשֶׂה שָׁלוֹם עָלֵינוּ וְעַל כָּל־יִשְׂרָאֵל,
וְאִמְרוּ אָמֵן.

An alternate closing prayer:

יְהִי רָצוֹן מִלְּפָנֶיךָ, יְיָ אֱלֹהֵינוּ, שֶׁתַּשְׁכֵּן בְּפוּרֵנוּ אַהֲבָה וְאַחֲוָה וְשָׁלוֹם
וְרֵיעוּת, וְתַרְבֶּה גְבוּלֵנוּ בְּתַלְמִידִים, וְתַצְלִיחַ סוֹפֵנוּ אַחֲרִית וְתִקְוָה,
וְתָשִׂים חֶלְקֵנוּ בְּגַן עֵדֶן, וְתַקְנֵנוּ בְּחָבֵר טוֹב וְיֵצֶר טוֹב בְּעוֹלָמְךָ,
וְנַשְׁכִּים וְנִמְצָא יְחוּל לְבָבֵנוּ לְיִרְאָה אֶת־שְׁמֶךָ, וְתָבוֹא לְפָנֶיךָ קוֹרַת
נַפְשֵׁנוּ לְטוֹבָה. יִהְיוּ לְרָצוֹן אִמְרֵי־פִי וְהֶגְיוֹן לִבִּי לְפָנֶיךָ, יְיָ צוּרִי
וְגֹאֲלִי.

Evening service

From Rosh Hashanah through Yom Kippur:

May we and the entire House of Israel be remembered and recorded in the Book of life, blessing, sustenance and peace. Praised are You, Lord, Source of peace.

Praised are You, Lord who blesses His people Israel with peace.

At the conclusion of the Amidah, personal prayers may be added, before or instead of the following.

My God, keep my tongue from telling evil, my lips from speaking lies. Help me ignore those who slander me. Let me be humble before all. Open my heart to Your Torah, so that I may pursue Your commandments. Frustrate the designs of those who plot evil against me. Make nothing of their schemes. Do so for the sake of Your power, Your holiness and Your Torah. Answer my prayer for the deliverance of Your people. May the words of my mouth and the meditations of my heart be acceptable to You, my Rock and my Redeemer. He who brings peace to His universe will bring peace to us, to the people Israel and to all mankind. Amen.

An alternate closing prayer:

May it be Your will, Lord our God, to cause love and friendship, peace and companionship to abide among us. Expand our influence with disciples, and prosper our latter end with good prospects and with hope. Set our portion in paradise, and help us to obtain a good companion and a good impulse in Your world. Thus we may rise early each morning with the yearning to revere Your name. And may You be pleased to grant us contentment. May the words of my mouth and the meditations of my heart be acceptable to You, Lord, my Rock and my Redeemer. Amen.

Evening service

Kaddish Shalem

Reader:

יִתְגַּדַּל וְיִתְקַדַּשׁ שְׁמֵהּ רַבָּא בְּעָלְמָא דִּי בְרָא כִרְעוּתֵהּ, וְיַמְלִיךְ מַלְכוּתֵהּ בְּחַיֵּיכוֹן וּבְיוֹמֵיכוֹן וּבְחַיֵּי דְכָל־בֵּית יִשְׂרָאֵל בַּעֲגָלָא וּבִזְמַן קָרִיב, וְאִמְרוּ אָמֵן.

Congregation and Reader:

יְהֵא שְׁמֵהּ רַבָּא מְבָרַךְ לְעָלַם וּלְעָלְמֵי עָלְמַיָּא.

Reader:

יִתְבָּרַךְ וְיִשְׁתַּבַּח וְיִתְפָּאַר וְיִתְרוֹמַם וְיִתְנַשֵּׂא וְיִתְהַדָּר וְיִתְעַלֶּה וְיִתְהַלָּל שְׁמֵהּ דְּקֻדְשָׁא בְּרִיךְ הוּא, לְעֵלָּא (לְעֵלָּא) מִן כָּל־ בִּרְכָתָא וְשִׁירָתָא תֻּשְׁבְּחָתָא וְנֶחֱמָתָא דַּאֲמִירָן בְּעָלְמָא, וְאִמְרוּ אָמֵן.

Omit these two lines in a House of Mourning:

תִּתְקַבֵּל צְלוֹתְהוֹן וּבָעוּתְהוֹן דְּכָל־יִשְׂרָאֵל קֳדָם אֲבוּהוֹן דִּי בִשְׁמַיָּא, וְאִמְרוּ אָמֵן.

יְהֵא שְׁלָמָא רַבָּא מִן־שְׁמַיָּא וְחַיִּים עָלֵינוּ וְעַל כָּל־יִשְׂרָאֵל, וְאִמְרוּ אָמֵן.

עֹשֶׂה שָׁלוֹם בִּמְרוֹמָיו הוּא יַעֲשֶׂה שָׁלוֹם עָלֵינוּ וְעַל כָּל־יִשְׂרָאֵל, וְאִמְרוּ אָמֵן.

From the eve of the second day of Pesaḥ until Shavuot eve, the Omer is counted. We rise and turn to page 214.

For Havdalah, we turn to page 218.

On Ḥanukkah, we turn to page 220.

Evening service

Kaddish Shalem

Reader:

Hallowed and enhanced may He be throughout the world of His own creation. May He cause His sovereignty soon to be accepted, during our life and the life of all Israel. And let us say: Amen.

Congregation and Reader:

Ye-hei shmei raba meva-rakh l'alam ul'almei 'almaya.

May He be praised throughout all time.

Reader:

Glorified and celebrated, lauded and praised, acclaimed and honored, extolled and exalted may the Holy One be, beyond all song and psalm, beyond all tributes which man can utter. And let us say: Amen.

Omit these two lines in a House of Mourning:

May the prayers and pleas of the whole House of Israel be accepted by our Father in Heaven. And let us say: Amen.

Let there be abundant peace from Heaven, with life's goodness for us and for all the people Israel. And let us say: Amen.

He who brings peace to His universe will bring peace to us and to all the people Israel. And let us say: Amen.

From the eve of the second day of Pesah until Shavuot eve, the Omer is counted. We rise and turn to page 214.

For Havdalah, we turn to page 219.

On Hanukkah, we turn to page 221.

Evening service

181

Aleinu

עָלֵֽינוּ לְשַׁבֵּֽחַ לַאֲדוֹן הַכֹּל, לָתֵת גְּדֻלָּה לְיוֹצֵר בְּרֵאשִׁית, שֶׁלֹּא עָשָֽׂנוּ כְּגוֹיֵי הָאֲרָצוֹת וְלֹא שָׂמָֽנוּ כְּמִשְׁפְּחוֹת הָאֲדָמָה, שֶׁלֹּא שָׂם חֶלְקֵֽנוּ כָּהֶם וְגוֹרָלֵֽנוּ כְּכָל־הֲמוֹנָם. וַאֲנַֽחְנוּ כּוֹרְעִים וּמִשְׁתַּחֲוִים וּמוֹדִים לִפְנֵי מֶֽלֶךְ מַלְכֵי הַמְּלָכִים הַקָּדוֹשׁ בָּרוּךְ הוּא, שֶׁהוּא נוֹטֶה שָׁמַֽיִם וְיוֹסֵד אָֽרֶץ וּמוֹשַׁב יְקָרוֹ בַּשָּׁמַֽיִם מִמַּֽעַל וּשְׁכִינַת עֻזּוֹ בְּגָבְהֵי מְרוֹמִים. הוּא אֱלֹהֵֽינוּ אֵין עוֹד. אֱמֶת מַלְכֵּֽנוּ אֶֽפֶס זוּלָתוֹ, כַּכָּתוּב בְּתוֹרָתוֹ: וְיָדַעְתָּ הַיּוֹם וַהֲשֵׁבֹתָ אֶל לְבָבֶֽךָ כִּי יְיָ הוּא הָאֱלֹהִים בַּשָּׁמַֽיִם מִמַּֽעַל וְעַל הָאָֽרֶץ מִתָּֽחַת, אֵין עוֹד.

עַל כֵּן נְקַוֶּה לְךָ יְיָ אֱלֹהֵֽינוּ לִרְאוֹת מְהֵרָה בְּתִפְאֶֽרֶת עֻזֶּֽךָ, לְהַעֲבִיר גִּלּוּלִים מִן הָאָֽרֶץ וְהָאֱלִילִים כָּרוֹת יִכָּרֵתוּן, לְתַקֵּן עוֹלָם בְּמַלְכוּת שַׁדַּי וְכָל־בְּנֵי בָשָׂר יִקְרְאוּ בִשְׁמֶֽךָ, לְהַפְנוֹת אֵלֶֽיךָ כָּל־רִשְׁעֵי־אָֽרֶץ. יַכִּֽירוּ וְיֵדְעוּ כָּל־יוֹשְׁבֵי תֵבֵל כִּי לְךָ תִּכְרַע כָּל־בֶּֽרֶךְ תִּשָּׁבַע כָּל־לָשׁוֹן. לְפָנֶֽיךָ יְיָ אֱלֹהֵֽינוּ יִכְרְעוּ וְיִפֹּֽלוּ וְלִכְבוֹד שִׁמְךָ יְקָר יִתֵּֽנוּ, וִיקַבְּלוּ כֻלָּם אֶת־עֹל מַלְכוּתֶֽךָ וְתִמְלֹךְ עֲלֵיהֶם מְהֵרָה לְעוֹלָם וָעֶד, כִּי הַמַּלְכוּת שֶׁלְּךָ הִיא וּלְעוֹלְמֵי עַד תִּמְלֹךְ בְּכָבוֹד, כַּכָּתוּב בְּתוֹרָתֶֽךָ: יְיָ יִמְלֹךְ לְעֹלָם וָעֶד.\וְנֶאֱמַר: וְהָיָה יְיָ לְמֶֽלֶךְ עַל כָּל־הָאָֽרֶץ, בַּיּוֹם הַהוּא יִהְיֶה יְיָ אֶחָד וּשְׁמוֹ אֶחָד.

Aleinu

We rise to our duty to praise the Lord of all the world, to acclaim the Creator. He made our lot unlike that of other people, assigning us a unique destiny. We bend the knee and bow, proclaiming Him as King of kings, the Holy One praised be He, who stretched forth the heavens and established the earth. He is God, our King. There is no other.

Va'anaḥnu kor'im u-mish-taḥavim u-modim
lifnei melekh malkhei ha-melakhim ha-kadosh barukh hu.

And so we hope in You, Lord our God, soon to see Your splendor, sweeping idolatry away so that false gods will be utterly destroyed, perfecting earth by Your kingship so that all mankind will invoke Your name, bringing all the earth's wicked back to You, repentant. Then all who live will know that to You every knee must bend, every tongue pledge loyalty. To You, Lord, may all men bow in worship, may they give honor to Your glory. May everyone accept the rule of Your kingship. Reign over all, soon and for all time. Sovereignty is Yours in glory, now and forever. Thus is it written in Your Torah: The Lord reigns for ever and ever. Such is the assurance of Your prophet Zechariah: The Lord shall be acknowledged King of all the earth. On that day the Lord shall be One and His name One.

Ve-ne'emar ve-haya Adonai le-melekh 'al kol ha-aretz, bayom
ha-hu yiyeh Adonai eḥad u-she-mo eḥad.

Evening service

Mourner's Kaddish

Mourners and those observing Yahrzeit rise:

יִתְגַּדַּל וְיִתְקַדַּשׁ שְׁמֵהּ רַבָּא בְּעָלְמָא דִּי בְרָא כִרְעוּתֵהּ, וְיַמְלִיךְ
מַלְכוּתֵהּ בְּחַיֵּיכוֹן וּבְיוֹמֵיכוֹן וּבְחַיֵּי דְכָל־בֵּית יִשְׂרָאֵל בַּעֲגָלָא
וּבִזְמַן קָרִיב, וְאִמְרוּ אָמֵן.

Congregation and Mourner:

יְהֵא שְׁמֵהּ רַבָּא מְבָרַךְ לְעָלַם וּלְעָלְמֵי עָלְמַיָּא.

Mourner:

יִתְבָּרַךְ וְיִשְׁתַּבַּח וְיִתְפָּאַר וְיִתְרוֹמַם וְיִתְנַשֵּׂא וְיִתְהַדָּר וְיִתְעַלֶּה
וְיִתְהַלָּל שְׁמֵהּ דְּקֻדְשָׁא בְּרִיךְ הוּא, לְעֵלָּא (לְעֵלָּא) מִן כָּל־
בִּרְכָתָא וְשִׁירָתָא תֻּשְׁבְּחָתָא וְנֶחֱמָתָא דַּאֲמִירָן בְּעָלְמָא, וְאִמְרוּ אָמֵן.

יְהֵא שְׁלָמָא רַבָּא מִן שְׁמַיָּא וְחַיִּים עָלֵינוּ וְעַל כָּל־יִשְׂרָאֵל,
וְאִמְרוּ אָמֵן.

עוֹשֶׂה שָׁלוֹם בִּמְרוֹמָיו הוּא יַעֲשֶׂה שָׁלוֹם עָלֵינוּ וְעַל כָּל־יִשְׂרָאֵל,
וְאִמְרוּ אָמֵן.

Mourner's Kaddish

Our Creator, the King of kings, delights in life. Because of His love for us and because we are so few, each of us is important in His kingdom. Though we are flesh and blood, we are irreplaceable. When one of the House of Israel dies, there is a loss of glory in His kingdom, and His grandeur is diminished. Therefore, brethren of the House of Israel, all of you who mourn and all of you who remember on this day, let us fix our hearts on our Father in Heaven, our King and our Redeemer, and let us pray for ourselves, and for Him too, that He and His kingdom be hallowed and enhanced, glorified and celebrated.

Mourners and those observing Yahrzeit rise.

Yit-gadal ve-yit-kadush shmei raba, b'alma divra khir'utei ve-yamlikh mal-khutei be-hayei-khon uve'yomei-khon uve-hayei di-khol beit yisrael ba-agala u-vizman kariv v'imru amen.

Congregation and Mourner:

Ye-hei shmei raba meva-rakh l'alam ul'almei 'almaya.

Mourner:

Yit-barakh ve-yish-tabah ve-vitpa'ar ve-yitromam ve-yitnasei ve-yit-hadar ve-yit'aleh ve-yit-halal shmei di-kudsha brikh hu, l'eila [l'eila] min kol bir-khata ve-shirata tush-be-hata ve-nehe-mata da-amiran b'alma, v'imru amen.

Ye-hei shlama raba min shmaya ve-hayim aleinu v'al kol yisrael v'imru amen.

Oseh shalom bimromav hu ya'aseh shalom aleinu v'al kol yisrael v'imru amen.

For translation, see the following page.

Evening service

185

Mourner's Kaddish

Mourners and those observing Yahrzeit rise.

Hallowed and enhanced may He be throughout the world of His own creation. May He cause His sovereignty soon to be accepted, during our life and the life of all Israel. And let us say: Amen.

Congregation and mourner:

May He be praised throughout all time.

Mourner:

Glorified and celebrated, lauded and praised, acclaimed and honored, extolled and exalted may the Holy One be, far beyond all song and psalm, beyond all tributes which man can utter. And let us say: Amen.

Let there be abundant peace from Heaven, with life's goodness for us and for all the people Israel. And let us say: Amen.

He who brings peace to His universe will bring peace to us and to all the people Israel. And let us say: Amen.

יְיָ רֹעִי לֹא אֶחְסָר. בִּנְאוֹת דֶּשֶׁא יַרְבִּיצֵנִי, עַל מֵי מְנֻחוֹת יְנַהֲלֵנִי. נַפְשִׁי
יְשׁוֹבֵב, יַנְחֵנִי בְמַעְגְּלֵי־צֶדֶק לְמַעַן שְׁמוֹ. גַּם כִּי אֵלֵךְ בְּגֵיא צַלְמָוֶת
לֹא אִירָא רָע כִּי אַתָּה עִמָּדִי, שִׁבְטְךָ וּמִשְׁעַנְתֶּךָ הֵמָּה יְנַחֲמֻנִי. תַּעֲרֹךְ
לְפָנַי שֻׁלְחָן נֶגֶד צֹרְרָי, דִּשַּׁנְתָּ בַשֶּׁמֶן רֹאשִׁי, כּוֹסִי רְוָיָה. אַךְ טוֹב
וָחֶסֶד יִרְדְּפוּנִי כָּל־יְמֵי חַיָּי, וְשַׁבְתִּי בְּבֵית יְיָ לְאֹרֶךְ יָמִים.

The Lord is my Shepherd, I shall not want.

He gives me repose in green meadows.

He leads me beside the still waters; He revives my spirit.

He guides me on the right path, for that is His nature.

Though I walk through the valley of the shadow of death,
I fear no harm, for You are with me.

Your staff and Your rod comfort me.

You prepare a banquet for me in the presence of my foes.

You anoint my head with oil; my cup overflows.

Surely goodness and kindness shall be my portion
all the days of my life.

And I shall dwell in the house of the Lord forever.

Evening service

We live in the light of God's compassion.

לְדָוִד. יְיָ אוֹרִי וְיִשְׁעִי מִמִּי אִירָא, יְיָ מָעוֹז חַיַּי מִמִּי אֶפְחָד.
בִּקְרֹב עָלַי מְרֵעִים לֶאֱכֹל אֶת־בְּשָׂרִי, צָרַי וְאֹיְבַי לִי הֵמָּה כָשְׁלוּ
וְנָפָלוּ. אִם תַּחֲנֶה עָלַי מַחֲנֶה לֹא יִירָא לִבִּי, אִם תָּקוּם עָלַי
מִלְחָמָה בְּזֹאת אֲנִי בוֹטֵחַ. אַחַת שָׁאַלְתִּי מֵאֵת יְיָ אוֹתָהּ אֲבַקֵּשׁ,
שִׁבְתִּי בְּבֵית יְיָ כָּל־יְמֵי חַיַּי, לַחֲזוֹת בְּנֹעַם יְיָ וּלְבַקֵּר בְּהֵיכָלוֹ.
כִּי יִצְפְּנֵנִי בְּסֻכֹּה בְּיוֹם רָעָה, יַסְתִּרֵנִי בְּסֵתֶר אָהֳלוֹ בְּצוּר יְרוֹמְמֵנִי.
וְעַתָּה יָרוּם רֹאשִׁי עַל אֹיְבַי סְבִיבוֹתַי, וְאֶזְבְּחָה בְאָהֳלוֹ זִבְחֵי
תְרוּעָה, אָשִׁירָה וַאֲזַמְּרָה לַיָיָ. שְׁמַע יְיָ קוֹלִי אֶקְרָא, וְחָנֵּנִי וַעֲנֵנִי.
לְךָ אָמַר לִבִּי בַּקְּשׁוּ פָנָי, אֶת־פָּנֶיךָ יְיָ אֲבַקֵּשׁ. אַל תַּסְתֵּר פָּנֶיךָ
מִמֶּנִּי אַל תַּט בְּאַף עַבְדֶּךָ, עֶזְרָתִי הָיִיתָ, אַל תִּטְּשֵׁנִי וְאַל תַּעַזְבֵנִי
אֱלֹהֵי יִשְׁעִי. כִּי אָבִי וְאִמִּי עֲזָבוּנִי, וַיְיָ יַאַסְפֵנִי. הוֹרֵנִי יְיָ דַּרְכֶּךָ
וּנְחֵנִי בְּאֹרַח מִישׁוֹר לְמַעַן שׁוֹרְרָי. אַל תִּתְּנֵנִי בְּנֶפֶשׁ צָרָי, כִּי קָמוּ
בִי עֵדֵי שֶׁקֶר וִיפֵחַ חָמָס.\לוּלֵא הֶאֱמַנְתִּי לִרְאוֹת בְּטוּב יְיָ בְּאֶרֶץ
חַיִּים. קַוֵּה אֶל יְיָ, חֲזַק וְיַאֲמֵץ לִבֶּךָ וְקַוֵּה אֶל יְיָ.

We live in the light of God's compassion.

A Psalm of David. The Lord is my light and my help. Whom shall I fear? The Lord is the strength of my life. Whom shall I dread? When evildoers draw near to devour me, when foes threaten, they stumble and fall. Though armies be arrayed against me, I have no fear. Though wars threaten, I remain steadfast in my faith.

One thing I ask of the Lord, for this I yearn: To dwell in the House of the Lord all the days of my life, to pray in His sanctuary, to behold the Lord's beauty. He will hide me in His shrine, safe from peril. He will shelter me, and put me beyond the reach of disaster. He will raise my head high above my enemies about me. I will bring Him offerings with shouts of joy. I will sing, I will chant praise to the Lord.

O Lord, hear my voice when I call; be gracious, and answer me. "It is You that I seek," says my heart. It is Your Presence that I crave, O Lord. Hide not Your Presence from me, reject not Your servant. You are my help, do not desert me. Forsake me not, God of my deliverance. Though my father and mother forsake me, the Lord will gather me in, and care for me. Teach me Your way, O Lord. Guide me on the right path, to confound those who mock me. Deceivers have risen against me, men who breathe out violence. Abandon me not to the will of my foes. Mine is the faith that I surely will see the Lord's goodness in the land of the living. Hope in the Lord and be strong. Hope in the Lord and take courage.

Psalm 27

Evening service

Aware of our mortality, we must embrace enduring values.

לַמְנַצֵּחַ לִבְנֵי־קֹרַח מִזְמוֹר. שִׁמְעוּ־זֹאת כָּל־הָעַמִּים, הַאֲזִינוּ כָּל־
יֹשְׁבֵי חָלֶד. גַּם בְּנֵי אָדָם גַּם בְּנֵי־אִישׁ, יַחַד עָשִׁיר וְאֶבְיוֹן. פִּי
יְדַבֵּר חָכְמוֹת, וְהָגוּת לִבִּי תְבוּנוֹת. אַטֶּה לְמָשָׁל אָזְנִי, אֶפְתַּח
בְּכִנּוֹר חִידָתִי. לָמָּה אִירָא בִּימֵי רָע, עֲוֹן עֲקֵבַי יְסוּבֵּנִי. הַבֹּטְחִים
עַל חֵילָם, וּבְרֹב עָשְׁרָם יִתְהַלָּלוּ. אָח לֹא פָדֹה יִפְדֶּה אִישׁ, לֹא
יִתֵּן לֵאלֹהִים כָּפְרוֹ. וְיֵקַר פִּדְיוֹן נַפְשָׁם, וְחָדַל לְעוֹלָם. וִיחִי־
עוֹד לָנֶצַח, לֹא יִרְאֶה הַשָּׁחַת. כִּי יִרְאֶה חֲכָמִים יָמוּתוּ, יַחַד
כְּסִיל וָבַעַר יֹאבֵדוּ, וְעָזְבוּ לַאֲחֵרִים חֵילָם. קִרְבָּם בָּתֵּימוֹ לְעוֹלָם,
מִשְׁכְּנֹתָם לְדוֹר וָדֹר, קָרְאוּ בִשְׁמוֹתָם עֲלֵי אֲדָמוֹת. וְאָדָם בִּיקָר
בַּל יָלִין, נִמְשַׁל כַּבְּהֵמוֹת נִדְמוּ. זֶה דַרְכָּם כֵּסֶל לָמוֹ, וְאַחֲרֵיהֶם
בְּפִיהֶם יִרְצוּ, סֶלָה. כַּצֹּאן לִשְׁאוֹל שַׁתּוּ מָוֶת יִרְעֵם וַיִּרְדּוּ־בָם
יְשָׁרִים לַבֹּקֶר וְצוּרָם לְבַלּוֹת שְׁאוֹל מִזְּבֻל לוֹ. אַךְ אֱלֹהִים
יִפְדֶּה נַפְשִׁי מִיַּד שְׁאוֹל, כִּי יִקָּחֵנִי, סֶלָה. אַל תִּירָא כִּי יַעֲשִׁר
אִישׁ, כִּי יִרְבֶּה כְּבוֹד בֵּיתוֹ. כִּי לֹא בְמוֹתוֹ יִקַּח הַכֹּל, לֹא יֵרֵד
אַחֲרָיו כְּבוֹדוֹ.\כִּי נַפְשׁוֹ בְּחַיָּיו יְבָרֵךְ, וְיוֹדֻךָ כִּי תֵיטִיב לָךְ.
תָּבוֹא עַד דּוֹר אֲבוֹתָיו, עַד נֵצַח לֹא יִרְאוּ־אוֹר. אָדָם בִּיקָר וְלֹא
יָבִין, נִמְשַׁל כַּבְּהֵמוֹת נִדְמוּ.

For an alternative psalm, turn to page 120.

Evening service

190

Aware of our mortality, we must embrace enduring values.

Hear this, all you nations; listen well, all who dwell on earth, the mighty as well as the lowly, the rich as well as the poor. My mouth will utter wisdom, the probings of a discerning heart. I will turn my attention now to teaching, present my lesson to the music of a harp.

Why should I be afraid in days of evil, even when surrounded by treacherous foes, men who put their trust in riches, who glory in their great wealth? Man cannot save a brother from death; there is no bribing God to recall His decree. The most costly ransom cannot save a life. There is no way to evade death forever.

Shall man live eternally? Shall he never see the grave? Wise men too must die, even as the foolish and the senseless, leaving their possessions to others. Their home eternal is the grave, though they were famous on the earth. For all the glory that they cherish, men die, even as the beasts that perish. Such is the fate of the foolishly self-satisfied, those who delight in their own speech. Like sheep are they marked for death, like sheep are they herded to their graves. Straight down into their tombs they go, where they remain to waste away. But God will ransom me from death; when He takes me, He will save my soul.

Envy not a man his riches, nor be jealous of his growing possessions. For in death he will take nothing with him, his wealth will not follow him to the grave. He may flatter himself in his lifetime because men praise him for his good fortune. Yet he must join his ancestors who will never again see the light of day. For all the glory that they cherish, men die, even as the beasts that perish.

Evening service   *Psalm 49*

Rosh Ḥodesh Musaf

*The first of each Hebrew month is Rosh Ḥodesh.
Since an additional sacrifice was offered at the ancient Temple in observance of this day, we offer an
additional prayer (Musaf), the Amidah on the following pages.*

Ḥatzi Kaddish

Reader:

יִתְגַּדַּל וְיִתְקַדַּשׁ שְׁמֵהּ רַבָּא בְּעָלְמָא דִּי בְרָא כִרְעוּתֵהּ, וְיַמְלִיךְ
מַלְכוּתֵהּ בְּחַיֵּיכוֹן וּבְיוֹמֵיכוֹן וּבְחַיֵּי דְכָל־בֵּית יִשְׂרָאֵל בַּעֲגָלָא
וּבִזְמַן קָרִיב, וְאִמְרוּ אָמֵן.

Congregation and Reader:

יְהֵא שְׁמֵהּ רַבָּא מְבָרַךְ לְעָלַם וּלְעָלְמֵי עָלְמַיָּא.

Reader:

יִתְבָּרַךְ וְיִשְׁתַּבַּח וְיִתְפָּאַר וְיִתְרוֹמַם וְיִתְנַשֵּׂא וְיִתְהַדָּר וְיִתְעַלֶּה
וְיִתְהַלָּל שְׁמֵהּ דְּקֻדְשָׁא בְּרִיךְ הוּא, לְעֵלָּא (לְעֵלָּא) מִן כָּל־
בִּרְכָתָא וְשִׁירָתָא תֻּשְׁבְּחָתָא וְנֶחֱמָתָא דַּאֲמִירָן בְּעָלְמָא, וְאִמְרוּ אָמֵן.

Rosh Ḥodesh Amidah

We stand in silent prayer, which ends on page 202.

כִּי שֵׁם יְיָ אֶקְרָא הָבוּ גֹדֶל לֵאלֹהֵינוּ.
אֲדֹנָי שְׂפָתַי תִּפְתָּח וּפִי יַגִּיד תְּהִלָּתֶךָ.

בָּרוּךְ אַתָּה יְיָ אֱלֹהֵינוּ וֵאלֹהֵי אֲבוֹתֵינוּ, אֱלֹהֵי אַבְרָהָם אֱלֹהֵי יִצְחָק
וֵאלֹהֵי יַעֲקֹב, הָאֵל הַגָּדוֹל הַגִּבּוֹר וְהַנּוֹרָא אֵל עֶלְיוֹן גּוֹמֵל חֲסָדִים
טוֹבִים וְקוֹנֵה הַכֹּל, וְזוֹכֵר חַסְדֵי אָבוֹת וּמֵבִיא גוֹאֵל לִבְנֵי בְנֵיהֶם
לְמַעַן שְׁמוֹ בְּאַהֲבָה.

מֶלֶךְ עוֹזֵר וּמוֹשִׁיעַ וּמָגֵן. בָּרוּךְ אַתָּה יְיָ מָגֵן אַבְרָהָם.

אַתָּה גִּבּוֹר לְעוֹלָם אֲדֹנָי מְחַיֶּה מֵתִים אַתָּה רַב לְהוֹשִׁיעַ.

From Shmini Atzeret to Pesaḥ:

מַשִּׁיב הָרוּחַ וּמוֹרִיד הַגָּשֶׁם.

מְכַלְכֵּל חַיִּים בְּחֶסֶד מְחַיֶּה מֵתִים בְּרַחֲמִים רַבִּים, סוֹמֵךְ נוֹפְלִים
וְרוֹפֵא חוֹלִים וּמַתִּיר אֲסוּרִים וּמְקַיֵּם אֱמוּנָתוֹ לִישֵׁנֵי עָפָר. מִי כָמוֹךָ
בַּעַל גְּבוּרוֹת וּמִי דּוֹמֶה לָּךְ, מֶלֶךְ מֵמִית וּמְחַיֶּה וּמַצְמִיחַ יְשׁוּעָה.

וְנֶאֱמָן אַתָּה לְהַחֲיוֹת מֵתִים. בָּרוּךְ אַתָּה יְיָ מְחַיֶּה הַמֵּתִים.

The Silent Amidah continues on page 198.

Rosh Ḥodesh musaf

Rosh Ḥodesh Amidah

We stand in silent prayer, which ends on page 203.

When I call upon the Lord, give glory to our God. Open my mouth, O Lord, and my lips will proclaim Your praise.

Praised are You, Lord our God and God of our fathers, God of Abraham, of Isaac and of Jacob, great, mighty, awesome, exalted God, bestowing lovingkindness and creating all things. You remember the pious deeds of our fathers, and will send a redeemer to their children's children because of Your love and for the sake of Your glory.

You are the King who helps and saves and shields. Praised are You, Lord, Shield of Abraham.

Your might, O Lord, is boundless. You give life to the dead; great is Your saving power.

From Shmini Atzeret to Pesaḥ:

You cause the wind to blow and the rain to fall.

Your lovingkindness sustains the living, Your great mercies give life to the dead. You support the falling, heal the ailing, free the fettered. You keep Your faith with those who sleep in dust. Whose power can compare with Yours? You are the master of life and death and deliverance.

Faithful are You in giving life to the dead. Praised are You, Lord, Master of life and death.

The Silent Amidah continues on page 199.

Rosh Ḥodesh musaf

Kedushah

When the Reader chants the Amidah aloud,
Kedushah is added. The congregation chants the
indented portions aloud.

נְקַדֵּשׁ אֶת־שִׁמְךָ בָּעוֹלָם כְּשֵׁם שֶׁמַּקְדִּישִׁים אוֹתוֹ בִּשְׁמֵי מָרוֹם כַּכָּתוּב
עַל יַד נְבִיאֶךָ, וְקָרָא זֶה אֶל זֶה וְאָמַר:

קָדוֹשׁ קָדוֹשׁ קָדוֹשׁ יְיָ צְבָאוֹת, מְלֹא כָל־הָאָרֶץ כְּבוֹדוֹ.

לְעֻמָּתָם בָּרוּךְ יֹאמֵרוּ:

בָּרוּךְ כְּבוֹד יְיָ מִמְּקוֹמוֹ.

וּבְדִבְרֵי קָדְשְׁךָ כָּתוּב לֵאמֹר:

יִמְלֹךְ יְיָ לְעוֹלָם אֱלֹהַיִךְ צִיּוֹן לְדֹר וָדֹר, הַלְלוּיָהּ.

לְדוֹר וָדוֹר נַגִּיד גָּדְלֶךָ, וּלְנֵצַח נְצָחִים קְדֻשָּׁתְךָ נַקְדִּישׁ. וְשִׁבְחֲךָ
אֱלֹהֵינוּ מִפִּינוּ לֹא יָמוּשׁ לְעוֹלָם וָעֶד כִּי אֵל מֶלֶךְ גָּדוֹל וְקָדוֹשׁ
אָתָּה. בָּרוּךְ אַתָּה יְיָ הָאֵל הַקָּדוֹשׁ.

Rosh Ḥodesh musaf

Kedushah

When the Reader chants the Amidah aloud,
Kedushah is added. The congregation chants the
indented portions aloud.

We proclaim Your holiness on earth as it is proclaimed in the heavens above. We sing the words of heavenly voices as recorded in Your prophet's vision:

Ka-dosh ka-dosh ka-dosh Ado-nai tz'va-ot, m'lo khol ha-aretz k'vodo.

Holy, holy, holy Lord of hosts. The whole world is filled with His glory.

Heavenly voices respond with praise:

Barukh k'vod Ado-nai mi-m'komo.

Praised is the Lord's glory throughout the universe.

And in Your holy psalms it is written:

Yim-lokh Ado-nai l'olam Elo-ha-yikh tzi-yon ledor va-dor ha-le-lu-yah.

The Lord shall reign through all generations; your God, Zion, shall reign forever. Halleluyah.

We declare Your greatness through all generations, hallow Your holiness to all eternity. Your praise will never leave our lips, for You are God and King, great and holy. Praised are You, Lord and holy God.

Rosh Ḥodesh musaf

197

אַתָּה קָדוֹשׁ וְשִׁמְךָ קָדוֹשׁ וּקְדוֹשִׁים בְּכָל־יוֹם יְהַלְלוּךָ סֶּלָה. בָּרוּךְ אַתָּה יְיָ הָאֵל הַקָּדוֹשׁ.

רָאשֵׁי חֳדָשִׁים לְעַמְּךָ נָתַתָּ, זְמַן כַּפָּרָה לְכָל־תוֹלְדוֹתָם. בִּהְיוֹתָם מַקְרִיבִים לְפָנֶיךָ זִבְחֵי רָצוֹן וּשְׂעִירֵי חַטָּאת לְכַפֵּר בַּעֲדָם, זִכָּרוֹן לְכֻלָּם יִהְיוּ וּתְשׁוּעַת נַפְשָׁם מִיַּד שׂוֹנֵא.

אַהֲבַת עוֹלָם תָּבִיא לָהֶם וּבְרִית אָבוֹת לַבָּנִים תִּזְכֹּר. וַהֲבִיאֵנוּ לְצִיּוֹן עִירְךָ בְּרִנָּה וְלִירוּשָׁלַיִם בֵּית מִקְדָּשְׁךָ בְּשִׂמְחַת עוֹלָם, שֶׁשָּׁם עָשׂוּ אֲבוֹתֵינוּ לְפָנֶיךָ אֶת־קָרְבְּנוֹת חוֹבוֹתֵיהֶם, תְּמִידִים כְּסִדְרָם וּמוּסָפִים כְּהִלְכָתָם, וְאֶת־מוּסַף יוֹם רֹאשׁ הַחֹדֶשׁ הַזֶּה עָשׂוּ וְהִקְרִיבוּ לְפָנֶיךָ בְּאַהֲבָה כְּמִצְוַת רְצוֹנֶךָ כַּכָּתוּב בְּתוֹרָתֶךָ. וְשָׁם אוֹתְךָ בְּיִרְאָה נַעֲבֹד.

אֱלֹהֵינוּ וֵאלֹהֵי אֲבוֹתֵינוּ, רַחֵם עַל אַחֵינוּ בֵּית יִשְׂרָאֵל הַנְּתוּנִים בְּצָרָה וְהוֹצִיאֵם מֵאֲפֵלָה לְאוֹרָה. וְקַבֵּל בְּרַחֲמִים אֶת־תְּפִלַּת עַמְּךָ בְּנֵי יִשְׂרָאֵל, בְּכָל־מְקוֹמוֹת מוֹשְׁבוֹתֵיהֶם, הַשּׁוֹפְכִים אֶת־לִבָּם לְפָנֶיךָ בְּיוֹם רֹאשׁ הַחֹדֶשׁ הַזֶּה.

אֱלֹהֵינוּ וֵאלֹהֵי אֲבוֹתֵינוּ, חַדֵּשׁ עָלֵינוּ אֶת־הַחֹדֶשׁ הַזֶּה לְטוֹבָה וְלִבְרָכָה, לְשָׂשׂוֹן וּלְשִׂמְחָה, לִישׁוּעָה וּלְנֶחָמָה, לְפַרְנָסָה וּלְכַלְכָּלָה, לְחַיִּים וּלְשָׁלוֹם, לִמְחִילַת חֵטְא וְלִסְלִיחַת עָוֹן [וּלְכַפָּרַת פָּשַׁע].

The silent Amidah continues here.

Holy are You and holy is Your name. Holy are those who praise You daily. Praised are You, Lord and holy God.

The beginning of each month have You assigned to Your people, for all their generations, as a time of atonement. On Rosh Ḥodesh, our ancestors brought free-will offerings and sin offerings to attain atonement and to overcome sin.

Bestow everlasting love upon Your people, and fulfill for their children Your covenant with the patriarchs. Lead us with song to Zion, Your city, with everlasting joy to Jerusalem, where Your Temple stood. There our forefathers sacrificed to You, with their daily offerings and with their special offerings for this day of Rosh Ḥodesh, as it is written in Your Torah. And there again in reverence may we worship You.

Our God and God of our fathers, be merciful to our brothers of the House of Israel who suffer persecution; deliver them from darkness to light. Accept with compassion the prayers of Your people Israel, wherever they dwell, as they stand before You on this Rosh Ḥodesh day.

Our God and God of our fathers, renew us with a new month of goodness and blessing, joy and gladness, deliverance and comfort, sustenance and support, life and peace and forgiveness of sin (*during a leap year add:* and atonement for wrongdoing).

כִּי בְעַמְּךָ יִשְׂרָאֵל בָּחַרְתָּ מִכָּל־הָאֻמּוֹת, וְחֻקֵּי רָאשֵׁי חֳדָשִׁים לָהֶם קָבָעְתָּ. בָּרוּךְ אַתָּה יְיָ מְקַדֵּשׁ יִשְׂרָאֵל וְרָאשֵׁי חֳדָשִׁים.

רְצֵה יְיָ אֱלֹהֵינוּ בְּעַמְּךָ יִשְׂרָאֵל וּבִתְפִלָּתָם וְהָשֵׁב אֶת־הָעֲבוֹדָה לִדְבִיר בֵּיתֶךָ וּתְפִלָּתָם בְּאַהֲבָה תְקַבֵּל בְּרָצוֹן וּתְהִי לְרָצוֹן תָּמִיד עֲבוֹדַת יִשְׂרָאֵל עַמֶּךָ.

וְתֶחֱזֶינָה עֵינֵינוּ בְּשׁוּבְךָ לְצִיּוֹן בְּרַחֲמִים. בָּרוּךְ אַתָּה יְיָ הַמַּחֲזִיר שְׁכִינָתוֹ לְצִיּוֹן.

During repetition of Amidah, read this paragraph silently, while Reader chants the next paragraph.

מוֹדִים אֲנַחְנוּ לָךְ שָׁאַתָּה הוּא יְיָ אֱלֹהֵינוּ וֵאלֹהֵי אֲבוֹתֵינוּ אֱלֹהֵי כָל־בָּשָׂר יוֹצְרֵנוּ יוֹצֵר בְּרֵאשִׁית. בְּרָכוֹת וְהוֹדָאוֹת לְשִׁמְךָ הַגָּדוֹל וְהַקָּדוֹשׁ עַל שֶׁהֶחֱיִיתָנוּ וְקִיַּמְתָּנוּ. כֵּן תְּחַיֵּנוּ וּתְקַיְּמֵנוּ וְתֶאֱסֹף גָּלֻיּוֹתֵינוּ לְחַצְרוֹת קָדְשֶׁךָ לִשְׁמֹר חֻקֶּיךָ וְלַעֲשׂוֹת רְצוֹנֶךָ וּלְעָבְדְּךָ בְּלֵבָב שָׁלֵם עַל שֶׁאֲנַחְנוּ מוֹדִים לָךְ. בָּרוּךְ אֵל הַהוֹדָאוֹת.

מוֹדִים אֲנַחְנוּ לָךְ שָׁאַתָּה הוּא יְיָ אֱלֹהֵינוּ וֵאלֹהֵי אֲבוֹתֵינוּ לְעוֹלָם וָעֶד, צוּר חַיֵּינוּ מָגֵן יִשְׁעֵנוּ אַתָּה הוּא. לְדוֹר וָדוֹר נוֹדֶה לְּךָ וּנְסַפֵּר תְּהִלָּתֶךָ עַל חַיֵּינוּ הַמְּסוּרִים בְּיָדֶךָ וְעַל נִשְׁמוֹתֵינוּ הַפְּקוּדוֹת לָךְ וְעַל נִסֶּיךָ שֶׁבְּכָל־יוֹם עִמָּנוּ וְעַל נִפְלְאוֹתֶיךָ וְטוֹבוֹתֶיךָ שֶׁבְּכָל־עֵת עֶרֶב וָבֹקֶר וְצָהֳרָיִם. הַטּוֹב כִּי לֹא כָלוּ רַחֲמֶיךָ וְהַמְרַחֵם כִּי לֹא תַמּוּ חֲסָדֶיךָ מֵעוֹלָם קִוִּינוּ לָךְ.

On Ḥanukkah, turn to page 204.

Rosh Ḥodesh musaf

You have chosen Israel from among all the nations to observe the precepts relating to the festival of the New Moon. Praised are You, Lord who hallows the people Israel and the New Moon.

Accept the prayer of Your people Israel as lovingly as it is offered. Restore worship to Your sanctuary. May the worship of Your people Israel always be acceptable to You.

May we bear witness to Your merciful return to Zion. Praised are You, Lord who restores His Presence to Zion.

During repetition of Amidah, read this paragraph
silently, while Reader chants the next paragraph.

We proclaim that You are the Lord our God and God of our fathers, Creator of all who created us, God of all flesh. We praise You and thank You for granting us life and for sustaining us. May You continue to do so, and may You gather our exiles, that we may all fulfill Your commandments and serve You wholeheartedly, doing Your will. For this shall we thank You. Praised be God to whom thanksgiving is due.

We proclaim that You are the Lord our God and God of our fathers throughout all time. You are the Rock of our lives, the Shield of our salvation. We thank You and praise You through all generations, for our lives are in Your hand, our souls are in Your charge. We thank You for Your miracles which daily attend us, for Your wondrous kindness, morning, noon and night. Your mercy and love are boundless. We have always placed our hope in You.

On Ḥanukkah, turn to page 205.

Rosh Ḥodesh musaf

וְעַל כֻּלָּם יִתְבָּרַךְ וְיִתְרוֹמַם שִׁמְךָ מַלְכֵּנוּ תָּמִיד לְעוֹלָם וָעֶד.

וְכֹל הַחַיִּים יוֹדוּךָ סֶּלָה וִיהַלְלוּ אֶת־שִׁמְךָ בֶּאֱמֶת הָאֵל יְשׁוּעָתֵנוּ וְעֶזְרָתֵנוּ סֶלָה. בָּרוּךְ אַתָּה יְיָ הַטּוֹב שִׁמְךָ וּלְךָ נָאֶה לְהוֹדוֹת.

שִׂים שָׁלוֹם בָּעוֹלָם, טוֹבָה וּבְרָכָה חֵן וָחֶסֶד וְרַחֲמִים עָלֵינוּ וְעַל כָּל־יִשְׂרָאֵל עַמֶּךָ. בָּרְכֵנוּ אָבִינוּ כֻּלָּנוּ כְּאֶחָד בְּאוֹר פָּנֶיךָ, כִּי בְאוֹר פָּנֶיךָ נָתַתָּ לָּנוּ, יְיָ אֱלֹהֵינוּ, תּוֹרַת חַיִּים וְאַהֲבַת חֶסֶד וּצְדָקָה וּבְרָכָה וְרַחֲמִים וְחַיִּים וְשָׁלוֹם. וְטוֹב בְּעֵינֶיךָ לְבָרֵךְ אֶת־עַמְּךָ יִשְׂרָאֵל בְּכָל־עֵת וּבְכָל־שָׁעָה בִּשְׁלוֹמֶךָ.

בָּרוּךְ אַתָּה יְיָ הַמְבָרֵךְ אֶת־עַמּוֹ יִשְׂרָאֵל בַּשָּׁלוֹם.

At the conclusion of the Amidah, personal
prayers may be added, before or instead
of the following.

אֱלֹהַי, נְצֹר לְשׁוֹנִי מֵרָע וּשְׂפָתַי מִדַּבֵּר מִרְמָה, וְלִמְקַלְלַי נַפְשִׁי תִדֹּם וְנַפְשִׁי כֶּעָפָר לַכֹּל תִּהְיֶה. פְּתַח לִבִּי בְּתוֹרָתֶךָ וּבְמִצְוֹתֶיךָ תִּרְדֹּף נַפְשִׁי. וְכָל הַחוֹשְׁבִים עָלַי רָעָה, מְהֵרָה הָפֵר עֲצָתָם וְקַלְקֵל מַחֲשַׁבְתָּם. עֲשֵׂה לְמַעַן שְׁמֶךָ, עֲשֵׂה לְמַעַן יְמִינֶךָ, עֲשֵׂה לְמַעַן קְדֻשָּׁתֶךָ, עֲשֵׂה לְמַעַן תּוֹרָתֶךָ, לְמַעַן יֵחָלְצוּן יְדִידֶיךָ הוֹשִׁיעָה יְמִינְךָ וַעֲנֵנִי. יִהְיוּ לְרָצוֹן אִמְרֵי־פִי וְהֶגְיוֹן לִבִּי לְפָנֶיךָ, יְיָ צוּרִי וְגֹאֲלִי. עוֹשֶׂה שָׁלוֹם בִּמְרוֹמָיו הוּא יַעֲשֶׂה שָׁלוֹם עָלֵינוּ וְעַל כָּל־יִשְׂרָאֵל, וְאִמְרוּ אָמֵן.

We continue on page 92.

For all these blessings we shall ever praise and exalt You.

May every living creature thank You and praise You faithfully, our deliverance and our help. Praised are You, beneficent Lord to whom all praise is due.

Grant peace, happiness and blessing to the world, with grace, love and mercy for us and for all the people Israel. Bless us, our Father, one and all, with Your light; for by that light did You teach us Torah and life, love and tenderness, justice, mercy and peace. May it please You to bless Your people Israel in every season and at all times with Your gift of peace. Praised are You, Lord who blesses His people Israel with peace.

At the conclusion of the Amidah, personal prayers
may be added, before or instead of the following.

My God, keep my tongue from telling evil, my lips from speaking lies. Help me ignore those who slander me. Let me be humble before all. Open my heart to Your Torah, so that I may pursue Your commandments. Frustrate the designs of those who plot evil against me. Make nothing of their schemes. Do so for the sake of Your power, Your holiness and Your Torah. Answer my prayer for the deliverance of Your people. May the words of my mouth and the meditations of my heart be acceptable to You, my Rock and my Redeemer. He who brings peace to His universe will bring peace to us, to the people Israel and to all mankind. Amen.

We continue on page 93.

Rosh Ḥodesh musaf

203

*On Ḥanukkah, on Purim and on Israel's Inde-
pendence Day, one of the following is added
as designated in each service.*

ON ḤANUKKAH:

עַל הַנִּסִּים וְעַל הַפֻּרְקָן וְעַל הַגְּבוּרוֹת וְעַל הַתְּשׁוּעוֹת וְעַל
הַמִּלְחָמוֹת, שֶׁעָשִׂיתָ לַאֲבוֹתֵינוּ בַּיָּמִים הָהֵם וּבַזְּמַן הַזֶּה.

בִּימֵי מַתִּתְיָהוּ בֶּן־יוֹחָנָן כֹּהֵן גָּדוֹל חַשְׁמוֹנַי וּבָנָיו, כְּשֶׁעָמְדָה מַלְכוּת
יָוָן הָרְשָׁעָה עַל עַמְּךָ יִשְׂרָאֵל לְהַשְׁכִּיחָם תּוֹרָתֶךָ, וּלְהַעֲבִירָם מֵחֻקֵּי
רְצוֹנֶךָ. וְאַתָּה בְּרַחֲמֶיךָ הָרַבִּים עָמַדְתָּ לָהֶם בְּעֵת צָרָתָם, רַבְתָּ
אֶת־רִיבָם, דַּנְתָּ אֶת־דִּינָם, נָקַמְתָּ אֶת־נִקְמָתָם, מָסַרְתָּ גִּבּוֹרִים
בְּיַד חַלָּשִׁים, וְרַבִּים בְּיַד מְעַטִּים, וּטְמֵאִים בְּיַד טְהוֹרִים, וּרְשָׁעִים
בְּיַד צַדִּיקִים, וְזֵדִים בְּיַד עוֹסְקֵי תוֹרָתֶךָ. וּלְךָ עָשִׂיתָ שֵׁם גָּדוֹל
וְקָדוֹשׁ בְּעוֹלָמֶךָ, וּלְעַמְּךָ יִשְׂרָאֵל עָשִׂיתָ תְּשׁוּעָה גְּדוֹלָה וּפֻרְקָן
כְּהַיּוֹם הַזֶּה. וְאַחַר כֵּן בָּאוּ בָנֶיךָ לִדְבִיר בֵּיתֶךָ וּפִנּוּ אֶת־הֵיכָלֶךָ
וְטִהֲרוּ אֶת־מִקְדָּשֶׁךָ, וְהִדְלִיקוּ נֵרוֹת בְּחַצְרוֹת קָדְשֶׁךָ, וְקָבְעוּ
שְׁמוֹנַת יְמֵי חֲנֻכָּה אֵלּוּ לְהוֹדוֹת וּלְהַלֵּל לְשִׁמְךָ הַגָּדוֹל.

*Morning service, continue on page 76.
Afternoon service, continue on page 142.
Evening service, continue on page 176.
On Rosh Hodesh, continue on page 202.*

Ḥanukkah

On Ḥanukkah, on Purim and on Israel's Independence Day, one of the following is added as designated in each service.

ON ḤANUKKAH:

We thank You for the heroism, for the triumphs, and for the miraculous deliverance of our fathers in other days and in our time.

In the days of Mattathias, the Hasmonean, son of Yohanan the renowned priest, in his days and in the days of his sons, a cruel power rose against Israel, demanding the abandonment of Your Torah and the violation of Your commandments. You, in great mercy, stood by Your people in time of trouble. You defended them, vindicated them, and avenged their wrongs. You delivered the strong into the hands of the weak, the many into the hands of the few, the corrupt into the hands of the pure in heart, the guilty into the hands of the innocent. You delivered the arrogant into the hands of those who were faithful to Your Torah. Because You wrought great victories and miraculous deliverance for Your people Israel to this very day, You revealed Your glory and Your holiness to all the world. Then Your children came into Your shrine, cleansed Your Temple, purified Your sanctuary, and kindled lights in Your sacred courts. They set aside these eight days as a season for giving thanks and reciting praises to You.

Morning service, continue on page 77.
Afternoon service, continue on page 143.
Evening service, continue on page 177.
On Rosh Ḥodesh, continue on page 203.

Ḥanukkah

205

עַל הַנִּסִּים וְעַל הַפֻּרְקָן וְעַל הַגְּבוּרוֹת וְעַל הַתְּשׁוּעוֹת וְעַל הַמִּלְחָמוֹת, שֶׁעָשִׂיתָ לַאֲבוֹתֵינוּ בַּיָּמִים הָהֵם וּבַזְּמַן הַזֶּה.

בִּימֵי מָרְדְּכַי וְאֶסְתֵּר בְּשׁוּשַׁן הַבִּירָה, כְּשֶׁעָמַד עֲלֵיהֶם הָמָן הָרָשָׁע, בִּקֵּשׁ לְהַשְׁמִיד לַהֲרֹג וּלְאַבֵּד אֶת־כָּל־הַיְּהוּדִים מִנַּעַר וְעַד זָקֵן, טַף וְנָשִׁים, בְּיוֹם אֶחָד, בִּשְׁלוֹשָׁה עָשָׂר לְחֹדֶשׁ שְׁנֵים עָשָׂר הוּא חֹדֶשׁ אֲדָר, וּשְׁלָלָם לָבוֹז. וְאַתָּה בְּרַחֲמֶיךָ הָרַבִּים הֵפַרְתָּ אֶת־ עֲצָתוֹ, וְקִלְקַלְתָּ אֶת־מַחֲשַׁבְתּוֹ, וַהֲשֵׁבוֹתָ מוּלוֹ בְּרֹאשׁוֹ, וְתָלוּ אוֹתוֹ וְאֶת־בָּנָיו עַל הָעֵץ.

Morning service, continue on page 76.
Afternoon service, continue on page 142.
Evening service, continue on page 176.

Purim

ON PURIM:

We thank You for the heroism, for the triumphs, and for the miraculous deliverance of our fathers in other days and in our time.

In the days of Mordekhai and Esther, in Shushan, the capital of Persia, the wicked Haman rose up against all Jews and plotted their destruction. In a single day, the thirteenth of Adar, the twelfth month of the year, Haman planned to annihilate all Jews, young and old, and to permit the plunder of their property. You, in great mercy, thwarted his designs, frustrated his plot, and visited upon him the evil he planned to bring on others. On the gallows he had made for Mordekhai, Haman, together with his sons, suffered death.

Morning service, continue on page 77.
Afternoon service, continue on page 143.
Evening service, continue on page 177.

Purim

עַל הַנִּסִּים וְעַל הַפֻּרְקָן, וְעַל הַגְּבוּרוֹת וְעַל הַתְּשׁוּעוֹת, וְעַל הַמִּלְחָמוֹת שֶׁעָשִׂיתָ לַאֲבוֹתֵינוּ בַּיָּמִים הָהֵם וּבַזְּמָן הַזֶּה.

בִּימֵי שִׁיבַת בָּנִים לִגְבוּלָם, בְּעֵת תְּקוּמַת עַם בְּאַרְצוֹ כִּימֵי קֶדֶם, נִסְגְּרוּ שַׁעֲרֵי אֶרֶץ אָבוֹת בִּפְנֵי אַחֵינוּ פְּלִיטֵי חֶרֶב, וְאוֹיְבִים בָּאָרֶץ וְשִׁבְעָה עֲמָמִים בַּעֲלֵי בְרִיתָם קָמוּ לְהַכְרִית עַמְּךָ יִשְׂרָאֵל, וְאַתָּה בְּרַחֲמֶיךָ הָרַבִּים עָמַדְתָּ לָהֶם בְּעֵת צָרָתָם, רַבְתָּ אֶת־רִיבָם, דַּנְתָּ אֶת־דִּינָם, חִזַּקְתָּ אֶת־לִבָּם לַעֲמֹד בַּשַּׁעַר, וְלִפְתֹּחַ שְׁעָרִים לַנִּרְדָּפִים וּלְגָרֵשׁ אֶת־צִבְאוֹת הָאוֹיֵב מִן הָאָרֶץ. מָסַרְתָּ רַבִּים בְּיַד מְעַטִּים, וּרְשָׁעִים בְּיַד צַדִּיקִים, וּלְךָ עָשִׂיתָ שֵׁם גָּדוֹל וְקָדוֹשׁ בְּעוֹלָמֶךָ, וּלְעַמְּךָ יִשְׂרָאֵל עָשִׂיתָ תְּשׁוּעָה גְדוֹלָה וּפֻרְקָן כְּהַיּוֹם הַזֶּה.

Morning service, continue on page 76.
Afternoon service, continue on page 142.
Evening service, continue on page 176.

We thank You for the heroism, for the triumphs, and for the miraculous deliverance of our ancestors in other days and in our time.

In the days when Your children were returning to their borders, at the time of a people revived in its land as in days of old, the gates to the land of our ancestors were closed before those who were fleeing the sword. When enemies from within the land together with seven neighboring nations sought to annihilate Your people, You, in Your great mercy, stood by them in time of trouble. You defended them and vindicated them. You gave them the courage to meet their foes, to open the gates to those seeking refuge, and to free the land of its armed invaders. You delivered the many into the hands of the few, the guilty into the hands of the innocent. You have wrought great victories and miraculous deliverance for Your people Israel to this day, revealing Your glory and Your holiness to all the world.

Morning service, continue on page 77.
Afternoon service, continue on page 143.
Evening service, continue on page 177.

נַחֵם, יְיָ אֱלֹהֵינוּ, אֶת־אֲבֵלֵי צִיּוֹן וְאֶת־אֲבֵלֵי יְרוּשָׁלַיִם וְאֶת־הָעִיר שֶׁחֲרֵבָה הָיְתָה וַאֲבֵלָה מִבְּלִי בָנֶיהָ. עַל עַמְּךָ יִשְׂרָאֵל שֶׁהוּטַל לַחֶרֶב וְעַל בָּנֶיהָ אֲשֶׁר מָסְרוּ נַפְשָׁם עָלֶיהָ צִיּוֹן בְּמַר תִּבְכֶּה וִירוּשָׁלַיִם תִּתֵּן קוֹלָהּ: לִבִּי לִבִּי עַל חַלְלֵיהֶם, מֵעַי מֵעַי עַל חַלְלֵיהֶם.

רַחֵם, יְיָ אֱלֹהֵינוּ, בְּרַחֲמֶיךָ הָרַבִּים עָלֵינוּ וְעַל יְרוּשָׁלַיִם עִירֶךָ הַנִּבְנֵית מֵחָרְבָּנָהּ וְהַמְיֻשֶּׁבֶת מִשּׁוֹמְמוּתָהּ. יְהִי רָצוֹן מִלְּפָנֶיךָ, מְשַׂמֵּחַ צִיּוֹן בְּבָנֶיהָ, שֶׁיִּשְׂמְחוּ אֶת־יְרוּשָׁלַיִם כָּל־אוֹהֲבֶיהָ וְיָשִׂישׂוּ אִתָּהּ כָּל־ הַמִּתְאַבְּלִים עָלֶיהָ, וְיִשְׁמְעוּ בְּעָרֵי יְהוּדָה וּבְחוּצוֹת יְרוּשָׁלַיִם קוֹל שָׂשׂוֹן וְקוֹל שִׂמְחָה, קוֹל חָתָן וְקוֹל כַּלָּה. תֵּן שָׁלוֹם לְעִירְךָ אֲשֶׁר פָּדִיתָ, וְהָגֵן עָלֶיהָ כָּאָמוּר: ,וַאֲנִי אֶהְיֶה לָּהּ, נְאֻם יְיָ, חוֹמַת אֵשׁ סָבִיב, וּלְכָבוֹד אֶהְיֶה בְתוֹכָהּ.' בָּרוּךְ אַתָּה יְיָ מְנַחֵם צִיּוֹן וּבוֹנֵה יְרוּשָׁלַיִם.

Continue on page 138.

Comfort, Lord our God, the mourners of Zion and those who grieve for Jerusalem, the city which was so desolate in mourning, like a woman bereft of her children. For Your people Israel smitten by the sword, and for her children who gave their lives for her, Zion cries with bitter tears, Jerusalem voices her anguish: My heart, my heart goes out for the slain. My entire being mourns for the slain.

Have mercy, Lord our God, in Your great compassion, for us and for Your city of Jerusalem, rebuilt from destruction and restored from desolation. Lord who causes Zion to rejoice at her children's return, may all who love Jerusalem exult in her, may all who mourn Jerusalem of old rejoice with her now. May they hear the cities of Judah, and in the streets of Jerusalem, sounds of joy and gladness, voices of bride and groom.

Grant peace to the city which You have redeemed, and protect her, as proclaimed by Your prophet: I will surround her, says the Lord, as a wall of fire, and I will be the glory in her midst. Praised are You, Lord who comforts Zion and rebuilds Jerusalem.

Continue on page 139.

עֲנֵנוּ יְיָ, עֲנֵנוּ בְּיוֹם צוֹם תַּעֲנִיתֵנוּ, כִּי בְצָרָה גְדוֹלָה אֲנָחְנוּ. אַל תֵּפֶן
אֶל רִשְׁעֵנוּ וְאַל תַּסְתֵּר פָּנֶיךָ מִמֶּנּוּ, וְאַל תִּתְעַלַּם מִתְּחִנָּתֵנוּ. הֱיֵה נָא
קָרוֹב לְשַׁוְעָתֵנוּ, יְהִי נָא חַסְדְּךָ לְנַחֲמֵנוּ. טֶרֶם נִקְרָא אֵלֶיךָ עֲנֵנוּ,
כַּדָּבָר שֶׁנֶּאֱמַר: ,וְהָיָה טֶרֶם יִקְרָאוּ וַאֲנִי אֶעֱנֶה, עוֹד הֵם מְדַבְּרִים
וַאֲנִי אֶשְׁמָע.׳ כִּי אַתָּה יְיָ, הָעוֹנֶה בְּעֵת צָרָה, פּוֹדֶה וּמַצִּיל בְּכָל־עֵת
צָרָה וְצוּקָה.

*Individuals, during Afternoon Service Silent
Amidah, continue on page 138.*

Reader only concludes:

בָּרוּךְ אַתָּה יְיָ הָעוֹנֶה בְּעֵת צָרָה.

Reader continues in Morning Service, page 70.
Reader continues in Afternoon Service, page 134.

Answer us, Lord, answer us on our Fast Day, for grievous anguish overwhelms us. Consider not our guilt, turn not away from us. Be mindful of our plea, and heed our supplication. Your love is our comfort; answer before we call. For this is the promise uttered by Your prophet: "I shall answer before they have spoken, I shall heed their call before it is uttered." You, Lord, do answer us in time of trouble; You rescue and redeem in time of distress.

Individuals, during Afternoon Service Silent Amidah, continue on page 139.

Reader only concludes:

Praised are You, Lord who answers the afflicted.

Reader continues in Morning Service, page 71.
Reader continues in Afternoon Service, page 135.

Fast Days

From the eve of the second day of Pesah until Shavuot eve, the Omer is counted at the end of the evening service.

Omer (literally "sheaf") refers to an offering from the new barley crop which was brought to the ancient Temple on the sixteenth of Nissan, the eve of the second day of Pesah. Omer has come to be the name of the period between Pesah and Shavuot. Counting the days of this period (sefirat ha-omer) relates the exodus from Egypt, commemorated by Pesah, to the giving of Torah at Mount Sinai, commemorated by Shavuot.

I am about to fulfill the commandment of Counting the Omer, as it is ordained in the Torah: You shall count from the eve of the second day of Pesah, when an Omer of grain was brought as an offering to the Temple, seven weeks and a day. Fifty days shall you count.

Praised are You, Lord our God, King of the universe who sanctified us with His commandments, and commanded us to count the Omer.

Counting the Omer

הִנְנִי מוּכָן וּמְזֻמָּן לְקַיֵּם מִצְוַת עֲשֵׂה שֶׁל סְפִירַת הָעֹמֶר, כְּמוֹ שֶׁכָּתוּב בַּתּוֹרָה: וּסְפַרְתֶּם לָכֶם מִמָּחֳרַת הַשַּׁבָּת, מִיּוֹם הֲבִיאֲכֶם אֶת־עֹמֶר הַתְּנוּפָה, שֶׁבַע שַׁבָּתוֹת תְּמִימֹת תִּהְיֶינָה עַד מִמָּחֳרַת הַשַּׁבָּת הַשְּׁבִיעִית תִּסְפְּרוּ חֲמִשִּׁים יוֹם.

בָּרוּךְ אַתָּה יְיָ אֱלֹהֵינוּ מֶלֶךְ הָעוֹלָם אֲשֶׁר קִדְּשָׁנוּ בְּמִצְוֹתָיו וְצִוָּנוּ עַל סְפִירַת הָעֹמֶר.

1 הַיּוֹם יוֹם אֶחָד לָעֹמֶר.

2 הַיּוֹם שְׁנֵי יָמִים לָעֹמֶר.

3 הַיּוֹם שְׁלֹשָׁה יָמִים לָעֹמֶר.

4 הַיּוֹם אַרְבָּעָה יָמִים לָעֹמֶר.

5 הַיּוֹם חֲמִשָּׁה יָמִים לָעֹמֶר.

6 הַיּוֹם שִׁשָּׁה יָמִים לָעֹמֶר.

7 הַיּוֹם שִׁבְעָה יָמִים, שֶׁהֵם שָׁבוּעַ אֶחָד לָעֹמֶר.

8 הַיּוֹם שְׁמֹנָה יָמִים, שֶׁהֵם שָׁבוּעַ אֶחָד וְיוֹם אֶחָד לָעֹמֶר.

9 הַיּוֹם תִּשְׁעָה יָמִים, שֶׁהֵם שָׁבוּעַ אֶחָד וּשְׁנֵי יָמִים לָעֹמֶר.

10 הַיּוֹם עֲשָׂרָה יָמִים, שֶׁהֵם שָׁבוּעַ אֶחָד וּשְׁלֹשָׁה יָמִים לָעֹמֶר.

11 הַיּוֹם אַחַד עָשָׂר יוֹם, שֶׁהֵם שָׁבוּעַ אֶחָד וְאַרְבָּעָה יָמִים לָעֹמֶר.

12 הַיּוֹם שְׁנֵים עָשָׂר יוֹם, שֶׁהֵם שָׁבוּעַ אֶחָד וַחֲמִשָּׁה יָמִים לָעֹמֶר.

13 הַיּוֹם שְׁלֹשָׁה עָשָׂר יוֹם, שֶׁהֵם שָׁבוּעַ אֶחָד וְשִׁשָּׁה יָמִים לָעֹמֶר.

14 הַיּוֹם אַרְבָּעָה עָשָׂר יוֹם, שֶׁהֵם שְׁנֵי שָׁבוּעוֹת לָעֹמֶר.

15 הַיּוֹם חֲמִשָּׁה עָשָׂר יוֹם, שֶׁהֵם שְׁנֵי שָׁבוּעוֹת וְיוֹם אֶחָד לָעֹמֶר.

16 הַיּוֹם שִׁשָּׁה עָשָׂר יוֹם, שֶׁהֵם שְׁנֵי שָׁבוּעוֹת וּשְׁנֵי יָמִים לָעֹמֶר.

17 הַיּוֹם שִׁבְעָה עָשָׂר יוֹם, שֶׁהֵם שְׁנֵי שָׁבוּעוֹת וּשְׁלֹשָׁה יָמִים לָעֹמֶר.

18 הַיּוֹם שְׁמֹנָה עָשָׂר יוֹם, שֶׁהֵם שְׁנֵי שָׁבוּעוֹת וְאַרְבָּעָה יָמִים לָעֹמֶר.

19 הַיּוֹם תִּשְׁעָה עָשָׂר יוֹם, שֶׁהֵם שְׁנֵי שָׁבוּעוֹת וַחֲמִשָּׁה יָמִים לָעֹמֶר.

20 הַיּוֹם עֶשְׂרִים יוֹם, שֶׁהֵם שְׁנֵי שָׁבוּעוֹת וְשִׁשָּׁה יָמִים לָעֹמֶר.

21 הַיּוֹם אֶחָד וְעֶשְׂרִים יוֹם, שֶׁהֵם שְׁלֹשָׁה שָׁבוּעוֹת לָעֹמֶר.

22 הַיּוֹם שְׁנַיִם וְעֶשְׂרִים יוֹם, שֶׁהֵם שְׁלֹשָׁה שָׁבוּעוֹת וְיוֹם אֶחָד לָעֹמֶר.

23 הַיּוֹם שְׁלֹשָׁה וְעֶשְׂרִים יוֹם, שֶׁהֵם שְׁלֹשָׁה שָׁבוּעוֹת וּשְׁנֵי יָמִים לָעֹמֶר.

24 הַיּוֹם אַרְבָּעָה וְעֶשְׂרִים יוֹם, שֶׁהֵם שְׁלֹשָׁה שָׁבוּעוֹת וּשְׁלֹשָׁה יָמִים לָעֹמֶר.

25 הַיּוֹם חֲמִשָּׁה וְעֶשְׂרִים יוֹם, שֶׁהֵם שְׁלֹשָׁה שָׁבוּעוֹת וְאַרְבָּעָה יָמִים לָעֹמֶר.

26 הַיּוֹם שִׁשָּׁה וְעֶשְׂרִים יוֹם, שֶׁהֵם שְׁלֹשָׁה שָׁבוּעוֹת וַחֲמִשָּׁה יָמִים לָעֹמֶר.

27 הַיּוֹם שִׁבְעָה וְעֶשְׂרִים יוֹם, שֶׁהֵם שְׁלֹשָׁה שָׁבוּעוֹת וְשִׁשָּׁה יָמִים לָעֹמֶר.

28 הַיּוֹם שְׁמֹנָה וְעֶשְׂרִים יוֹם, שֶׁהֵם אַרְבָּעָה שָׁבוּעוֹת לָעֹמֶר.

29 הַיּוֹם תִּשְׁעָה וְעֶשְׂרִים יוֹם, שֶׁהֵם אַרְבָּעָה שָׁבוּעוֹת וְיוֹם אֶחָד לָעֹמֶר.

30 הַיּוֹם שְׁלֹשִׁים יוֹם, שֶׁהֵם אַרְבָּעָה שָׁבוּעוֹת וּשְׁנֵי יָמִים לָעֹמֶר.

31 הַיּוֹם אֶחָד וּשְׁלֹשִׁים יוֹם, שֶׁהֵם אַרְבָּעָה שָׁבוּעוֹת וּשְׁלֹשָׁה יָמִים לָעֹמֶר.

32 הַיּוֹם שְׁנַיִם וּשְׁלֹשִׁים יוֹם, שֶׁהֵם אַרְבָּעָה שָׁבוּעוֹת וְאַרְבָּעָה יָמִים לָעֹמֶר.

33 הַיּוֹם שְׁלֹשָׁה וּשְׁלֹשִׁים יוֹם, שֶׁהֵם אַרְבָּעָה שָׁבוּעוֹת וַחֲמִשָּׁה יָמִים לָעֹמֶר.

34 הַיּוֹם אַרְבָּעָה וּשְׁלֹשִׁים יוֹם, שֶׁהֵם אַרְבָּעָה שָׁבוּעוֹת וְשִׁשָּׁה יָמִים לָעֹמֶר.

35 הַיּוֹם חֲמִשָּׁה וּשְׁלֹשִׁים יוֹם, שֶׁהֵם חֲמִשָּׁה שָׁבוּעוֹת לָעֹמֶר.

36 הַיּוֹם שִׁשָּׁה וּשְׁלֹשִׁים יוֹם, שֶׁהֵם חֲמִשָּׁה שָׁבוּעוֹת וְיוֹם אֶחָד לָעֹמֶר.

37 הַיּוֹם שִׁבְעָה וּשְׁלֹשִׁים יוֹם, שֶׁהֵם חֲמִשָּׁה שָׁבוּעוֹת וּשְׁנֵי יָמִים לָעֹמֶר.

38 הַיּוֹם שְׁמֹנָה וּשְׁלֹשִׁים יוֹם, שֶׁהֵם חֲמִשָּׁה שָׁבוּעוֹת וּשְׁלֹשָׁה יָמִים לָעֹמֶר.

39 הַיּוֹם תִּשְׁעָה וּשְׁלֹשִׁים יוֹם, שֶׁהֵם חֲמִשָּׁה שָׁבוּעוֹת וְאַרְבָּעָה יָמִים לָעֹמֶר.

40 הַיּוֹם אַרְבָּעִים יוֹם, שֶׁהֵם חֲמִשָּׁה שָׁבוּעוֹת וַחֲמִשָּׁה יָמִים לָעֹמֶר.

41 הַיּוֹם אֶחָד וְאַרְבָּעִים יוֹם, שֶׁהֵם חֲמִשָּׁה שָׁבוּעוֹת וְשִׁשָּׁה יָמִים לָעֹמֶר.

42 הַיּוֹם שְׁנַיִם וְאַרְבָּעִים יוֹם, שֶׁהֵם שִׁשָּׁה שָׁבוּעוֹת לָעֹמֶר.

43 הַיּוֹם שְׁלֹשָׁה וְאַרְבָּעִים יוֹם, שֶׁהֵם שִׁשָּׁה שָׁבוּעוֹת וְיוֹם אֶחָד לָעֹמֶר.

44 הַיּוֹם אַרְבָּעָה וְאַרְבָּעִים יוֹם, שֶׁהֵם שִׁשָּׁה שָׁבוּעוֹת וּשְׁנֵי יָמִים לָעֹמֶר.

45 הַיּוֹם חֲמִשָּׁה וְאַרְבָּעִים יוֹם, שֶׁהֵם שִׁשָּׁה שָׁבוּעוֹת וּשְׁלֹשָׁה יָמִים לָעֹמֶר.

46 הַיּוֹם שִׁשָּׁה וְאַרְבָּעִים יוֹם, שֶׁהֵם שִׁשָּׁה שָׁבוּעוֹת וְאַרְבָּעָה יָמִים לָעֹמֶר.

47 הַיּוֹם שִׁבְעָה וְאַרְבָּעִים יוֹם, שֶׁהֵם שִׁשָּׁה שָׁבוּעוֹת וַחֲמִשָּׁה יָמִים לָעֹמֶר.

48 הַיּוֹם שְׁמֹנָה וְאַרְבָּעִים יוֹם, שֶׁהֵם שִׁשָּׁה שָׁבוּעוֹת וְשִׁשָּׁה יָמִים לָעֹמֶר.

49 הַיּוֹם תִּשְׁעָה וְאַרְבָּעִים יוֹם, שֶׁהֵם שִׁבְעָה שָׁבוּעוֹת לָעֹמֶר.

The service concludes with Aleinu, pages 182–183,
On Saturday night, continue with Havdalah,
pages 218–219.

הִנֵּה אֵל יְשׁוּעָתִי, אֶבְטַח וְלֹא אֶפְחָד. כִּי עָזִּי וְזִמְרָת יָהּ יְיָ, וַיְהִי לִי
לִישׁוּעָה. וּשְׁאַבְתֶּם מַיִם בְּשָׂשׂוֹן מִמַּעַיְנֵי הַיְשׁוּעָה. לַיְיָ הַיְשׁוּעָה, עַל
עַמְּךָ בִרְכָתֶךָ, סֶּלָה. יְיָ צְבָאוֹת עִמָּנוּ, מִשְׂגָּב לָנוּ אֱלֹהֵי יַעֲקֹב, סֶּלָה.
יְיָ צְבָאוֹת, אַשְׁרֵי אָדָם בֹּטֵחַ בָּךְ. יְיָ הוֹשִׁיעָה, הַמֶּלֶךְ יַעֲנֵנוּ בְיוֹם
קָרְאֵנוּ.

לַיְּהוּדִים הָיְתָה אוֹרָה וְשִׂמְחָה וְשָׂשׂוֹן וִיקָר. כֵּן תִּהְיֶה לָנוּ.

כּוֹס יְשׁוּעוֹת אֶשָּׂא וּבְשֵׁם יְיָ אֶקְרָא.

בָּרוּךְ אַתָּה יְיָ אֱלֹהֵינוּ מֶלֶךְ הָעוֹלָם, בּוֹרֵא פְּרִי הַגָּפֶן.

בָּרוּךְ אַתָּה יְיָ אֱלֹהֵינוּ מֶלֶךְ הָעוֹלָם, בּוֹרֵא מִינֵי בְשָׂמִים.

בָּרוּךְ אַתָּה יְיָ אֱלֹהֵינוּ מֶלֶךְ הָעוֹלָם, בּוֹרֵא מְאוֹרֵי הָאֵשׁ.

בָּרוּךְ אַתָּה יְיָ אֱלֹהֵינוּ מֶלֶךְ הָעוֹלָם, הַמַּבְדִּיל בֵּין קֹדֶשׁ לְחוֹל, בֵּין
אוֹר לְחשֶׁךְ, בֵּין יִשְׂרָאֵל לָעַמִּים, בֵּין יוֹם הַשְּׁבִיעִי לְשֵׁשֶׁת יְמֵי
הַמַּעֲשֶׂה. בָּרוּךְ אַתָּה יְיָ, הַמַּבְדִּיל בֵּין קֹדֶשׁ לְחוֹל.

On Hanukkah, turn to page 220.
We conclude with Alienu, page 182.

Havdalah

God is my deliverance; confident is my trust in Him. The Lord is my strength, my song, my deliverance. Joyfully shall you drink from the fountains of deliverance. The Lord will rescue; the Lord will bless His people. Selah. The Lord of hosts is with us, the God of Jacob is our fortress. Lord of hosts, blessed is the person who trusts in You. Lord and King, answer us when we call, and rescue us.

Grant us the blessing of light, of gladness and of honor, which the miracle of deliverance brought to our ancestors. I lift the cup of deliverance; I call upon the Lord.

Praised are You, Lord our God, King of the universe who creates the fruit of the vine.

Praised are You, Lord our God, King of the universe who creates fragrant spices.

Praised are You, Lord our God, King of the universe who creates the lights of fire.

Praised are You, Lord our God, King of the universe who has endowed all creation with distinctive qualities and differentiated between light and darkness, between sacred and profane, between the people Israel and other people, and between the seventh day and the other days of the week. Praised are You, Lord who differentiates between the sacred and the profane.

On Ḥanukkah, we turn to page 221.
We conclude with Aleinu, page 183.

Havdalah

בָּרוּךְ אַתָּה יְיָ אֱלֹהֵינוּ מֶלֶךְ הָעוֹלָם, אֲשֶׁר קִדְּשָׁנוּ בְּמִצְוֹתָיו וְצִוָּנוּ לְהַדְלִיק נֵר שֶׁל חֲנֻכָּה.

בָּרוּךְ אַתָּה יְיָ אֱלֹהֵינוּ מֶלֶךְ הָעוֹלָם, שֶׁעָשָׂה נִסִּים לַאֲבוֹתֵינוּ בַּיָּמִים הָהֵם בַּזְּמַן הַזֶּה.

On the first night only:

בָּרוּךְ אַתָּה יְיָ אֱלֹהֵינוּ מֶלֶךְ הָעוֹלָם, שֶׁהֶחֱיָנוּ וְקִיְּמָנוּ וְהִגִּיעָנוּ לַזְּמַן הַזֶּה.

After lighting the lights:

הַנֵּרוֹת הַלָּלוּ אֲנַחְנוּ מַדְלִיקִין עַל הַנִּסִּים וְעַל הַנִּפְלָאוֹת, וְעַל הַתְּשׁוּעוֹת וְעַל הַמִּלְחָמוֹת, שֶׁעָשִׂיתָ לַאֲבוֹתֵינוּ בַּיָּמִים הָהֵם בַּזְּמַן הַזֶּה עַל יְדֵי כֹּהֲנֶיךָ הַקְּדוֹשִׁים.

וְכָל־שְׁמֹנַת יְמֵי חֲנֻכָּה הַנֵּרוֹת הַלָּלוּ קֹדֶשׁ הֵם, וְאֵין לָנוּ רְשׁוּת לְהִשְׁתַּמֵּשׁ בָּהֶם אֶלָּא לִרְאוֹתָם בִּלְבָד, כְּדֵי לְהוֹדוֹת וּלְהַלֵּל לְשִׁמְךָ הַגָּדוֹל עַל נִסֶּיךָ וְעַל נִפְלְאוֹתֶיךָ וְעַל יְשׁוּעָתֶךָ.

We continue with Aleinu, page 182.

Ḥanukkah lights

Praised are You, Lord our God, King of the universe who sanctified us with His commandments, and commanded us to kindle the lights of Ḥanukkah.

Praised are You, Lord our God, King of the universe who performed wondrous deeds for our ancestors in ancient days at this season.

On the first night only:

Praised are You, Lord our God, King of the universe who kept us in life, sustained us and enabled us to reach this season.

After lighting the lights:

These lights we kindle to recall the wondrous triumphs and the miraculous victories wrought through Your holy *kohanim* for our ancestors in ancient days at this season.

These lights are sacred through all the eight days of Ḥanukkah. We may not put them to ordinary use, but are to look upon them and thus be reminded to thank and praise You for the wondrous miracle of our deliverance.

We continue with Aleinu, page 183.

Ḥanukkah lights